THE BEDFORD SERIES IN HISTORY AND CULTURE

Martin Luther King Jr., Malcolm X, and the Civil Rights Struggle of the 1950s and 1960s

A Brief History with Documents

Related Titles in
THE BEDFORD SERIES IN HISTORY AND CULTURE
Advisory Editors: Lynn Hunt, *University of California, Los Angeles*
David W. Blight, *Yale University*
Bonnie G. Smith, *Rutgers University*
Natalie Zemon Davis, *Princeton University*
Ernest R. May, *Harvard University*

THE CONFESSIONS OF NAT TURNER *and Related Documents*
Edited with an Introduction by Kenneth S. Greenberg, *Suffolk University*

NARRATIVE OF THE LIFE OF FREDERICK DOUGLASS, AN AMERICAN SLAVE, WRITTEN BY HIMSELF, Second Edition
Edited with an Introduction by David W. Blight, *Yale University*

SOUTHERN HORRORS AND OTHER WRITINGS: *The Anti-Lynching Campaign of Ida B. Wells, 1892–1900*
Edited with an Introduction by Jacqueline Jones Royster, *Ohio State University*

PLESSY V. FERGUSON: *A Brief History with Documents*
Edited with an Introduction by Brook Thomas, *University of California, Irvine*

UP FROM SLAVERY *by Booker T. Washington with Related Documents*
Edited with an Introduction by W. Fitzhugh Brundage, *University of North Carolina at Chapel Hill*

THE SOULS OF BLACK FOLK *by W. E. B. Du Bois*
Edited with an Introduction by David W. Blight, *Yale University,* and Robert Gooding-Williams, *Northwestern University*

Black Protest and the Great Migration: A Brief History with Documents
Eric Arnesen, *University of Illinois at Chicago*

TO SECURE THESE RIGHTS: *The Report of Harry S Truman's Committee on Civil Rights*
Edited with an Introduction by Steven F. Lawson, *Rutgers University*

BROWN V. BOARD OF EDUCATION: *A Brief History with Documents*
Waldo E. Martin Jr., *University of California, Berkeley*

Lyndon B. Johnson and American Liberalism: A Brief Biography with Documents
Bruce J. Schulman, *Boston University*

THE BEDFORD SERIES IN HISTORY AND CULTURE

Martin Luther King Jr., Malcolm X, and the Civil Rights Struggle of the 1950s and 1960s
A Brief History with Documents

David Howard-Pitney
De Anza College

BEDFORD/ST. MARTIN'S   Boston ♦ New York

For Bedford/St. Martin's
Publisher for History: Patricia A. Rossi
Director of Development for History: Jane Knetzger
Developmental Editor: Carina Schoenberger
Assistant Editor, Publishing Services: Maria Burwell
Senior Production Supervisor: Joe Ford
Production Assistant: Nancy DiCostanzo-Chillemi
Senior Marketing Manager: Jenna Bookin Barry
Project Management: Books By Design, Inc.
Text Design: Claire Seng-Niemoeller
Indexer: Books By Design, Inc.
Cover Design: Billy Boardman
Cover Photo: Malcolm X with Dr. Martin Luther King Jr. © Bettmann/CORBIS.
Composition: Stratford Publishing Services, Inc.
Printing and Binding: Haddon Craftsmen, an RR Donnelley & Sons Company

President: Joan E. Feinberg
Editorial Director: Denise B. Wydra
Director of Marketing: Karen Melton Soeltz
Director of Editing, Design, and Production: Marcia Cohen
Manager, Publishing Services: Emily Berleth

Library of Congress Control Number: 2003109929

Copyright © 2004 by Bedford/St. Martin's

All rights reserved. No part of this book may be reproduced, stored in a retrieval system, or transmitted in any form or by any means, electronic, mechanical, photocopying, recording, or otherwise, except as may be expressly permitted by the applicable copyright statutes or in writing by the Publisher.

Manufactured in the United States of America.

5 4 3 2 1 0
l k j

For information, write: Bedford/St. Martin's, 75 Arlington Street, Boston, MA 02116 (617-399-4000)

ISBN-10: 0-312-39505-1
ISBN-13: 978-0-312-39505-6

Acknowledgments

Acknowledgments and copyrights appear at the back of the book on page 200, which constitutes an extension of the copyright page.

Foreword

The Bedford Series in History and Culture is designed so that readers can study the past as historians do.

The historian's first task is finding the evidence. Documents, letters, memoirs, interviews, pictures, movies, novels, or poems can provide facts and clues. Then the historian questions and compares the sources. There is more to do than in a courtroom, for hearsay evidence is welcome, and the historian is usually looking for answers beyond act and motive. Different views of an event may be as important as a single verdict. How a story is told may yield as much information as what it says.

Along the way the historian seeks help from other historians and perhaps from specialists in other disciplines. Finally, it is time to write, to decide on an interpretation and how to arrange the evidence for readers.

Each book in this series contains an important historical document or group of documents, each document a witness from the past and open to interpretation in different ways. The documents are combined with some element of historical narrative—an introduction or a biographical essay, for example—that provides students with an analysis of the primary source material and important background information about the world in which it was produced.

Each book in the series focuses on a specific topic within a specific historical period. Each provides a basis for lively thought and discussion about several aspects of the topic and the historian's role. Each is short enough (and inexpensive enough) to be a reasonable one-week assignment in a college course. Whether as classroom or personal reading, each book in the series provides firsthand experience of the challenge—and fun—of discovering, recreating, and interpreting the past.

Lynn Hunt
David W. Blight
Bonnie G. Smith
Natalie Zemon Davis
Ernest R. May

Preface

Martin Luther King Jr. and Malcolm X were the most effective and lasting voices of the civil rights revolution of the 1950s and 1960s. While King spoke and wrote from a southern, Baptist sermonic tradition, influenced by his extensive theological and philosophical training, Malcolm named the grievances of the dispossessed with an eloquence forged in poverty, hardship, prison, and social alienation. Both were brilliant protest leaders—men of ideas and personal courage who devoted their lives to creating change in America.

King and Malcolm represented distinct wings of the movement they helped to lead. King and the civil rights activists in the South gained national attention in the hard-won struggle to abolish de jure, or legal, discrimination. Malcolm, on the other hand, represented America's northern urban ghettos where de jure racial proscription was less common but where de facto discrimination prevailed, enforced not by law but by social norms and inherited prejudice. While King preached nonviolent resistance, Malcolm stressed blacks' right to self-defense and demanded freedom "by any means necessary."

Their differences, however, do not tell the entire story. Often considered adversaries, King and Malcolm each found the other's presence strategically useful for advancing their own ends in the Civil Rights movement. Living within the same era and struggling against the same prejudices, their leadership and destinies were inevitably entwined. It is important, therefore, to study these leaders in relation to each other. Because King and Malcolm continue to affect people potently and because of the conflicting purposes for which their legacies may be used, it is vital to understand the historical range and depth of their thought and leadership.

The following selection of speeches, essays, and excerpts from Malcolm X's autobiography and King's sermons reveals the range of each man's ideology, demonstrating their differences, similarities, and evolution over time. Organized into six topical chapters—"Formative Influences and Ideas," "Social Ends," "Means of Struggle," "On America," "Critiques of Rival Racial Programs and Philosophies," and "Eras of Convergence"—the documents provide the tools for thoughtful discussion and informed evaluation of some of the central questions King and Malcolm faced, such as the ends of integration or black nationalism and the most effective and acceptable means of struggle by oppressed groups.

This volume offers these documents in an accessible, compact, and readily usable form. The documents can be read alone or together with outside sources. The introduction, document headnotes, and chronology provide background and contextual information, while a list of questions for consideration encourages readers to engage in focused examination of these leaders' words and ideas. A selected bibliography guides readers to further sources on these men and the era they represented.

Although their approaches differed, Martin Luther King Jr. and Malcolm X shared a common weapon: language. Only by studying the words of these two great leaders can we understand their impact on America's continuing struggle to achieve genuine equality under law, in living conditions, and in each individual's spirit.

A NOTE ABOUT THE TEXT

Malcolm inherited the surname Little, but after joining the Nation of Islam, he replaced his "slave name" Little with an X to symbolize his lost African family name. Upon accepting Sunni Islam in 1964, he adopted the name El–Hajj Malik El-Shabazz. As he was and remains far best known as Malcolm X, I customarily use that name for him.

Malcolm produced fewer written texts than King did, which is one reason I frequently cite *The Autobiography of Malcolm X*. Journalist Alex Haley played an important role in producing that book, compiling the manuscript from hundreds of interview sessions he held with Malcolm. While conveying Malcolm's authentic voice, *The Autobiography of Malcolm X* owes its status as a literary classic significantly to Haley's talents—although even more so to its subject's compelling story and personality.

ACKNOWLEDGMENTS

I wish to thank the many people at Bedford/St. Martin's whose labor and expertise were indispensable for producing this volume. I particularly wish to express gratitude to history publisher Patricia Rossi, developmental editor Carina Schoenberger, and editorial advisor David W. Blight for their invaluable help and guidance every step of the way. Thanks also to Marcia Cohen and Emily Berleth, who managed the production of this book; Billy Boardman, who designed the cover; and Sandy Schechter, who managed the permissions. I am grateful as well to professors Lewis V. Baldwin at Vanderbilt University, Clayborne Carson at Stanford University, James H. Cone at Union Theological Seminary, Stephen G. Hall at Ohio State University, Walter A. Jackson at North Carolina State University, and Lee Williams II at University of Alabama in Huntsville for their insightful reviews of the manuscript.

Closer to home, I benefited in my labors from the services of De Anza College research librarian Pauline Yeckley and Kathy Munson in the Inter-Library Loan Division of the Robert De Hart Learning Center. I thank, from the bottom of my heart, all the students, colleagues, staff, and administrators at De Anza College, who make it a wonderful place to work. Thanks and hugs to my wife, Beth, and sons, Christopher and Sean, for putting up with "distant Dad" while I worked on this book.

David Howard-Pitney

Contents

Foreword   v

Preface   vii

LIST OF ILLUSTRATIONS   xv

PART ONE

Introduction: Martin Luther King Jr. and Malcolm X in the African American Freedom Struggle of the 1950s and 1960s   1

PART TWO

The Documents: Words and Themes of Martin Luther King Jr. and Malcolm X   31

1. Formative Influences and Ideas   33
    Martin Luther King Jr.   34
    An Autobiography of Religious Development, 1950   34
    Pilgrimage to Nonviolence, 1960   40

    Malcolm X   46
    From Nightmare to Salvation, 1965   47

2. **Social Ends: Racial Integration versus Separation** — 57

   Martin Luther King Jr. — 58
   The Ethical Demands for Integration, 1963 — 58

   Malcolm X — 67
   From *The Black Revolution*, 1963 — 67
   Independence, Not Separation, 1964 — 70

3. **Means of Struggle: Nonviolent Resistance versus "By Any Means Necessary"** — 73

   Martin Luther King Jr. — 74
   Letter from Birmingham Jail, 1963 — 74
   From *Nonviolence: The Only Road to Freedom*, 1966 — 90

   Malcolm X — 96
   From *The Afro-American's Right to Self-Defense*, 1964 — 96
   From *On Revolution*, 1963 — 99

4. **On America: Dream or Nightmare?** — 102

   Martin Luther King Jr. — 103
   I Have a Dream, 1963 — 103

   Malcolm X — 107
   The White Man Is a Devil: Statements on Whites, 1965 — 108
   From *God's Judgment of White America*, 1963 — 113

5. **Critiques of Rival Racial Programs and Philosophies** — 117

   Martin Luther King Jr. — 118
   Three Responses of Oppressed Groups, 1958 — 118
   On Black Nationalists and Malcolm X, 1965 — 121
   The Nightmare of Violence: Regarding the Death of Malcolm X, 1965 — 124

Malcolm X	**127**
Black Bodies with White Heads! 1965	127
From *Message to the Grassroots,* 1963	128
King Is the White Man's Best Weapon, 1963	134
6. Eras of Convergence	**136**
Martin Luther King Jr.	**137**
From *Beyond Vietnam,* 1967	138
From *Where Do We Go from Here?* 1967	147
Malcolm X	**156**
Press Conference on Return from Africa, 1964	157
Sincere Whites (That Coed Again), 1964	160
I'm Not a Racist, 1964	162
America Can Have a Bloodless Revolution, 1964	164
From *The Ballot or the Bullet,* 1964	165
All of Us Should Be Critics of Each Other, 1964	176
My Voice Helped Save America, 1965	178

APPENDIXES

A Martin Luther King Jr. and Malcolm X Chronology (1925–1968)   180

Questions for Consideration   192

Selected Bibliography   194

Index   201

Illustrations

King in his "second home," the black church, in 1960.	5
King waving to the crowd at the 1963 March on Washington.	7
King mishandled by police during his arrest for loitering outside a courthouse in 1958.	7
Malcolm X speaks at a Harlem civil rights rally in 1963.	11
A quiet, pensive Malcolm in an interview with Alex Haley in 1963.	15
Malcolm's electric persona made him a thrilling figure when he spoke in public.	15

PART ONE

Introduction
Martin Luther King Jr. and Malcolm X in the African American Freedom Struggle of the 1950s and 1960s

THE MEETING

It was news on March 26, 1964, when the nation's preeminent civil rights leader, Martin Luther King Jr., and his harshest black critic, Malcolm X, met for the first time face-to-face. Reporters' surprise was amplified when the two opposing leaders chatted amiably and shook hands. Each had earlier observed some of that day's U.S. Senate debate on what would become the historic 1964 Civil Rights Act, which largely dismantled legal racial segregation and discrimination in the United States. Each was intensely interested in the bill and wished to show support by attending the debate. After observing part of the floor debate and conferring with key senators supporting the bill, Dr. King held a press conference elsewhere in the Capitol building to urge the civil rights bill's passage. Unknown to King and his staff, Malcolm entered the room and took a seat in the back.

After finishing his statement, King, amid a cloud of reporters, began to exit. Meanwhile, Malcolm ducked out a side door, putting himself directly in King's path in the corridor, and extended his hand. "Well, Malcolm, good to see you," King smiled, taking the proffered hand. "Good to see you," Malcolm replied, grinning widely. As reporters begged for pictures, the leaders posed and made pleasant small talk amid rapidly flashing cameras. "Now you're going to get investigated," Malcolm kidded just before they separated. Thus did these two key leaders and symbols of the era's African American freedom struggle briefly meet and part, never (though they had no way of knowing it) to meet again.[1]

The press clamored for pictures that day mainly for the shock effect of capturing a friendly image of two leaders widely thought to embody the opposite ends of their era's surging African American protest. The media was fascinated by Malcolm's contrast with King— especially their markedly different attitudes toward whites. Whereas King and his compatriots fought for the goal of racial integration, Malcolm's Muslims spurned integration with "white devils" and urged separation. African Americans who desired integration, he charged, were ashamed of their race and wished they were white. King urged blacks to resist white racism through nonviolent actions undertaken in a spirit of love. Malcolm mocked nonviolence, deriding it as cowardly. He said it played into the enemy's hands by keeping blacks helpless before white abuse. Malcolm expressed hatred for the white oppressors and openly rejoiced in their coming destruction, which Malcolm's religious group, the Nation of Islam, prophesied. Finally King, while criticizing white Americans' racist acts, enthusiastically endorsed America's highest religious and democratic ideals. Malcolm, on the other hand, considered white Christian America evil to its core and felt whites behaved demonically because they were *made* that way.

During the early sixties, King and Malcolm themselves seem to have seen each other as completely opposed leaders. King had deep misgivings about many of Malcolm's words and views and resented the many slighting remarks that Malcolm had made against the integrationist, nonviolent Civil Rights movement and about him personally. Malcolm had called King, among other things, "a fool," "a chump," "a clown," "a traitor," "a false shepherd," "a Rev. Dr. Chickenwing," and "a twentieth-century religious Uncle Tom."[2]

Martin Luther King and Malcolm X rose to fame amid the new mass African American protest and social movement during the 1950s and 1960s. International trends at mid century, such as decolonization in Africa and Asia and cold war competition between the Soviet Union and the United States for these new nations' support, combined with domestic developments, such as the ongoing migration of African Americans to urban areas and the growing importance of the black vote to national politics, contributed to the U.S. Supreme Court's historic *Brown v. Board of Education of Topeka, Kansas* decision, which outlawed legal racial segregation in public education (even though it initially continued unabated).

Subsequent events, including a black bus boycott in Montgomery, Alabama, which King helped lead and which ended segregated seating on the city's buses, set in motion the Civil Rights movement, a rising tide of social activism and protest among blacks that began in the South and spread across the nation. Civil rights demonstrations and violent racist resistance rocked the South and challenged the nation's conscience. For more than a decade, many thousands of African Americans determinedly marched, demonstrated, broke discriminatory laws, willingly went to jail, and otherwise challenged racist systems and practices and militantly pushed for change.

The southern movement's dramatic victories for civil and political equality raised expectations for improvement among African Americans everywhere; but the oppressive realities of black ghetto life—slums, unemployment, substandard education, and substantial, if not necessarily legally enforced, segregation—were untouched and worsening. The denied expectations of black ghetto dwellers began exploding in outbursts of rage and violence directed at white-owned property in America's urban cores from 1964 to 1968. The African American mass revolt and rising impatience and anger at white racist treatment was the hurricane both King and Malcolm rode and tried to guide. King worked to channel blacks' explosive discontent into nonviolent campaigns for social reform while Malcolm tried to turn black people's dissatisfaction with whites into support for, first, the Nation of Islam and, later, Malcolm's more general secular brand of black nationalism.

KING'S BACKGROUND AND RISE

Martin Luther King Jr. was born in Atlanta, Georgia, on January 15, 1929, into a prominent middle-class family. Both his maternal grandfather, A. D. Williams, and his father, Martin Luther King Sr., pastored the upscale Ebenezer Baptist Church and were prominent in their denomination's largest organization, the National Baptist Convention, making young King a virtual prince of the black church. King's upbringing was materially secure and anchored in strong African American institutions of family, church, and community. King benefited from an extensive higher education, first from 1944 to 1948 at Morehouse College, a black institution in Atlanta. From 1948 to 1951, he attended Pennsylvania's predominantly white Crozer Seminary, then Boston University from 1951 to 1953, where he earned a Ph.D. in philosophy. As a student King studied, besides the Bible, theories for social change advanced by such thinkers as socialist Karl Marx and Mohandas Gandhi, the Indian independence leader and proponent of nonviolent civil disobedience as a tool for social-political change.[3]

In 1954, at age twenty-six, Martin Luther King became pastor of Dexter Avenue Baptist Church in Montgomery, Alabama. This was the year of the *Brown* decision and the bus boycott in Montgomery, which began when Rosa Parks refused to give her seat to a white person. King's work in the Montgomery movement was an extension of earlier black activism by persons such as labor leader E. D. Nixon of the Brotherhood of Sleeping Car Porters and Maids and Jo Anne Robinson of the Women's Political Council. During the boycott, King, partly at Nixon's instigation, became president of the organization heading the boycott, the Montgomery Improvement Association. In this position, in the glare of national and international publicity, King swiftly emerged as the movement's most compelling and articulate figure.[4] After a yearlong struggle often marred by white segregationist violence that received national and international media coverage, Montgomery's bus lines were reopened on a nondiscriminatory basis.

In 1957, King and other African American leaders, mostly ministers, founded the Atlanta-based Southern Christian Leadership Conference (SCLC) to mount and coordinate civil rights activities using mass nonviolent actions and civil disobedience across the South. King headed the SCLC the rest of his life. He also became co-pastor with his father of Ebenezer Baptist Church in Atlanta. For a crushingly busy decade or so, King traveled and spoke extensively around the country, drumming up support for African Americans' equal rights cause and raising large sums of money for the SCLC and other civil rights groups. In mass protest campaigns, King constantly risked prison, injury, and death as he helped lead the swelling American social movement against racial discrimination and inequality.

King in his "second home," the black church, in 1960.
Donald Uhrbrock/Time Life Pictures/Getty Images.

KING'S ROLE IN THE MOVEMENT

King not only led many specific civil disobedience campaigns, but he also served as the movement's foremost strategist, theorist, interpreter, and symbol maker. His charismatic leadership and inspirational oratory helped create black unity and resolve to keep demonstrating, often amid danger and adversity. Equally crucially, King became the movement's chief interpreter to white Americans. Television was still a novelty in the 1950s and early 1960s, and King proved adept at its use for affecting social opinion and bringing about change. By artfully presenting local civil rights campaigns to distant third parties through the media, King and others could leverage sympathetic outside opinion to increase pressure against local segregation forces. From the mid fifties to early sixties, King, more than any other single person, led many Americans to view the peaceful black Civil Rights movement as morally right (he explicitly defined it as Christian and democratic) and consonant with America's highest ideals of freedom and equality.[5]

MALCOLM'S RISE AND INFLUENCE

As Americans by the early 1960s were newly focusing on the Civil Rights movement and especially on King's moral demands and peaceful means of achieving them, they began to hear a far more alarming voice of black discontent, that of extreme black nationalism as articulated by the Nation of Islam's fiery national spokesman, Malcolm X.

The leader that made Americans so uneasy was born Malcolm Little to Earl and Louise Little in 1925 in Omaha, Nebraska. His father was economically self-sufficient and, among other things, an itinerant Baptist preacher. He was also an organizer for Marcus Garvey's black nationalist organization, the Universal Negro Improvement Association (UNIA), which stressed black pride and independence, separation from whites, and an internationalist Pan-African identity among blacks everywhere. For Earl's Garveyite preaching and recruiting activities, the Little family was repeatedly harassed by the Ku Klux Klan and other white supremacist groups. Their house in Lansing, Michigan, was burned down when Malcolm was four years old, and his father was murdered in what was made to look like a streetcar accident when Malcolm was six.[6]

Malcolm lived with his widowed mother and numerous siblings, who barely managed to scrape by during the Great Depression of the 1930s. The Littles eventually had to go on public relief. Louise, a proud

King triumphant (*right*): waving to the crowd at the 1963 March on Washington.

Hulton Archive/Getty Images.

In the valley of struggle (*below*): King mishandled by police during his arrest for loitering outside a courthouse in 1958.

Charles Moore/Black Star/Timepix.

woman, gradually deteriorated mentally, her descent speeded, Malcolm always believed, by intrusive white welfare workers' belittling behavior. After a nervous breakdown, Louise was committed to Michigan's state mental hospital in 1939. Malcolm and the other children, now wards of the state, were separated. Malcolm lived in white foster homes and attended predominantly white public schools until finishing eighth grade, which was the end of his formal education. At about fifteen, he moved in with his sister Ella in Boston, where he gradually descended into a life of urban crime and vice. During his criminal years, living primarily in Boston, Detroit, and Harlem, Malcolm was a predatory hustler who pimped, peddled illicit drugs and alcohol, ran gambling, and generally did anything he could to gain money or advantage. He survived by his wits in this harsh social jungle until imprisoned for burglary between 1946 and 1952.

MALCOLM'S CONVERSION TO THE NATION OF ISLAM

While serving time in prison, Malcolm discovered the Nation of Islam (NOI). The NOI originated in Detroit in the 1930s under W. D. Fard, then was reconstituted and newly based in Chicago during the 1940s under Elijah Muhammad. The Nation had emerged as a splinter group from the Moorish Science Temple led by Noble Drew Ali, and both movements reflected the interests in Eastern mysticism, Islam, Pan-Africanism, and Garveyism among many migrants from the South. The NOI most potently appealed to lower-class, urban African Americans, especially migrants from the South who had been sorely disappointed by the northern "promised land" and found themselves trapped in racial ghettos with little hope of social-economic advancement.

Mr. Muhammad taught his followers that their race was "original man" with Asiatic roots and that Islam was the black man's "natural" religion. Once, he taught, the world was under black original man's happy rule, but whites (mutants created by a mad scientist) had succeeded over eons in overturning this black Muslim golden age and instituting white Christian imperialism's rule. Now Allah, through his divine messenger Elijah Muhammad, was calling his black chosen people in North America, long blind to their own and whites' true natures, back to their Islamic identity. Fast approaching was the final judgment day when Allah would destroy white society and restore righteous Muslim world rule. Indeed, the giant spaceship from which Allah would launch white Christians' annihilation was already hidden in the air, ready to strike. In view of all this, African Americans should isolate themselves from the white devils, both in order to purify themselves to fulfill their divine mission *and* to escape the holocaust about to descend on whites.

Two precepts at the heart of this black nationalist doomsday sect were pride in black racial identity and culture and identification of whites as the demonic cause of blacks'—and the entire nonwhite world's—woes. The Nation's assertion of black divinity and white devilry reversed dominant white society's notion of white and black persons' worth. On the more practical level, the NOI demanded that followers adhere to a strict moral standard, avoiding all drugs, pork, and sexual immoralities, and stressed the need to build independent black social institutions and businesses. Its ultimate social goal was separation from whites in order to achieve independent black nationhood.[7] This was the fundamental NOI gospel Malcolm so zealously and effectively spread, first as a prison inmate, then, following his 1952 parole, in general society.

Becoming an NOI minister in 1953, Malcolm was utterly devoted to this nationalist religious group and its leader, Elijah Muhammad, whom he, like other NOI members, considered Allah incarnate. Even before converting, Malcolm had begun improving himself educationally by taking correspondence courses in writing and Latin, for example, and by reading widely in the prison library. After joining the NOI, he accelerated his heavy reading and continued improving his language and reasoning skills, mainly toward the end of better serving Mr. Muhammad. He followed the NOI's custom and replaced his "slave name," Little, with an X to symbolize his ancestors' lost African name. Malcolm's personal dynamism and ready familiarity with ghetto ways made his evangelism among members of the black urban underclass spectacularly successful. Besides winning many individual converts, Malcolm started many new NOI temples in major cities. Malcolm's charismatic presence and electrifying speeches and his utter devotion to the NOI quickly established him as Muhammad's most valuable disciple.[8]

MALCOLM'S PSYCHOLOGICAL AND CULTURAL IMPACT

It was as the Nation of Islam's national spokesman in the early sixties that Malcolm first came to national notoriety. He was on countless TV and radio shows and gave many interviews and speeches defending his group and leader's views. He was a master debater whose sharp tongue, magnetic personality, and astounding mental agility soon made most people in the Civil Rights movement reluctant to appear with him. He was one of the nation's most sought-after speakers.

Malcolm's attitude toward whites was unremittingly alienated, angry, and hostile, sharply contrasting with that of King and the (mainly) nonviolent southern movement. America, indeed the whole white race, according to Malcolm, was by nature irredeemably evil. The black masses were turning away from the delusional goals of racial integration and civil rights to the NOI's answer of complete separation from the white oppressors. If King delivered a challenging message of "tough love" to his white countrymen, Malcolm's harsh diatribes against whites were unalloyed (until very late) with any prospect for white redemption or interracial reconciliation. For African Americans to *love* those who had for centuries committed unspeakable crimes against them would be abnormal human behavior—indeed, would be outright insane. Does the lamb love the wolf devouring it? he asked rhetorically; does a person being raped love the rapist? Malcolm's answer was obvious, his logic hard to question.

Malcolm had a strongly positive psychological impact on many non-NOI African Americans, even while still delivering the straight NOI gospel. His obvious pride in himself and his people and in the worthiness of black culture proved powerfully attractive to people whose self-esteem had been damaged by the pervasive contempt for blackness promulgated by the surrounding white racist society.

Part of Malcolm's allure for African Americans, too, was his daredevil swagger and bristling, defiant manner before whites. Many non-NOI blacks (particularly, but not just ghetto residents) admired his courage and got a vicarious thrill watching him fearlessly denounce whites for their depravity. Many were gratified when hearing him forcefully, brilliantly articulate the bitter resentments and rage that most African Americans felt on some level toward whites but were too afraid or politic to express—and from seeing the visible discomfort and alarm register on the faces of his shocked white listeners.

A master propagandist, Malcolm had a genius for making even those cultic beliefs that struck most outsiders as bizarre sound reasonable and have the ring of truth. Malcolm drew on his vast reading for social-historical facts about slavery and lynching to build a virtually undeniable case about the evil of whites and their conduct toward blacks. Even many mainstream civil rights activists, who adamantly disagreed with him about the problem's solution, basically agreed with

Malcolm X, fiery orator, bristling with indignation, speaks at a Harlem civil rights rally in 1963.
Bettmann/CORBIS.

his diagnosis of the chief problem facing African Americans: whites' evil racism.

MALCOLM'S REORIENTATION

Even while advocating the NOI, however, Malcolm began to chafe under Elijah Muhammad's strict prohibitions against his followers engaging in any protests against white authorities. By 1963, Malcolm wished seriously to engage in the cresting Civil Rights movement, but, despite the NOI's denunciations of whites, like many sectarian groups, it instructed believers to withdraw from, not engage with, the larger society. It was for Allah, not *them,* to take vengeance on the white race.

Jealousy over Malcolm's celebrity and concern about his potential for independent power began to grow within Muhammad's Chicago-based inner circle. Malcolm's relationship with the NOI was further strained when Malcolm heard reports that Muhammad himself had been breaking the NOI's strict moral code by having children by several young women. Following the assassination of John F. Kennedy in November 1963, Muhammad used the opportunity to silence Malcolm, saying that the minister's remark that the incident was evidence of "chickens coming home to roost" violated Muhammad's instructions not to speak ill of the slain president.

While under official NOI discipline, Malcolm traveled abroad to Africa and the Middle East, which broadened his perspective on his faith and on the international struggle of darker peoples. In 1964, Malcolm made a hajj, the Muslim pilgrimage to the holy city of Mecca. There he was moved by the sight of Muslims of all colors from many nations meeting in common devotion to Allah. During this period of profound religious and ideological reorientation, Malcolm converted to orthodox Sunni Islam. Just weeks before shaking hands with King at the U.S. Capitol (see front cover photograph), Malcolm publicly broke with Elijah Muhammad's Nation of Islam.

Founding Muslim Mosque, Inc. (later replaced by the Organization of Afro-American Unity), Malcolm announced his intent to form a nonsectarian black nationalist movement aimed at heightening political consciousness and activity among African Americans. Malcolm's new program included supporting the activities of the southern Civil Rights movement—aligning himself especially with local grassroots activists and the movement's more militant groups such as SNCC, the Student Nonviolent Coordinating Committee.

MALCOLM REACHES OUT TO THE CIVIL RIGHTS MOVEMENT

Malcolm's conversion to true Islam, his rejection of the NOI tenets of white devilry and black divinity, and his desire to be more politically active all figured into his decision to go to the Capitol and seek out King. Their encounter, he hoped, would convey and symbolize his new support for mainstream black protest and willingness to cooperate with all forces sincerely working for black people's liberation.

Though still voicing important differences with King and other moderate and conservative black civil rights leaders, in his last year or so Malcolm ceased his former ferocious verbal assaults on the leaders of the national civil rights organizations. He announced his willingness to join with all African American groups seeking to better blacks' conditions. Although Malcolm continued to spurn integration as a goal, he was even willing to join other African Americans in protesting segregation, he now announced, since it was imposed on blacks by whites rather than voluntarily chosen.

During King-led civil disobedience campaigns in 1964 and 1965, Malcolm offered to provide armed defense for the black activists against the violent racist repression they faced. On June 30, 1964, Malcolm sent King a telegram in St. Augustine, Florida, which read:

> If the Federal Government will not send troops to your aid, just say the word and we will immediately dispatch some of our brothers there to organize self defense units among our people, and the Ku Klux Klan will then receive a taste of its own medicine.

Malcolm made similar remarks during the subsequent campaign in Selma, Alabama, stating that "if I were there with King and I saw someone knocking on him, I'd come to his rescue."[9]

After the 1964 Civil Rights Act substantially ended legal segregation, King and the movement's next main objective became securing voting rights. Malcolm publicly endorsed this goal, too, the centerpiece of King and the SCLC's 1965 campaign in Selma. Unable to resist being near the action, Malcolm surprised King and the SCLC by visiting Selma during the campaign, having received an invitation from SNCC members to speak there. While declaring himself in favor of the Selma civil rights forces' voting rights goal, Malcolm pointedly still refused to commit to nonviolence.

King and most of his SCLC colleagues were displeased by Malcolm's unexpected Selma appearance. Nevertheless, after his talk,

Malcolm had a few words with King's wife and fellow activist, Coretta Scott King. He told her:

> I want Dr. King to know that I didn't come to Selma to make his job difficult. I really did come thinking that I could make it easier. If the white people realize what the alternative is, perhaps they will be more willing to hear Dr. King.

Mrs. King said he stressed that he wanted "to work with Dr. King, and not against him."[10] She also recalls that King deeply appreciated Malcolm's relayed message. Yet, as of the time of the Selma protest, King still considered Malcolm's leadership (especially talk about violence) irresponsible and incendiary and would not let Malcolm participate in any public action in which King took part.

TOWARD ANOTHER MEETING?

Nonetheless, Malcolm's continual attempts to offer the olive branch—combined with an important shift in King and the SCLC's objectives following Selma—may have been leading them toward some kind of accord. Both leaders could sense the growing momentum of the mass revolt among African Americans, and the anger and militance percolating up from the bottom compelled them to alter some of their earlier positions. Malcolm was forced to recognize that the mostly nonviolent mass movement in the South had changed the American legal and political order and created much greater opportunity for his kind of nationalist politics. King had to respond to the grassroots approach of SNCC, to the desire of younger blacks for greater solidarity and identification with Africa, and to uprisings by poor blacks in northern ghettos. By the mid sixties such trends were starting to push Malcolm and King in similar directions.

King's top goal after Selma was to address inner-city poverty. The SCLC knew that if King's antislum crusade ever reached Malcolm's turf in New York, their efforts could benefit enormously from Malcolm's rapport with Harlem's black poor. This strategic consideration and the "new" Malcolm's oft-stated wish to join in civil rights demonstrations were nudging the two nearer—but not enough time remained to see how this process would play out. Some of Malcolm and King's common influential acquaintances and supporters in New York, such as the writer James Baldwin, actor Ossie Davis, and lawyer Clarence B. Jones, believed that some type of upcoming cooperative relation between them was likely. During Malcolm's final days, both

A quiet, pensive Malcolm (*right*) in an interview with Alex Haley in 1963.

Reproduced by special permission of *Playboy* magazine. Copyright © 1963 by *Playboy*. From the "*Playboy* Interview: Malcolm X" with Alex Haley (May 1963).

Malcolm's electric persona (*below*) made him a thrilling figure when he spoke in public.

Reproduced by permission of O'Neal L. Abel.

camps were sending out feelers about arranging a meeting between the two men sometime soon in New York City. King and Malcolm had spoken by phone about it. But on February 21, 1965, just two days before a scheduled meeting for exploring collaborative possibilities between them, assassins' bullets cut down Malcolm.[11]

Malcolm's inability to complete his attempted transition from a public moralist-commentator to an effective political leader in no way diminishes his gigantic cultural contributions and impact. Malcolm's true genius, his biographer Peter Goldman notes, was as an artist of the spoken word. He was an inspirational cultural-psychological revivalist who aimed to convert souls and minds as much as to make or overthrow kingdoms. Malcolm believed that until an interior change, until the "decolonization of the black mind" occurred, external acts to change the world could never materialize. Mental liberation had to precede social liberation. Consequently his greatest success lay in his ability, through his inspiring personal example and moving words, to awaken a proud new consciousness of color in African Americans. Civil rights strategist Bayard Rustin insightfully remarked that, in the final analysis, Malcolm's accomplishments must

> be seen over and above...the struggle for concrete objectives. King has to be measured by his victories. But what King did, what the NAACP did, what the March on Washington did...all that was for the benefit of the Southern Negro. There were no obtainable, immediate results for the Northern ghettoized black, whose house is getting worse; who is unable to find work; whose schools are deteriorating; who sees constantly more rats and roaches and more garbage in the streets. He, because he is human, must find victory somewhere, and he finds his victory within. He needed Malcolm, who brought him an internal victory, precisely because the external victory was beyond his reach. What can bring satisfaction is the feeling that he is a man, he is internally free. King had to win victories in the real world. Malcolm's were the kind you can create yourself.[12]

KING AND MALCOLM: BEYOND MERE DUALISM

How can these great leaders of the modern African American freedom struggle—and their relation to each other—be most accurately understood? When the two were first well known together in the early 1960s, they were viewed by virtually everyone—by supporters and detractors, by the vast majority of whites, by most blacks, and by themselves—as ideological nemeses and antagonists on all important questions involving race in America. This view of King and Malcolm as exact opposites continues to have many adherents today (certainly in white-dominated "mainstream" opinion, considerably less so among African Americans).[13] The dualistic view portrays them as "adversaries in a great Manichaean [cosmic] contest," one scholar writes, pitting "the forces of light against the forces of darkness, with the future course of black protest at stake."[14]

There are reasons, some good, for the predominant dualistic image of King and Malcolm. Strongest is that, through most of their careers, Rev. King and Minister Malcolm had very substantial disagreements. A partial list of their areas of major dispute includes: the goals of interracial integration versus black separatism, using only nonviolent means of struggle versus seeking freedom "by any means necessary," and commitments to Christianity versus Islam. In these and other key areas large gaps separated their positions, especially early on, some of which persisted even in their late periods, when their political ideologies began to grow closer.

A second reason for their portrayal as opposites—chiefly, then and now, created and perpetuated by the white-controlled media—resides in widespread white phobias about blacks' feelings toward whites. Part of slavery's psychological inheritance in America is whites' (sometimes repressed) guilty knowledge that their kind has done abominable things to African Americans. This knowledge makes many whites fearful that blacks hate them and wish to take revenge on them. Alternately, whites yearn to believe that, notwithstanding past and present oppression, blacks forgive and accept them. Viewed through the lens of white racial guilt and phobias, King and Malcolm appear as symbols of these two opposite black responses toward whites, Malcolm representing an avenging angel, spewing hatred, and King a saintly figure who would lovingly correct and forgive whites.

In background and temperament, the two men were quite dissimilar. King was a moderate consensus builder, both within the often conflicting opinions of civil rights forces and with white opinion and power holders. Malcolm, by inclination and purposeful design, was more often a polarizing firebrand given to burning bridges with opponents by vehemently denouncing and scorning those whom he considered black people's enemies (chiefly middle-class integrationist blacks and all whites).

Sociologically, too, Martin and Malcolm were quite dissimilar—other than both being black men in white supremacist America. King was born comfortably middle-class and received exceptional educational opportunities, whereas Malcolm came from a poor broken home, then lived as a semi-illiterate criminal and prisoner before commencing his life's reformation. King was the kind of respectable bourgeois Negro for whom Malcolm always had contempt; Martin and his wife Coretta regarded the NOI teachings spouted by Malcolm as bizarre and "so different from our thinking."[15]

Another reason the dualistic vision of these men's relationship still circulates is that too little focus tends to be given to each leader's most advanced, latest thinking. Too many commentators dwell almost exclusively on the men's early careers in the 1950s and early 1960s, when they functioned mainly as foils to each other. After Malcolm's acceptance of true Islam and departure from the NOI, he began to favor blacks pursuing traditional civil rights goals of desegregation and voting rights, and he no longer *automatically* defined whites as unchangeably evil. In his own last years, circa 1966–68, King nearly as dramatically revised his own views on such things as the nature and tenacity of white racism, which was far deeper and harder to remove than he had earlier imagined, and on the extent of the many systematic changes that needed to be made in U.S. society to eradicate racism and remedy its damage. As far as the dominant collective memory of King goes, however, he might as well have died in 1963 as in 1968.

As King widened his view of the structural evils plaguing American society by stressing the evils of poverty and imperialism and went beyond civil rights in identifying their solution, he moved rapidly toward views and rhetoric more associated with Malcolm than himself. King and Malcolm's late agreement on civil rights; concern for the urban poor; and opposition to racism, capitalism, and imperialism were broadly parallel. After 1965, voicing ever stronger criticisms of U.S. domestic and foreign policy, King's popularity declined sharply, and he was increasingly seen by whites as an unpatriotic rabble-rouser. As King's critique of American society grew unmistakably more radical, his tone also turned harsher and more pessimistic. Journalist David Halberstam, who covered King in 1967, wrote that by that year King sounded "like a nonviolent Malcolm X."[16] A widespread tendency to ignore or minimize the later "moderate Malcolm" and "militant Martin" remains a major reason for the common misrepresentation of them as total opposites.

UNDERLYING SIMILARITIES

Throughout their careers, Martin Luther King and Malcolm X had both great differences and important similarities. They shared roles as inspirational leaders of black struggle. They both loved their people and were committed to realizing African Americans' full freedom. They both battled against vicious racist oppression and urged blacks to defend their rights and confront their oppressors. Both indicted white racism and demanded its end. As Malcolm put it late in his career, really "King and I have nothing to debate about. We are both indicting. I would say to him: You indict and give them hope. I'll indict and give them no hope."[17] At the most fundamental level, King and Malcolm were fellow freedom fighters in the cause of African American liberation.

By 1964, Malcolm claimed that his remaining disagreements with traditional civil rights leaders and organizations were not over the final end but over the best way of achieving it, claiming that the goal of all the forces of black resistance was not necessarily either integration or separatism, but African Americans' full freedom and dignity. While King, of course, always advocated nonviolent struggle as the best tool of resistance, he also consistently held that the *most* immoral response to injustice was failing to resist it—in other words, even hateful, violent resistance was preferable to no resistance at all.[18] Without doubt, King and Malcolm stood resolutely together in calling for black resistance to racial oppression.

James Cone and Lewis Baldwin make the scholarly case as well as any for King and Malcolm's crucial similarities. In *Martin & Malcolm & America,* Cone holds that the two men "complemented and corrected each other." For Cone, "they were like two soldiers fighting their enemies from different angles of vision, each pointing out the other's blind spots and correcting the other's errors." Far from harming the effectiveness of each other's activities, he asserts, "they needed each other, for they represented—and continue to represent—the 'yin and yang' deep in the soul of black America." Baldwin writes equally perceptively about "the King/Malcolm dialectic" that was healthy ultimately for them, the black freedom struggle, and America. "Despite their many differences," Baldwin stresses, "they *needed* each other, *learned* from each other, and helped *make* each other."[19]

King and Malcolm themselves understood the "good cop/bad cop" aspect of their relation. They grasped the value to civil rights forces of having the "scary" nationalists around to point to as the alternative if whites refused to deal forthrightly with more reasonable, "responsible Negro leaders." King often made references to the NOI and nationalists with the implied threat that blacks might turn to such philosophies if the nonviolent movement's demands for change were not met. Characteristically, Malcolm put it most bluntly (while seeking some acknowledgment of his contribution to King's success): He and the NOI, he claimed, had "made the whole civil rights movement become more militant, and more acceptable to the white power structure. The white man would rather have them than us."[20]

Cone states that, although King and Malcolm represented two distinct historic streams of black social assertion in America—integrationism and nationalism—each figure was influenced to some degree by both traditions, arguing that "no black thinker has been a pure integrationist or nationalist, but rather all black intellectuals have represented aspects of each." Clayborne Carson likewise rejects the "false dichotomy" of nationalism versus integrationism as "inadequate terms to describe the vast range of political insights" developed by blacks in the struggle. Carson also argues that debates over the use of violence "are unproductive without a recognition that all effective political movements combine elements of persuasion and coercion."[21] Cone, Carson, Baldwin, and other leading black scholars tend to hold that King's and Malcolm's approaches, at once sharply different yet integrally related, together formed a whole and effective African American freedom struggle.

Another basic similarity is that both King and Malcolm were religious leaders and deeply spiritual men. Raised in religiously devout social-activist families, each responded first to a religious calling from which their larger public leadership and significance emerged. Each came to the fore voicing essentially a theology of liberation. Each spoke prophetically what they believed was God's word against social injustice. A positive trend in the study of these two men is deepening awareness of just how elementary religion was to their personal lives and public leadership.[22]

Further, even though King and Malcolm belonged to different religious communities, their versions of their faiths shared one key trait: they embraced socially and politically active forms of their religion. Genuine religion, for them, necessarily involved every aspect of life and had to serve people's everyday needs. King often stated his belief that the Christian gospel deals with the whole man, not only his soul but his body, not only his spiritual well-being, but his material well-being. Any religion that professes to be concerned about the souls of men and is not concerned about the slums that damn them ... and the social conditions that cripple them is a spiritually moribund religion awaiting burial.

Malcolm likewise declared that his understanding of religion was not limited "just to praying and things of that sort, but my concept of religion included every aspect of one's life—economic, political, social."[23]

Similarities between Malcolm and King are most striking when viewing their respective late eras (Malcolm's in 1964–65, King's in 1965–68), when the two shared commitments to the poor and opposition to racism, capitalism, and imperialism.

But has scholarship on these leaders, then, gone from presenting an image of them as polar opposites to portraying them as virtual identical twins? Not at all. The writers of what one might call the "convergence school" on King and Malcolm do not fail to note their many real, often very substantial differences.[24] Rather, these writers simply assert that these leaders' significance should, in the end, be defined more by their commonalities than by their differences.

Indeed, in evaluating King and Malcolm's relation one must acknowledge that significant clashes of opinion continued between them, even during their most compatible phases. When journalist David Halberstam told King in 1967 that he "sounded like a nonviolent Malcolm X," King disagreed, saying that he could "never go along with black separatism."[25] King's disagreement underscores the centrality to their differences of Malcolm's overriding commitment to black nationalism, which diminished little, if at all, to the end.

Equally perceptive was Halberstam's qualifying adjective in stating that the radical King sounded like a *"nonviolent"* Malcolm, for the issue of physical force's place in the African American freedom struggle was the greatest single issue on which neither man ever moved significantly in the other's direction. Malcolm remained adamant about black people's absolute right to self-defense and to wage their freedom struggle "by any means necessary." Even if he did hedge slightly in his new moderate image by suggesting that retributive violence *might* conceivably prove unnecessary, Malcolm never wavered in asserting the simple intelligence, in any event, of being seen as ready and willing to use it. For his part, King likewise never retreated from his unconditional commitment, morally and tactically, to nonviolence.

It is difficult to see how this impasse between King and Malcolm on violence's role in the liberation movement could ever have been bridged. At the time of his death, Malcolm's refusal to reject the possibility of physical retaliation during demonstrations still kept King from permitting Malcolm to participate in any event in which King took part. Peter Goldman and James Cone are among those writers who doubt that King and Malcolm would have ever actually allied. Of course, it is possible that one or both of them might yet have gone on to revise significantly their positions on that contentious issue. Even if no such compromise ever occurred, they could conceivably have found a way to agree to disagree on that and still explore areas for cooperation, particularly in inner-city settings. It must be remembered that each side was taking steps toward opening a dialogue between the leaders to explore just such possibilities. It looked like Malcolm's overtures to King, which started with that brief handshake in the Capitol, were finally about to pay off—at least as far as getting a substantial audience with King. But then, two days before they were scheduled finally to meet again, Malcolm was tragically cut down in a hail of bullets, leaving everyone afterward with only tantalizing "what ifs" and irresolvable conjecture about the future course of these great leaders' relations.[26]

KING AND MALCOLM IN AMERICAN MYTH AND MEMORY

The impact of Martin Luther King's and Malcolm X's work did not end with their lives, for they have achieved mythic status and their images carry enormous symbolic weight. As Lewis Baldwin notes:

> Throughout black America, streets, parks, schools, libraries, community centers, public housing developments, social service and cultural centers, and works of art bear their names. Their pictures hang on the walls of countless homes . . . lines from their speeches are included in rap and gospel lyrics, [and] their names and words are marketed . . . and branded on hats and T-shirts.[27]

Although white Americans show considerably more confusion and ambiguous attitudes toward these men and their legacies, large segments of the white public also accept one or both of them as heroic. Both leaders' images appear on commemorative U.S. postage stamps. When King's birthday became a national holiday in 1983, he joined

George Washington, Thomas Jefferson, and Abraham Lincoln as the only Americans so honored. Despite a few extreme conservatives who insist that King was a Communist stooge, or agent, or a moral reprobate undeserving of public esteem,[28] King's stature as a heroic icon is nearly as universal among whites as blacks. Groups as diverse as feminists, gay rights activists, peace forces, the pro-life movement, and affirmative action's friends and foes all regularly invoke King to support their causes. Although among African Americans Malcolm is as revered as King, Malcolm's iconic stature among whites is far less universal, as many whites still see Malcolm as a ranting, crazed white-hater.

Despite King's greater overall popularity, Malcolm has made the greatest mark on recent popular culture and entertainment. Perhaps this is because he can be more readily reduced to a mere attitude, or "edgy" image, attractive to youth and suitable for selling consumer goods. From the late 1980s through the mid 1990s, there was an explosion of Malcolm-mania in what has been variously termed his "cultural renaissance" and "second coming." Interest in Malcolm surged in such areas as black hip-hop culture, rap music, and clothing fashion. Baseball hats, clothes, book packs, and even hairdos were emblazoned with the ubiquitous "X," and film director Spike Lee shot a major Hollywood movie version of Malcolm's life.[29]

While King became a powerful social symbol during his lifetime, Malcolm's apotheosis occurred overwhelmingly after his death in early 1965—particularly some months later with publication of his powerful and highly acclaimed *Autobiography*. Cowriter Alex Haley's literary skill and adept editing enhanced the text's power while preserving the authenticity of Malcolm's voice, ideas, and personality. Malcolm's death and the book's appearance coincided with the urban racial explosions that Malcolm had predicted, giving his words added prophetic quality. His posthumous celebrity dovetailed with the rise of "Black Power" and black nationalism's growing popularity among African Americans in the late sixties. His autobiography's great popularity thus set off a scramble by various black (even white) groups to claim him as one of their own. Because he spoke so widely and evolved so much politically and ideologically, groups as varied as revolutionary nationalists, middle-of-the-road integrationists, radical socialists, and capitalist conservatives could all quote him selectively and purportedly show that the "real" Malcolm endorsed their ideas and programs.

The popular images of mythic figures typically get flattened and drained of living complexity. Symbols can be simplified and distorted to serve any number of purposes. Whether it stems from wishful thinking, ignorance, or willful distortion, different parties shape and present icons differently to further their agendas. The fate of Malcolm X and Martin Luther King in contemporary society has been widespread social appropriation and distortion of their words and work.

Since King's stature is greatest in the general society, political-ideological struggles to define King and his legacy are most common in contemporary America. King was actually well to the left politically—somewhere in the vicinity of an American liberal or Western European social democrat. The views of contemporary African American progressives such as Jesse Jackson, Michael Eric Dyson, Vincent Harding, and Lewis Baldwin, therefore, probably most closely approximate King's own views.

Longtime social-political activist Rev. Jesse L. Jackson, as much as any public figure, uses the mythic memory of Martin Luther King to legitimize his ongoing political agenda. Jackson, who worked with King in the SCLC, consistently links his own long-term goal of having the U.S. government advance economic rights to King's final call for a National Poor People's Campaign and related (mainly economic) "Revolution of Values." Jackson teaches that America's unfinished business is "the struggle to provide shared economic security" for all; it is to complete "the movement begun by Dr. King just before his death."[30]

In academia, historian Vincent Harding (another King SCLC colleague) has long advanced the thesis that it is the late radical King whose prophetic voice speaks most meaningfully to contemporary America's challenges. The greatest obstacle to understanding the meaning of King's leadership, he argues, "is our apparent determination to forget—or ignore—the last years of his life." America suffers from severe selective amnesia (partly innocent, partly willful) about King. The post-1965 King is the "inconvenient hero," Harding claims, whom most Americans would prefer (and pretend) never existed. Ironically, King's magnificent "I Have a Dream" oration at the March on Washington has imprisoned King, in the nation's dominant image and memory, as he existed in 1963. The "unremitting focus" and "never-ending repetition" of that speech, Harding laments, has boxed King "into the relatively safe categories of 'Civil Rights leader,' 'great orator,' [and] harmless dreamer of black and white children [holding hands] on the hillside."[31] Powerful parties prefer to promote this mild, unchallenging hero over the mature *inconvenient* King who challenged more than celebrated society and disturbed more than soothed its conscience. It is as though King, in memory, has suffered a second assassination—that of his last five years.

A similar interpretation of King comes from black cultural critic Michael Eric Dyson. His book's title—*I May Not Get There with You: The True Martin Luther King Jr.*—takes a line from King's final speech. Dyson's "true" King, like Harding's, is the mature later leader who was a radical critic of U.S. domestic injustice and global militarism. Dyson, too, sees harm done to our understanding of King, and to society's uses of him, by the repression of this most relevant King in our collective memory. Dyson energetically takes on those whom he thinks have distorted King's legacy, including both his most unfairly critical detractors and his extreme venerators, who want nothing unflattering about him, such as his marital infidelity and plagiarism on some student papers, ever acknowledged.[32]

But it is "the misappropriations of King's words" by political conservatives which draws Dyson's heaviest fire. By being represented as *the* definitive statement of his ideas, King's "I Have a Dream" speech, Dyson claims, has actually become a hindrance to apprehending the totality of his thought. So successful has been the speech's abuse and overuse by conservatives who opposed nearly all that the real King fought for, that Dyson (only half seriously) proposes "a ten-year moratorium on listening to or reading 'I Have a Dream'" to correct the imbalance. The "great consolation" in temporarily giving up this famed speech, Dyson suggests, would be that people might pay greater attention to King's many other, relatively neglected, statements, "especially his trenchant later speeches."[33]

Outside academia, progressives have had far less success shaping the image of a man who was, after all, one of their own. Rather, American conservatives have most energetically and ingeniously cited King's authority in the general culture on their side in such contemporary policy debates as Affirmative Action. Affirmative Action (AA) is the term for public policies giving nonwhites and women favorable consideration in such areas as hiring, college admissions, and receiving government contracts to compensate for societal discrimination. Conservatives' success using King's legacy and words in the fight against AA is somewhat ironic, given that King himself advocated "compensatory or preferential treatment for the Negro" (the term Affirmative Action was not yet in use) and argued that a "society that has done something *against* the Negro for hundreds of years must now do something *for* him ... to equip him to compete on a just and equal basis."[34]

Proving his appeal and utility across the political spectrum, King has become virtually the patron saint of the movement to abolish AA. For example, during the 1990s California businessman-turned-activist Ward Connerly became the most visible and outspoken representative for the campaigns that ended all public AA programs, first at University of California campuses, then in all areas by the state of California.

In 1996, Republican supporters of California's ballot initiative to end all state AA programs (Prop. 209, or the CCRI, California Civil Rights Initiative) produced a television advertisement in favor of Prop. 209 "starring" King! The ad contained eight recorded seconds of King's most iconic words and images from his "I Have a Dream" speech at the 1963 March on Washington, citing these thirty-four uplifting words: "I have a dream my four little children will one day live in a nation where they will not be judged by the color of their skin but by the content of their character."

Although the ad was eventually pulled before running widely, state and national Democrats and civil rights activists howled in protest at what they considered the ad's dishonest use of King. A San Francisco supervisor called it "sacrilegious to take Martin Luther King's sacred words out of context and use it for evil, sinister, divisive ends."[35]

Ward Connerly aggressively defended the properness of citing King and his ideals in the anti-AA movement. He shot back at critics who charged that doing so grossly distorted King's views for trying to keep King's mantle all to themselves: "They say, 'How dare you,'" Connerly said. "Well, how dare them.... The words that he said are right," so "from now on, I'm going to use them with far more frequency." Connerly declared, "I think it is outrageous for Jesse Jackson and all of those from the past, the 1960s ... to somehow suggest that it is inappropriate for any of us [believers in true race-neutral equality] to use Dr. King's memory: He belongs to us all."[36]

BEYOND CARICATURE

Americans naturally may differ about the proper understanding of King's and Malcolm's ideas and deeds and about what current courses of action are truest to them. That is potentially healthy and probably inevitable. Powerful symbols, such as these figures, have multiple levels of meaning and are open-ended enough to allow different interpretations. Precisely because King and Malcolm continue to influence people potently, however, and because of the conflicting purposes for which they are used, it is vital for educated people to know some of the real range and depth of their thought and leadership. Otherwise, how can one help but be misled and manipulated by simplistic or outright false images of them put out by interested parties with an agenda? No one-dimensional, frozen snapshots of them viewed outside the totality of their evolving lives and ideas will do. How tragic it would be if most people never got beyond crude caricatures: Malcolm as raving racial fanatic and King as mild, harmless saint. If Martin Luther King's and Malcolm X's messages and lives still hold relevance for a society not completely delivered from racism and a world still with too many people who are unfree and poor, if we can learn anything worthwhile from them in a world of rising ethnic, racial, and religious conflict and hatred, then we owe it to ourselves and posterity to look at these leaders and their ideas in a manner approaching their true depth and complexity.

NOTES

[1] For other accounts of their Washington meeting, see James H. Cone, *Martin & Malcolm & America: A Dream or a Nightmare* (Maryknoll, N.Y.: Orbis Books, 1991), 2–3; Lewis V. Baldwin, "Reluctant Admiration," in Lewis V. Baldwin and Amiri Yasin Al-Hadid, *Between Cross and Crescent: Christian and Muslim Perspectives on Malcolm and Martin* (Gainesville: University Press of Florida, 2002), 306–7; and Peter Goldman, *The Death and Life of Malcolm X* (Urbana: University of Illinois Press, 1979), 95.

[2] C. Eric Lincoln, *The Black Muslims in America* (Boston: Beacon Press, 1961; reprint, Trenton, N.J.: Africa World Press, 1994), 161; Stephen B. Oates, *Let the Trumpet Sound: The Life of Martin Luther King Jr.* (New York: Harper & Row, 1982), 251–52; Malcolm X, *Malcolm X Speaks: Selected Speeches and Statements*, ed. George Breitman (New York: Merit Publishers, 1965), 12–13; Louis E. Lomax, *When the Word Is Given: A Report on Elijah Muhammad, Malcolm X, and the Black Muslim World* (1963; reprint, Westport, Conn.: Greenwood Press, 1979), 174; Malcolm X, *The End of White World Supremacy: Four Speeches by Malcolm X*, ed. Imam Benjamin Karim (New York: Merlin House/Seaver Books, 1971), 68, 109, 115–17, 135, 140; Malcolm X, "Emancipation II," *America*, CVIII (June 1, 1963): 790–91; and Kenneth B. Clark, ed., *King, Malcolm, Baldwin: Three Interviews* (Boston: Beacon Press, 1963; reprint, Middletown, Conn.: Wesleyan University Press, 1985), 42–47; all cited in Lewis V. Baldwin, "A Reassessment of the Relationship between Malcolm X and Martin Luther King Jr.," *Western Journal of Black Studies* 13, no. 2 (Summer 1989): 104, 111n15.

[3] Works detailing the influence of Western philosophies on King include Kenneth L. Smith and Ira G. Zepp Jr., *Search for the Beloved Community: The Thinking of Martin Luther King Jr.* (Valley Forge, Pa.: Judson Press, 1974, 1998); and John J. Ansbro, *Martin Luther King Jr: The Making of a Mind* (Maryknoll, N.Y.: Orbis Books, 1982). Works stressing the black church's crucial influence on King include James H. Cone, "The Theology of Martin Luther King Jr.," *Union Seminary Quarterly Review* 40, no. 4 (1986): 21–36; and Lewis V. Baldwin, *There Is a Balm in Gilead: The Cultural Roots of Martin Luther King Jr.* (Minneapolis: Fortress Press, 1991).

[4] For good substantial accounts of King's leadership in the Montgomery bus boycott, see David J. Garrow, *Bearing the Cross: Martin Luther King Jr., and the Southern Christian Leadership Conference* (New York: William Morrow, 1986), chap. 1; and Taylor Branch, *Parting the Waters: America in the King Years, 1954–63* (New York: Simon & Schuster, 1988), chap. 5.

[5] On King and the Civil Rights movement's skillful use of symbols and of the media in winning public support, see David Garrow, *Protest at Selma: Martin Luther King Jr. and the Voting Rights Act of 1965* (New Haven, Conn.: Yale University Press, 1978); Roger Cobb and Charles Elder, *Participation in American Politics: The Dynamic of Agenda-Building* (Baltimore, Md.: Johns Hopkins University Press, 1972), chaps. 8 and 9; and Richard Lentz, *Symbols, the News Magazines, and Martin Luther King* (Baton Rouge: Louisiana State University Press, 1990).

[6] For an outstanding biography of Malcolm, see Goldman, *The Death and Life of Malcolm X*. See also Cone, *Martin & Malcolm & America*. Malcolm X's own, with Alex Haley, *Autobiography of Malcolm X* (hereafter *AMX*) (New York: Ballantine Books, 1999), remains indispensable biographical reading on Malcolm.

[7] The classic scholarly work on the Nation of Islam is Lincoln, *The Black Muslims in America*; see also E. U. Essien-Udom, *Black Nationalism: The Search for Identity in America* (Chicago: University of Chicago Press, 1962). More recent helpful overviews of NOI cosmology and beliefs appear in Louis A. DeCaro Jr., *Malcolm and the Cross: The Nation of Islam, Malcolm X, and Christianity* (New York: New York University Press, 1998), chap. 4; and in Claude Andrew Clegg III, *An Original Man: The Life and Times of Elijah Muhammad* (New York: St. Martin's Griffin, 1997), chap. 3.

[8] Malcolm's early prison ministry as well as evangelistic efforts after release are well presented in Louis A. DeCaro Jr., *On the Side of My People: A Religious Life of Malcolm X* (New York and London: New York University Press, 1996), chaps. 7 and 8. DeCaro's book is the best and most thorough study of Malcolm's religious experiences and development.

[9] "A Telegram from Malcolm X to Dr. Martin Luther King Jr.," St. Augustine, Fla. (June 30, 1964), King Library and Archives, Martin Luther King Jr., Center for Nonviolent Social Change, Atlanta, Ga.; Malcolm X, *Malcolm X on Afro-American History* (New York: Pathfinder Press, 1970), 44.

[10] Coretta Scott King, *My Life with Martin Luther King Jr.* (New York: Holt, Rinehart & Winston, 1969), 261–62.

[11] For accounts of attempts to arrange a meeting between them, see Baldwin, "Reluctant Admiration," 310–11; Cone, *Martin & Malcolm & America,* 207–8; and Taylor Branch, *Pillar of Fire: America in the King Years, 1963–65* (New York: Simon & Schuster, 1998), 345–46, 381.

[12] Peter Goldman and Bayard Rustin quotations are from Goldman, "Malcolm X, Witness for the Prosecution," in David Gallen, ed., *Malcolm X: As They Knew Him* (New York: Ballantine Books, 1996), 220–21.

[13] Typical dualistic comparisons of the leaders appear in Peter J. Paris, *Black Leaders in Conflict: Martin Luther King Jr., Malcolm X, Joseph H. Jackson, and Adam Clayton Powell Jr.* (New York: Pilgrim Press, 1978), 9ff.; and Jim Bishop, *The Days of Martin Luther King Jr.* (New York: G. P. Putnam's Sons, 1971), 379.

[14] Goldman, *The Death and Life of Malcolm X,* 79.

[15] Malcolm X, *AMX*, 42–43; Coretta Scott King, *My Life with Martin Luther King,* 259–60.

[16] David Halberstam, "The Second Coming of Martin Luther King," *Harper's* (Aug. 1967), reprinted in C. Eric Lincoln, ed., *Martin Luther King Jr.: A Profile* (New York: Hill & Wang, 1970), 201. Writers such as Michael Eric Dyson and Vincent Harding have been working to rectify the traditional slighting of King's radical final phase.

[17] Malcolm quoted in George Plimpton, "Miami Notebook: Cassius Clay and Malcolm X," *Harper's* (June 1964), 57.

[18] For examples of statements by Malcolm and King of these views, see Malcolm X, "The Ballot or the Bullet," in chap. 6, and King, "Three Responses of Oppressed Groups," in chap. 5 in this book.

[19] Cone, *Martin & Malcolm & America,* 246, 270–71; Baldwin, "Reassessment," 110; Baldwin, "Reluctant Admiration," 305. (Italics in the original.)

[20] Malcolm X, *Malcolm X Speaks,* 172; see, e.g., King's reference to black nationalists in Martin Luther King Jr., *Why We Can't Wait* (New York: New American Library, 1964), 87.

[21] Cone, *Martin & Malcolm & America,* 2; Clayborne Carson, "Malcolm and the American State," part 1 of *Malcolm X: The FBI File* (New York: Carroll & Graf, 1991), 48–49. Carson is, besides the author of this book, director of the Martin Luther King, Jr. Papers Project at Stanford University.

[22] Researchers such as Cone, Baldwin, and David Garrow have helped remedy the early lack of close scholarly attention to King's religiosity. See, e.g., Garrow's stress on King's Montgomery "Kitchen" conversion experience and on King's essentially religious self-conception in "Martin Luther King Jr. and the Spirit of Leadership," in *We Shall Overcome: Martin Luther King Jr. and the Black Freedom Struggle,* ed. Peter J. Albert and Ronald Hoffman (New York: Pantheon Books, 1990), 11–34, and *Bearing the Cross,* 56–58. There was a similar lack of serious study of Malcolm's spiritual experiences in the opening decades of Malcolm scholarship. Louis A. DeCaro Jr.'s books, *On the Side of My People* and *Malcolm and the Cross* have helped close this gap.

[23] King, "Pilgrimage to Nonviolence"—see chap. 1 of this book. Malcolm's statement is from Malcolm X, interview by Douglass Geoffrey Bridson, London, BBC Broadcasting House, 2 Dec. 1964, transcribed and edited by Paul Lee (Highland Park, Mich.: Best Efforts, Inc.), cited in DeCaro, *On the Side of My People,* 76.

[24] See, e.g., Baldwin, "Reluctant Admiration," 311.

[25] Halberstam, "The Second Coming," 201.

[26] On the unlikeliness of King and Malcolm allying, see Peter Goldman, "Malcolm X: Witness for the Prosecution," in Gallen, *Malcolm X: As They Knew Him,* 46–47; and Cone, *Martin & Malcolm & America,* 208, 259. On the general topic of their relation at the time of Malcolm's death, see also Clayborne Carson, "A 'Common Solution': Martin and Malcolm's Gulf Was Closing, but the Debate Lives On," *Emerge* 9, no. 4 (Feb. 1998): 44–46, 48–52.

[27] Lewis V. Baldwin, "Out of the Dark Past," in Baldwin and Al-Hadid, *Between Cross and Crescent,* 43–44.

[28] For a slam on King's fitness for hero status, see Patrick Buchanan, "A Rascal's Bedroom Escapades Diminish His Status as a Saint," *Tennessean,* 22 Oct. 1989, 5G. Also see Taylor Branch, "Uneasy Holiday," *The New Republic,* 3 Feb. 1983, 22–27

[29] Michael Eric Dyson, *Making Malcolm: The Myth and Meaning of Malcolm X* (New York: Oxford University Press, 1995), xiii, 79–184; Lee Bey, "The Renaissance of Malcolm X," *Chicago Sun Times,* 8 Nov. 1992, 38–39; Vern E. Smith et. al., "Rediscovering Malcolm X: Twenty-Five Years after His Murder, His Message Has New Resonance for Blacks," *Newsweek,* 26 Feb. 1990, 68–69; Spike Lee, with Ralph Wiley, *By Any Means Necessary: The Trials and Tribulations of the Making of Malcolm X* (New York: Hyperion, 1992).

[30] Jesse L. Jackson, "Rebuilding the House: The Fourth Movement of the Freedom Symphony," Remarks of the Reverend Jesse L. Jackson at the NAACP 90th Annual Convention, 14 July 1999, Online: Rainbow/Push Coalition [www home page]: http://www.rainbowpush.org/speech/index.html [23 Sept. 1999].

[31] Vincent Harding, *Martin Luther King: The Inconvenient Hero* (Maryknoll, N.Y.: Orbis Books, 1996), vii, 58.

[32] On King's extramarital affairs see, e.g., Garrow, *Bearing the Cross,* 361–62, 374–75; Michael Eric Dyson, *I May Not Get There with You: The* True *Martin Luther King Jr.* (New York: Free Press, 2000), chap. 8; and Ralph D. Abernathy, *And the Walls Came*

Tumbling Down: An Autobiography (New York: Harper & Row, 1989), 434–36, 470–75. On King's plagiarism in some of his student work, including his doctoral thesis and in early sermons, see, e.g., Clayborne Carson, "Documenting Martin Luther King's Importance—and His Flaws," *Chronicle of Higher Education,* 16 Jan. 1991, A52; Peter Waldman, "To Their Dismay, King Scholars Find a Troubling Pattern: Civil Rights Leader Was Lax in Attributing Some Parts of His Academic Papers," *Wall Street Journal,* 9 Nov. 1990, A1, A6; and David J. Garrow, "How King Borrowed: Reading the Truth between the Sermons and Footnotes," *Washington Post,* 18 Nov. 1990, C1, C5.

[33] Dyson, *I May Not Get There with You,* 15–16.

[34] King, *Why We Can't Wait,* 134; Martin Luther King Jr., *Where Do We Go from Here: Chaos or Community?* (Boston: Beacon Press, 1968), 106.

[35] The TV spot was pulled mainly because the King estate insisted that it infringed on its copyright to King's words and threatened to sue the Republicans if they ran it. Larry D. Hatfield and Annie Nakao, "Stations Pulling TV Ad Quoting Dr. King," *San Francisco Examiner,* 23 Oct. 1996, Online: SF Gate [www home page]: http://www.sfgate.com/examiner/archive/1996/10/23.html.

[36] Ward Connerly quoted in Annie Nakao, "Furor over Dr. King Ad Ignites 209 Fight," *San Francisco Examiner,* 24 Oct. 1996, Online: SF Gate [www home page]: http://www.sfgate.com/examiner/archive/1996/10/2.html, and in Dave Lesher, "Prop. 209 Backer Defends Use of King in Ad," *Los Angeles Times,* 24 Oct. 1996, Online: Los Angeles Times Archives [www home page]: http://www.pqasb.pqarchiver.com/latimes/main/doc.html.

PART TWO

The Documents

Words and Themes of Martin Luther King Jr. and Malcolm X

1
Formative Influences and Ideas

People are always speculating—why am I as I am? To understand that of any person, his whole life, from birth, must be reviewed. All of our experiences fuse into our personality. Everything that has happened to us is an ingredient. —Malcolm X

It is quite easy for me to think of a God of love mainly because I grew up in a family where ... lovely relationships were ever present.... It is quite easy for me to lean more toward optimism than pessimism about human nature mainly because of my childhood experiences.
—Martin Luther King

"I don't completely trust anyone,... not even myself." Malcolm X looked squarely at me. "You I trust about twenty-five percent."
—Alex Haley, quoting Malcolm X

I had sunk to the very bottom of the American white man's society when—in prison—I found Allah and the religion of Islam and it completely transformed my life. —Malcolm X

At that moment... I could hear an inner voice say to me, "Martin Luther, stand up for righteousness, stand up for justice, stand up for truth. And lo, I will be with you, even until the end of the world." ... I heard the voice of Jesus saying still to fight on.
—Martin Luther King

Besides being black in white-dominated America and having received from their families socially aware religion, Martin Luther King and Malcolm X had little in common during their formative years. King came from the black professional classes and experienced material comfort and social stability. By contrast, Malcolm Little as a child experienced much conflict, violence, and instability. In the urban petty-criminal world, he saw the worst of human nature and grew suspicious of people's self-interested motives.

As young men, King received an extensive higher education that equipped him to serve his people, while Malcolm was surrounded by crime and violence, which eventually led him to prison. There Malcolm encountered Allah, radically reordered his life, and became, like King, a brave and selfless African American leader. Despite these men's dramatically different backgrounds, their experiences led them both to become highly influential, spiritually motivated liberation leaders.

MARTIN LUTHER KING JR.

All influences on King built upon the foundation laid by his family, church, and community. His favorable formative conditions disposed him toward a positive outlook. Later encounters with philosophies stressing the reality of human evil and his own sobering experiences with others' cruelty during social protests led him to qualify, but never abandon, his essential optimism.

King attended Morehouse College, a historically black undergraduate institution in Atlanta from 1944 through 1948. From 1948 through 1951 he studied theology at predominantly white Crozer Theological Seminary in Pennsylvania and then attended Boston University, where he earned his Ph.D. in philosophy in 1953. From his extensive studies, King absorbed a wide array of Western and other intellectual traditions.

An Autobiography of Religious Development
1950

King wrote this essay as a young man for one of his seminary courses. It is a revealing self-statement.[1] In it, King stressed the profound influence that family and religion had on him all his life. He described his home life with his parents, siblings, and grandmother as warm and loving; char-

---

[1] In this document, spelling, grammar, and punctuation errors are neither corrected nor indicated by *sic*. Insertions, usually handwritten, by King into the text are placed within curly braces ({}).

Clayborne Carson, ed., *The Papers of Martin Luther King Jr.*, vol. 1, *Called to Serve, January 1929–June 1951* (Berkeley: University of California Press, 1992), 359–63.

acterized his middle-class neighborhood and community; and related his social and spiritual development in his "second home," the black church.

A precocious youth, King came to question—and ultimately discard—many of the conservative theological teachings of his childhood religious environment. He told here of shocking his Sunday school class when he was thirteen by denying the bodily resurrection of Jesus. Although King would move on to far wider social and intellectual circles, he would always feel "the affects of the noble moral and ethical ideals that I grew up under. They have been real and precious to me, and . . . I could never turn away from them."

My birthplace was Atlanta Georgia, the capital of the state and the so-called "gate-way to the south." I was born in the late twenties on the verge of the great depression, which was to spread its disastrous arms into every corner of this nation for over a decade. I was much too young to remember the beginning of this depression, but I do recall how I questioned my parent about the numerous people standing in bread lines when I was about five years of age. I can see the effects of this early childhood experience on my present anti capitalistic feelings.

I was the second child of a family of three children, having one brother and one sister. Because of {our} relative closeness of ages we all grew up together, and to this day there still exist that intimate relationship which existed between us in childhood. Our parents themselves were very intimate, and they always maintained an intimate relationship with us. In our immediate family there was also a saintly grandmother (my mother's mother) whose husband had died when I was one years old. She was {very} dear to each of us, but especially to me. I sometimes think that I was his favorite grandchild. I can remember very vividly how she spent many evenings telling us interesting stories.

From the very beginning I was an extraordinarily healthy child. It is said that at my birth the doctors pronounced me a one hundred percent perfect child, from a physical point of view. Even today this physical harmony still abides, in that I hardly know how an ill moment feels. I guess the same thing would apply to my mental life. I have always been somewhat precocious, both physically and mentally. My I.Q. stands somewhat above the average. So it seems that from a hereditary point of view nature was very kind to me.

The same applies to my environment. I was born in a very congenial home situation. My parents have always lived together very intimately, and I can hardly remember a time that they ever argued. (My father happens to be the kind who just wont argue), or had any great fall out. I have never experienced the feeling of not having the basic necessities of life. These things were always provided by a father who always put his family first. My father has always been a real father. This is not to say that I was born with a silver spoon in my mouth; far from it. My father has never made more than an ordinary salary, but the secret is that he knows the art of saving and budgeting. He never wastes his money at the expense of his family. He has always had sense enough not to live beyond his means. So for this reason He has been able to provide us with the basic necessities of life with little strain. For the past three years he has had the tremendous responsibility of keeping all of us in school, (my brother in college, my sister in graduate school, and me in the Seminary) and although it has been somewhat a burden from a financial angle, he has done it with a smile. Our mother has also been behind the scene setting forth those motherly cares, the lack of which leaves a missing link in life.

The community in which I was born was quite ordinary in terms of social status. No one in our community had attained any great wealth. Most of the Negroes in my home town who had attained wealth lived in a section of town known as "Hunter Hills." The community in which I was born was characterized with a sought of unsophisticated simplicity. No one in our community was in the extremely poor class. This community was not the slum district. It is probably fair to class the people of this community as those of average income. Yet I insist that this was a wholesome community, notwithstanding the fact that none of us were ever considered member of the "upper upper class." Crime was at a minimum in our community, and most of our neighbors were deeply religious. I can well remember that all of my childhood playmates were regular Sunday School goers, not that I chose them on that basis, but because it was very difficult to find playmates in my community who did not attend Sunday School.

I was exposed to the best educational conditions in my childhood. At three I entered nursery school. This great childhood contact had a tremendous effect on the development of my personality. At five I entered kindergarten and there I remained for one year until I entered the first grade.

One may ask at this point, why discuss such factors as the above in a paper dealing with ones religious development? The answer to this question lies in the fact that the above factors were highly significant in determining my religious attitudes. It is quite easy for me to think of a God of love mainly because I grew up in a family where love was central and where lovely relationships were ever present. It is quite easy for me to think of the universe as basically friendly mainly because of my uplifting hereditary and environmental circumstances. It is quite easy for me to lean more toward optimism than pessimism about human nature mainly because of my childhood experiences. It is impossible to get at the roots of ones religious attitudes without taking in account the psychological and historical factors that play upon the individual. So that the above biographical factors are absolutely necessary in understanding my religious development.

Now for a more specific phase of my religious development. It was at the age of five that I joined the church. I well remember how this event occurred. Our church was in the midst of the spring revival, and a guest evangelist had come down from Virginia. On Sunday morning the guest evangelist came into our Sunday School to talk to us about salvation, and after a short talk on this point he extended an invitation to any of us who wanted to join the church. My sister was the first one to join the church that morning, and after seeing her join I decided that I would not let her get ahead of me, so I was the next. I had never given this matter a thought, and even at the time of {my} baptism I was unaware of what was taking place. From this it seems quite clear that I joined the church not out of any dynamic conviction, but out of a childhood desire to keep up with my sister.

Conversion for me was never an abrupt something. I have never experienced the so called "crisis moment." Religion has just been something that I grew up in. Conversion for me has been the gradual intaking of the noble {ideals} set forth in my family and my environment, and I must admit that this intaking has been largely unconscious.

The church has always been a second home for me. As far back as I can remember I was in church every Sunday. I guess this was inevitable since my father was the pastor of my church, but I never regretted going to church until I passed through a state of scepticism in my second year of college. My best friends were in Sunday School, and it was the Sunday School that helped me to build the capacity for getting along with people.

The lessons which I taught in Sunday School were quite in the fundamentalist line. None of my teachers ever doubted the infallibility of the Scriptures. Most of them were unlettered and had never heard of Biblical criticism. Naturally I accepted the teachings as they were being given to me. I never felt any need to doubt them, at least at that time I didn't. I guess I accepted Biblical studies uncritically until I was about twelve years old. But this uncritical attitude could not last long, for it was contrary to the very nature of my being. I had always been the questioning and precocious type. At the age of 13 I shocked my Sunday School class by denying the bodily resurrection of Jesus. From the age of thirteen on doubts began to spring forth unrelentingly. At the age of fifteen I entered college and more and more could I see a gap between what I had learned in Sunday School and what I was learning in college. This conflict continued until I studied a course in Bible in which I came to see that behind the legends and myths of the Book were many profound truths which one could not escape.

One or two incidents happened in my late childhood and early adolescence that had tremendous effect on my religious development. The First was the death of my grandmother when I was about nine years old. I was particularly hurt by this incident mainly because of the extreme love I had for her. As stated above, she assisted greatly in raising all of us. It was after this incident for the first time that I talked at any length on the doctrine of immortality. My parents attempted to explain it to me and I was assured that somehow my grandmother still lived. I guess this is why today I am such a strong believer in personal immortality.

The second incident happened when I was about six years of age. From about the age of three up until this time I had had a white playmate who was about my age. We always felt free to play our childhood games together. He did not live in our community, but he was usually around every day until about 6:00; his father owned a store just across the streets from our home. At the age of six we both entered school—separate schools of course. I remember how our friendship began to break as soon as we entered school, of course this was not my desire but his. The climax came when he told me one day that his father had demanded that he would play with me no more. I never will forget what a great shock this was to me. I immediately asked my parents about the motive behind such a statement. We were at the dinner table when the situation was discussed, and here for the first time I was made aware of the existence of a race problem. I had never been conscious of it before. As my parents discussed some of the tragedies that had resulted from this problem and some of the insults they themselves had confronted on account of it, I was greatly shocked, and from that moment on I was determined to hate every white person. As I grew older and older this feeling continued to grow. My parents would always tell me that I should not hate the white {man}, but that it was my duty as a Christian to love him. At this point the religious element came in. The question arose in my mind, how could I love a race of people {who} hated me and who had been responsible for breaking me up with one of my best childhood friends? This was a great question in my mind for a number of years. I did not conquer this anti White feeling until I entered college and came in contact with white students through working in interracial organizations.

My days in college were very exciting ones. As stated above, my college training, especially the first two years, brought many doubts into my mind. It was at this period that the shackles of fundamentalism were removed from my body. This is why, when I came to Crozer, I could accept the liberal interpretation with relative ease.

It was in my senior year of college that I entered the ministry. I had felt the urge to enter the ministry from my latter high school days, but accumulated doubts had somewhat blocked the urge. Now it appeared again with an inescapable drive. My call to the ministry was not a miraculous or supernatural something, on the contrary it was an inner urge calling me to serve humanity. I guess the influence of my father also had a great deal to do with my going in the ministry. This is not to say that he ever spoke to me in terms of being a minister, but that my admiration for him was the great moving factor; He set forth a noble example that I didn't mind following. Today I differ a great deal with my father theologically, but that admiration for a real father still remains.

At the age of 19 I finished college and was ready to enter the seminary. On coming to the seminary I found it quite easy to fall in line with the liberal tradition there found, mainly because I had been prepared for it before coming.

At present I still feel the affects of the noble moral and ethical ideals that I grew up under. They have been real and precious to me, and even in moments of theological doubt I could never turn away from them. Even though I have never had an abrupt conversion experience, religion has been real to me and closely knitted to life. In fact the two cannot be separated; religion for me is life.

Pilgrimage to Nonviolence
1960

In this essay, King traced the development of the major theological and philosophical ideas underlying his ministry and leadership. His intellectual journey began when he rejected certain strict fundamentalist beliefs and embraced liberal Christianity. King's keen interest in social ethics is pronounced, especially his "serious intellectual quest for a method to eliminate social evil."

A number of King's most distinctive traits as a social-religious thinker are well illustrated by this document, including his social gospel insistence on serving "the whole man"—not only spiritually but also materially, socially, and politically; his use of varied intellectual sources and tendency to synthesize opposing ideas; his belief that human personality is sacred; and his rejection of the argument that nonviolent resistance really constituted passive nonresistance to evil.

Ten years ago I was just entering my senior year in theological seminary....

At this stage of my development I was a thoroughgoing liberal. Liberalism provided me with an intellectual satisfaction that I could never find in fundamentalism. I became so enamored of the insights of liberalism that I almost fell into the trap of accepting uncritically everything that came under its name. I was absolutely convinced of the natural goodness of man and the natural power of human reason.

The basic change in my thinking came when I began to question some of the theories that had been associated with so-called liberal theology. Of course there is one phase of liberalism that I hope to cherish always: its devotion to the search for truth, its insistence on an open and analytical mind, its refusal to abandon the best light of reason. Liberalism's contribution to the philological-historical criticism of biblical literature has been of immeasurable value and should be defended with religious and scientific passion.

It was mainly the liberal doctrine of man that I began to question.

Christian Century 77 (13 April 1960): 439–41; reprinted in James M. Washington, ed., *A Testament of Hope: The Essential Writings and Speeches of Martin Luther King Jr.* (San Francisco: HarperCollins, 1986; HarperCollins Paperback ed., 1991), 35–40.

The more I observed the tragedies of history and man's shameful inclination to choose the low road, the more I came to see the depths and strength of sin. My reading of the works of Reinhold Niebuhr made me aware of the complexity of human motives and the reality of sin on every level of man's existence. Moreover, I came to recognize the complexity of man's social involvement and the glaring reality of collective evil. I came to feel that liberalism had been all too sentimental concerning human nature and that it leaned toward a false idealism.

I also came to see that liberalism's superficial optimism concerning human nature caused it to overlook the fact that reason is darkened by sin. The more I thought about human nature the more I saw how our tragic inclination for sin causes us to use our minds to rationalize our actions. Liberalism failed to see that reason by itself is little more than an instrument to justify man's defensive ways of thinking. Reason, devoid of [the] purifying power of faith, can never free itself from distortions and rationalizations.

In spite of the fact that I had to reject some aspects of liberalism, I never came to an all-out acceptance of neo-orthodoxy.[1] While I saw neo-orthodoxy as a helpful corrective for a liberalism that had become all too sentimental, I never felt that it provided an adequate answer to the basic questions. If liberalism was too optimistic concerning human nature, neo-orthodoxy was too pessimistic. Not only on the question of man but also on other vital issues neo-orthodoxy went too far in its revolt. In its attempt to preserve the transcendence of God, which had been neglected by liberalism's overstress of his immanence, neo-orthodoxy went to the extreme of stressing a God who was hidden, unknown and "wholly other." In its revolt against liberalism's overemphasis on the power of reason, neo-orthodoxy fell into a mood of antirationalism and semifundamentalism, stressing a narrow, uncritical biblicism. This approach, I felt, was inadequate both for the church and for personal life.

So although liberalism left me unsatisfied on the question of the nature of man, I found no refuge in neo-orthodoxy. I am now convinced that the truth about man is found neither in liberalism nor in neo-orthodoxy. Each represents a partial truth. A large segment of Protestant liberalism defined man only in terms of his essential nature,

---

[1] *Neo-orthodoxy:* A theological movement that arose during the first half of the twentieth century that countered liberal Christianity's optimism about human nature and social perfectibility. It was associated with such theologians as Reinhold Niebuhr and dominated Protestant theology at mid century, when King did his advanced studies.

his capacity for good. Neo-orthodoxy tended to define man only in terms of his existential nature, his capacity for evil. An adequate understanding of man is found neither in the thesis of liberalism nor in the antithesis of neo-orthodoxy, but in a synthesis which reconciles the truths of both. . . .

Although most of my formal study during this decade has been in systematic theology and philosophy, I have become more and more interested in social ethics. Of course my concern for social problems was already substantial before the beginning of this decade. From my early teens in Atlanta I was deeply concerned about the problem of racial injustice. I grew up abhorring segregation, considering it both rationally inexplicable and morally unjustifiable. I could never accept the fact of having to go to the back of a bus or sit in the segregated section of a train. The first time that I was seated behind a curtain in a dining car I felt as if the curtain had been dropped on my selfhood. I had also learned that the inseparable twin of racial injustice is economic injustice. I saw how the systems of segregation ended up in the exploitation of the Negro as well as the poor whites. Through these early experiences I grew up deeply conscious of the varieties of injustice in our society.

Not until I entered theological seminary, however, did I begin a serious intellectual quest for a method to eliminate social evil. I was immediately influenced by the social gospel. In the early fifties I read Rauschenbusch's *Christianity and the Social Crisis,* a book which left an indelible imprint on my thinking. Of course there were points at which I differed with Rauschenbusch. I felt that he had fallen victim to the nineteenth century "cult of inevitable progress," which led him to an unwarranted optimism concerning human nature. Moreover, he came perilously close to identifying the kingdom of God with a particular social and economic system—a temptation which the church should never give in to. But in spite of these shortcomings Rauschenbusch gave to American Protestantism a sense of social responsibility that it should never lose. The gospel at its best deals with the whole man, not only his soul but his body, not only his spiritual well-being, but his material well-being. Any religion that professes to be concerned about the souls of men and is not concerned about the slums that damn them, the economic conditions that strangle them and the social conditions that cripple them is a spiritually moribund religion awaiting burial.

After reading Rauschenbusch I turned to a serious study of the social and ethical theories of the great philosophers. During this period I had almost despaired of the power of love in solving social problems. The "turn the other cheek" philosophy and the "love your enemies" philosophy are only valid, I felt, when individuals are in conflict with other individuals; when racial groups and nations are in conflict a more realistic approach is necessary. Then I came upon the life and teachings of Mohandas Gandhi. As I read his works I became deeply fascinated by his campaigns of nonviolent resistance. The whole Gandhian concept of *satyagraha* (*satya* is truth which equals love, and *graha* is force; *satyagraha* thus means truth-force or love-force) was profoundly significant to me. As I delved deeper into the philosophy of Gandhi my skepticism concerning the power of love gradually diminished, and I came to see for the first time that the Christian doctrine of love operating through the Gandhian method of nonviolence was one of the most potent weapons available to oppressed people in their struggle for freedom. At this time, however, I had a merely intellectual understanding and appreciation of the position, with no firm determination to organize it in a socially effective situation.

When I went to Montgomery, Alabama, as a pastor in 1954, I had not the slightest idea that I would later become involved in a crisis in which nonviolent resistance would be applicable. After I had lived in the community about a year, the bus boycott began. The Negro people of Montgomery, exhausted by the humiliating experiences that they had constantly faced on the buses, expressed in a massive act of noncooperation their determination to be free. They came to see that it was ultimately more honorable to walk the streets in dignity than to ride the buses in humiliation. At the beginning of the protest the people called on me to serve as their spokesman. In accepting this responsibility my mind, consciously or unconsciously, was driven back to the Sermon on the Mount and the Gandhian method of nonviolent resistance. This principle became the guiding light of our movement. Christ furnished the spirit and motivation while Gandhi furnished the method.

The experience in Montgomery did more to clarify my thinking on the question of nonviolence than all of the books that I had read. As the days unfolded I became more and more convinced of the power of nonviolence. Living through the actual experience of the protest, nonviolence became more than a method to which I gave intellectual assent; it became a commitment to a way of life. Many issues I had not cleared up intellectually concerning nonviolence were now solved in the sphere of practical action.

A few months ago I had the privilege of traveling to India. The trip had a great impact on me personally and left me even more convinced of the power of nonviolence. It was a marvelous thing to see the amazing results of a nonviolent struggle. India won her independence, but without violence on the part of Indians. The aftermath of hatred and bitterness that usually follows a violent campaign is found nowhere in India. Today a mutual friendship based on complete equality exists between the Indian and British people within the commonwealth.

I do not want to give the impression that nonviolence will work miracles overnight. Men are not easily moved from their mental ruts or purged of their prejudiced and irrational feelings. When the underprivileged demand freedom, the privileged first react with bitterness and resistance. Even when the demands are couched in nonviolent terms, the initial response is the same. I am sure that many of our white brothers in Montgomery and across the South are still bitter toward Negro leaders, even though these leaders have sought to follow a way of love and nonviolence. So the nonviolent approach does not immediately change the heart of the oppressor. It first does something to the hearts and souls of those committed to it. It gives them new self-respect; it calls up resources of strength and courage that they did not know they had. Finally, it reaches the opponent and so stirs his conscience that reconciliation becomes a reality.

During recent months I have come to see more and more the need for the method of nonviolence in international relations. While I was convinced during my student days of the power of nonviolence in group conflicts within nations, I was not yet convinced of its efficacy in conflicts between nations. I felt that while war could never be a positive or absolute good, it could serve as a negative good in the sense of preventing the spread and growth of an evil force. War, I felt, horrible as it is, might be preferable to surrender to a totalitarian system. But more and more I have come to the conclusion that the potential destructiveness of modern weapons of war totally rules out the possibility of war ever serving again as a negative good. If we assume that mankind has a right to survive then we must find an alternative to war and destruction. In a day when sputniks[2] dash through outer space and guided ballistic missiles are carving highways of death through the stratosphere, nobody can win a war. The choice today is no longer between violence and nonviolence. It is either nonviolence or nonexistence.

---

[2]*Sputnik:* The first space satellite, launched in 1957 by the Soviet Union.

I am no doctrinaire pacifist. I have tried to embrace a realistic pacifism. Moreover, I see the pacifist position not as sinless but as the lesser evil in the circumstances. Therefore I do not claim to be free from the moral dilemmas that the Christian nonpacifist confronts. But I am convinced that the church cannot remain silent while mankind faces the threat of being plunged into the abyss of nuclear annihilation. If the church is true to its mission it must call for an end to the arms race.

In recent months I have also become more and more convinced of the reality of a personal God. True, I have always believed in the personality of God. But in past years the idea of a personal God was little more than a metaphysical category which I found theologically and philosophically satisfying. Now it is a living reality that has been validated in the experiences of everyday life. Perhaps the suffering, frustration and agonizing moments which I have had to undergo occasionally as a result of my involvement in a difficult struggle have drawn me closer to God. Whatever the cause, God has been profoundly real to me in recent months. In the midst of outer dangers I have felt an inner calm and known resources of strength that only God could give. In many instances I have felt the power of God transforming the fatigue of despair into the buoyancy of hope. I am convinced that the universe is under the control of a loving purpose and that in the struggle for righteousness man has cosmic companionship. Behind the harsh appearances of the world there is a benign power. To say God is personal is not to make him an object among other objects or attribute to him the finiteness and limitations of human personality; it is to take what is finest and noblest in our consciousness and affirm its perfect existence in him. It is certainly true that human personality is limited, but personality as such involves no necessary limitations. It simply means self-consciousness and self-direction. So in the truest sense of the word, God is a living God. In him there is feeling and will, responsive to the deepest yearnings of the human heart: this God both evokes and answers prayers.

The past decade has been a most exciting one. In spite of the tensions and uncertainties of our age something profoundly meaningful has begun. Old systems of exploitation and oppression are passing away and new systems of justice and equality are being born. In a real sense ours is a great time in which to be alive. Therefore I am not yet discouraged about the future. Granted that the easygoing optimism of yesterday is impossible. Granted that we face a world crisis which often leaves us standing amid the surging murmur of life's restless sea. But every crisis has both its dangers and its opportunities. Each can spell either salvation or doom. In a dark, confused world the spirit of God may yet reign supreme.

MALCOLM X

All Malcolm documents in this chapter are from his famous *The Autobiography of Malcolm X* and illustrate major formative influences on his life and outlook. Malcolm's father was murdered by white supremacists when Malcolm was only six. While his mother, Louise, struggled alone to support her large family during the Great Depression, Malcolm observed white officials belittle her and undermine her self-respect. After Louise was committed to a state mental hospital, Malcolm and his siblings were dispersed to different white foster families and schools. At age fourteen, Malcolm went to live in Boston with his eldest sister, Ella. From there, he gradually entered the criminal underworld in the black ghettos of Boston, Detroit, and New York until imprisoned for burglary in 1946.

Virtually nothing in Malcolm's life up to then had led him to think well of others and society. In this phase of his life, Malcolm had contempt for conventional society's mores; he especially despised organized religion.

Malcolm's prison-time conversion to a black nationalist religious and social movement, the Nation of Islam led by Elijah Muhammad, was the catalyst for his resurgence. Malcolm's desire to serve Muhammad's Nation was the motivating force behind his drive for self-education and reformation. Nevertheless, as the following autobiographical excerpts show, long before his exposure to the NOI, Malcolm's family had instilled in him an internationalist racial consciousness, a deep spirituality, and a sharp awareness of white racism, all of which were powerfully reawakened in the NOI.

From Nightmare to Salvation
1965

The first selection from the Autobiography *indicates Malcolm and his family's recurrent experiences with white racist violence; it also shows Malcolm's exposure to conflict and violence within his family. This selection shows his parents' wish to instill religion and racial pride in their children.*

Nightmare

... When my mother was pregnant with me, she told me later, a party of hooded Ku Klux Klan riders galloped up to our home in Omaha, Nebraska, one night. Surrounding the house, brandishing their shotguns and rifles, they shouted for my father to come out. My mother went to the front door and opened it. Standing where they could see her pregnant condition, she told them that she was alone with her three small children, and that my father was away, preaching, in Milwaukee. The Klansmen shouted threats and warnings at her that we had better get out of town because "the good Christian white people" were not going to stand for my father's "spreading trouble" among the "good" Negroes of Omaha with the "back to Africa" preachings of Marcus Garvey.[1]

My father, the reverend Earl Little, was a Baptist minister, a dedicated organizer for Marcus Aurelius Garvey's U.N.I.A. (Universal Negro Improvement Association). With the help of such disciples as my father, Garvey, from his headquarters in New York City's Harlem, was raising the banner of black-race purity and exhorting the Negro masses to return to their ancestral African homeland—a cause which had made Garvey the most controversial black man on earth.

Still shouting threats, the Klansmen finally spurred their horses and galloped around the house, shattering every window pane with

---

[1] *Marcus Garvey:* Founder of the Universal Negro Improvement Association, who led a mass "Back to Africa" movement during the 1920s.

All selections from the *Autobiography* in this volume follow the text in Malcolm X, with Alex Haley, *The Autobiography of Malcolm X* (New York: Ballantine Books, 1999), 1–4, 6–7, 10, 12–13, 17–18, 21–22, 37–49, 55–57, 152–53, 162–73.

their gun butts. Then they rode off into the night, their torches flaring, as suddenly as they had come.

My father was enraged when he returned. He decided to wait until I was born—which would be soon—and then the family would move.... He believed, as did Marcus Garvey, that freedom, independence and self-respect could never be achieved by the Negro in America, and that therefore the Negro should leave America to the white man and return to his African land of origin. Among the reasons my father had decided to risk and dedicate his life to help disseminate this philosophy among his people was that he had seen four of his six brothers die by violence, three of them killed by white men, including one by lynching. What my father could not know then was that of the remaining three, including himself, only one, my Uncle Jim, would die in bed, of natural causes. Northern white police were later to shoot my Uncle Oscar. And my father was finally himself to die by the white man's hands.

It has always been my belief that I, too, will die by violence....

Our family stayed only briefly in Milwaukee.... We went next, for some reason, to Lansing, Michigan. My father bought a house and soon, as had been his pattern, he was doing free-lance Christian preaching in local Negro Baptist churches, and during the week he was roaming about spreading word of Marcus Garvey....

... This time, the get-out-of-town threats came from a local hate society called The Black Legion. They wore black robes instead of white. Soon, nearly everywhere my father went, Black Legionnaires were reviling him as an "uppity nigger" for wanting to own a store, for living outside the Lansing Negro district, for spreading unrest and dissention among "the good niggers."

... [Next] came the nightmare night in 1929, my earliest vivid memory. I remember being suddenly snatched awake into a frightening confusion of pistol shots and shouting and smoke and flames. My father had shouted and shot at the two white men who had set the fire and were running away. Our home was burning down around us. We were lunging and bumping and tumbling all over each other trying to escape. My mother, with the baby in her arms, just made it into the yard before the house crashed in, showering sparks. I remember we were outside in the night in our underwear, crying and yelling our heads off. The white police and firemen came and stood around watching as the house burned down to the ground.

My father ... moved us into another house on the outskirts of East

Lansing.... East Lansing harassed us so much that we had to move again....

After that, my memories are of the friction between my father and mother. They seemed to be nearly always at odds. Sometimes my father would beat her. It might have had something to do with the fact that my mother had a pretty good education. Where she got it I don't know. But an educated woman, I suppose, can't resist the temptation to correct an uneducated man. Every now and then, when she put those smooth words on him, he would grab her.

My father was also belligerent toward all of the children, except me. The older ones he would beat almost savagely if they broke any of his rules—and he had so many rules it was hard to know them all. Nearly all my whippings came from my mother. I've thought a lot about why. I actually believe that as anti-white as my father was, he was subconsciously so afflicted with the white man's brainwashing of Negroes that he inclined to favor the light ones, and I was his lightest child....

... The image of him that made me proudest was his crusading and militant campaigning with the words of Marcus Garvey. As young as I was then, I knew from what I overheard that my father was saying something that made him a "tough" man. I remember an old lady, grinning and saying to my father, "You're scaring these white folks to death!"...

I remember seeing the big, shiny photographs of Marcus Garvey that were passed from hand to hand. My father had a big envelope of them that he always took to these meetings. The pictures showed what seemed to me millions of Negroes thronged in parade behind Garvey riding in a fine car, a big black man dressed in a dazzling uniform with gold braid on it, and he was wearing a thrilling hat with tall plumes. I remember hearing that he had black followers not only in the United States but all around the world, and I remember how the meetings always closed with my father saying, several times, and the people chanting after him, "Up, you mighty race, you can accomplish what you will!"

... She told me later, my mother did, that she had a vision of my father's end....

I remember waking up to the sound of my mother's screaming again. When I scrambled out, I saw the police in the living room....

My mother was taken by the police to the hospital, and to a room where a sheet was over my father in a bed, and she wouldn't look, she was afraid to look. Probably it was wise that she didn't. My father's skull, on one side, was crushed in, I was told later. Negroes in Lansing have always whispered that he was attacked, and then laid across some tracks for a streetcar to run over him. His body was cut almost in half....

... He was dead. I was six. I can remember a vague commotion, the house filled up with people crying, saying bitterly that the white Black Legion had finally gotten him....

[Malcolm bitterly recalled the destructive role of the white system and its public officials in his family's demise.]

Vicious as Vultures

... When the state Welfare people began coming to our house, we would come from school sometimes and find them talking with our mother, asking a thousand questions. They acted and looked at her, and at us, and around in our house, in a way that had about it the feeling—at least for me—that we were not people. In their eyesight we were just *things,* that was all.

My mother began to receive two checks—a Welfare check and, I believe, widow's pension. The checks helped. But they weren't enough, as many of us as there were....

We began to go swiftly downhill. The physical downhill wasn't as quick as the psychological. My mother was, above everything, a proud woman, and it took its toll on her that she was accepting charity....

Meanwhile, the state Welfare people kept after my mother. By now, she didn't make it any secret that she hated them, and didn't want them in her house. But they exerted their right to come, and I have many, many times reflected upon how, talking to us children, they began to plant the seeds of division in our minds. They would ask such things as who was smarter than the other. And they would ask me why I was "so different."

I think they felt that getting children into foster homes was a legitimate part of their function, and the result would be less troublesome, however they went about it.

And when my mother fought them, they went after her—first, through me. I was the first target. I stole; that implied that I wasn't being taken care of by my mother....

I'm not sure just how or when the idea was first dropped by the Welfare workers that our mother was losing her mind....

They were as vicious as vultures. They had no feelings, understanding, compassion, or respect for my mother. They told us, "She's crazy for refusing food." Right then was when our home, our unity, began to disintegrate....

Eventually my mother suffered a complete breakdown, and the court orders were finally signed. They took her to the State Mental Hospital at Kalamazoo.

... A Judge McClellan in Lansing had authority over me and all of my brothers and sisters. We were "state children," court wards; he had the full say-so over us. A white man in charge of a black man's children! Nothing but legal, modern slavery....

[In the predominantly white institutions in which Malcolm spent early adolescence, he initially got on well with his white foster family, teachers, and schoolmates. However, he gradually grew alienated from them. Malcolm cited an incident with his eighth-grade English teacher, Mr. Ostrowski, as pivotal in his evolving attitudes toward the whites who surrounded and controlled him during his parentless late childhood.]

Mr. Ostrowski

... And then one day, just about when those of us who had passed were about to move up to 8-A, from which we would enter high school the next year, something happened which was to become the first major turning point of my life.

Somehow, I happened to be alone in the classroom with Mr. Ostrowski, my English teacher. He was a tall, rather reddish white man and he had a thick mustache. I had gotten some of my best marks under him, and he had always made me feel that he liked me. He was, as I have mentioned, a natural-born "advisor." ...

I know that he probably meant well in what he happened to advise me that day. I doubt that he meant any harm. It was just in his nature as an American white man. I was one of his top students, one of the school's top students—but all he could see for me was the kind of future "in your place" that almost all white people see for black people.

He told me, "Malcolm, you ought to be thinking about a career. Have you been giving it thought?"

The truth is, I hadn't. I never have figured out why I told him, "Well, yes, sir, I've been thinking I'd like to be a lawyer." ...

Mr. Ostrowski looked surprised, I remember, and leaned back in his chair and clasped his hands behind his head. He kind of half-smiled and said, "Malcolm, one of life's first needs is for us to be realistic.

Don't misunderstand me, now. We all here like you, you know that. But you've got to be realistic about being a nigger. A lawyer—that's no realistic goal for a nigger. You need to think about something you *can* be. You're good with your hands—making things. Everybody admires your carpentry shop work. Why don't you plan on carpentry? People like you as a person—you'd get all kinds of work."

The more I thought afterwards about what he said, the more uneasy it made me. It just kept treading around in my mind.

What made it really begin to disturb me was Mr. Ostrowski's advice to others in my class—all of them white. Most of them had told him they were planning to become farmers. But those who wanted to strike out on their own, to try something new, he had encouraged. Some, mostly girls, wanted to be teachers. A few wanted other professions, such as one boy who wanted to become a county agent; another, a veterinarian; and one girl wanted to be a nurse. They all reported that Mr. Ostrowski had encouraged what they had wanted. Yet nearly none of them had earned marks equal to mine.

It was a surprising thing that I had never thought of it that way before, but I realized that whatever I wasn't, I *was* smarter than nearly all of those white kids. But apparently I was still not intelligent enough, in their eyes, to become whatever *I* wanted to be.

It was then that I began to change—inside.

I drew away from white people. . . .

[Getting a "conk," or hair treatment that straightened one's hair to look "white," was surely not the gravest misdeed Malcolm committed in his inner-city hoodlum days—indeed, it was not even a crime. However, it was, to his mind later, among the most degrading and stupid things he did during this sordid phase of his life. Malcolm's friend Shorty gave him his first conk, which entailed a painful application of chemicals to his scalp.]

Conked

. . . The congolene just felt warm when Shorty started combing it in. But then my head caught fire.

I gritted my teeth and tried to pull the sides of the kitchen table together. The comb felt as if it was raking my skin off.

My eyes watered, my nose was running. I couldn't stand it any longer; I bolted to the washbasin. I was cursing Shorty with every name I could think of when he got the spray going and started soap-lathering my head.

He lathered and spray-rinsed, lathered and spray-rinsed, maybe ten or twelve times, each time gradually closing the hot-water faucet, until the rinse was cold, and that helped some.

"You feel any stinging spots?"

"No," I managed to say. My knees were trembling. . . .

My first view in the mirror blotted out the hurting. I'd seen some pretty conks, but when it's the first time, on your *own* head, the transformation, after the lifetime of kinks, is staggering.

The mirror reflected Shorty behind me. We both were grinning and sweating. And on top of my head was this thick, smooth sheen of shining red hair—real red—as straight as any white man's.

How ridiculous I was! Stupid enough to stand there simply lost in admiration of my hair now looking "white," reflected in the mirror in Shorty's room. I vowed that I'd never again be without a conk, and I never was for many years.

This was my first really big step toward self-degradation: when I endured all of that pain, literally burning my flesh to have it look like a white man's hair. I had joined that multitude of Negro men and women in America who are brainwashed into believing that the black people are "inferior"—and white people "superior"—that they will even violate and mutilate their God-created bodies to try to look "pretty" by white standards. . . .

[Malcolm's career as a criminal ended when he was arrested while trying to sell a stolen wristwatch in a pawnshop. Malcolm had formed, with two more black men and two white women, an effective burglary ring. The young white women, because they aroused no suspicion, cased homes in wealthy neighborhoods for subsequent burglary. In this excerpt, Malcolm related white authorities' fixation during the trial on the presence of white women in his interracial burglary ring.]

Caught

The cops found the apartment loaded with evidence—fur coats, some jewelry, other small stuff—plus the tools of our trade. A jimmy, a lockpick, glass cutters, screwdrivers, pencil-beam flashlights, false keys . . . and my small arsenal of guns.

The girls got low bail. They were still white—burglars or not. Their worst crime was their involvement with Negroes. . . .

The social workers worked on us. White women in league with Negroes was their main obsession. The girls weren't so-called "tramps," or "trash," they were well-to-do upper-middle-class whites.

That bothered the social workers and the forces of the law more than anything else.

How, where, when, had I met them? Did we sleep together? Nobody wanted to know anything at all about the robberies. All they could see was that we had taken the white man's women.

I just looked at the social workers: "Now, what do *you* think?"

Even the court clerks and the bailiffs: "Nice white girls... goddamn niggers—" It was the same even from our court-appointed lawyers as we sat down, under guard, at a table, as our hearing assembled. Before the judge entered, I said to one lawyer, "We seem to be getting sentenced because of those girls." He got red from the neck up and shuffled his papers: "You had no business with white girls!"

Later, when I had learned the full truth about the white man, I reflected many times that the average burglary sentence for a first offender, as we all were, was about two years. But we[2] weren't going to get the average—not for *our* crime....

[In the chapter's last autobiographical excerpt, Malcolm related his first exposure to the ideas of the Nation of Islam through his brother Philbert, his initial reaction to the Nation's teachings about whites and blacks, and how hard it was for him at first to humble himself by kneeling before Allah.]

Saved

One day in 1948, after I had been transferred to Concord Prison, my brother Philbert, who was forever joining something, wrote me this time that he had discovered the "natural religion for the black man." He belonged now, he said, to something called "the Nation of Islam." He said I should "pray to Allah for deliverance."...

He told me that this God had come to America, and that he had made himself known to a man named Elijah—"a black man, just like us." This God had let Elijah know, Reginald said, that the devil's "time was up."

I didn't know what to think. I just listened.

"The devil is also a man," Reginald said.

"What do you mean?"

---

[2] Malcolm was sentenced to ten years in prison; he was paroled in 1952 after serving six years.

With a slight movement of his head, Reginald indicated some white inmates and their visitors talking, as we were, across the room.

"Them," he said. "The white man is the devil." . . .

After Reginald left, I thought. I thought. Thought.

I couldn't make of it head, or tail, or middle.

The white people I had known marched before my mind's eye. From the start of my life. The state white people always in our house after the other whites I didn't know had killed my father . . . the white people who kept calling my mother "crazy" to her face and before me and my brothers and sisters, until she finally was taken off by white people to the Kalamazoo asylum . . . the white judge and others who had split up the children. . . .

When Reginald left, he left me rocking with some of the first serious thoughts I had ever had in my life: that the white man was fast losing his power to oppress and exploit the dark world; that the dark world was starting to rise to rule the world again, as it had before; that the white man's world was on the way down, it was on the way out.

"You don't even know who you are," Reginald had said. "You don't even know, the white devil has hidden it from you, that you are of a race of people of ancient civilizations, and riches in gold and kings. You don't even know your true family name, you wouldn't recognize your true language if you heard it. You have been cut off by the devil white man from all true knowledge of your own kind. You have been a victim of the evil of the devil white man ever since he murdered and raped and stole you from your native land in the seeds of your forefathers. . . ."

Many a time, I have looked back, trying to assess, just for myself, my first reactions to all this. Every instinct of the ghetto jungle streets, every hustling fox and criminal wolf instinct in me, which would have scoffed at and rejected anything else, was struck numb. It was as though all of that life merely was back there, without any remaining effect, or influence. . . .

The very enormity of my previous life's guilt prepared me to accept the truth.

Not for weeks yet would I deal with the direct, personal application to myself, as a black man, of the truth. It still was like a blinding light. . . .

The hardest test I ever faced in my life was praying. You understand. My comprehending, my believing the teachings of Mr. Muhammad had only required my mind's saying to me, "That's right!" or "I never thought of that."

But bending my knees to pray—that *act*—well, that took me a week.

You know what my life had been. Picking a lock to rob someone's house was the only way my knees had ever been bent before.

I had to force myself to bend my knees. And waves of shame and embarrassment would force me back up.

For evil to bend its knees, admitting its guilt, to implore the forgiveness of God, is the hardest thing in the world. It's easy for me to see and to say that now. But then, when I was the personification of evil, I was going through it. Again, again, I would force myself back down into the praying-to-Allah posture. . . .

2
Social Ends: Racial Integration versus Separation

King consistently identified his ultimate social goal as realizing the "beloved community." King's conception of the beloved community was a society in which all members related to each other with the attitude of agape, or unconditional love. Achieving social justice and reconciliation were prerequisites for realizing a community in which, at both personal and institutional levels, love would be the regulating ideal. King was unswervingly committed to racial integration, since any loving community had necessarily to include all members of the human family, regardless of race, class, gender, or nation.

King's immediate goals and priorities changed considerably over time. His main goals gradually shifted from ending segregation to gaining black voting rights and political power, and finally to abolishing war and poverty. His tactics for achieving his goals also evolved. During the fifties and early sixties, he counted on white northern and federal government goodwill, whereas by the late sixties he believed that only forceful pressure could move a basically uncaring white public and government to respond. Always, even amid significant change, King remained totally committed to nonviolent means of resistance and to the final goal of an all-inclusive beloved community.

Malcolm, by contrast, became infamous for spurning the goal of racial integration. As a minister of the Nation of Islam, Malcolm energetically preached the group's teaching of black self-development and establishment of independent institutions controlled by blacks. Complete withdrawal and separation from white society was the NOI program. Although never forsaking the principle of nationalist group development, Malcolm would later significantly modify his position on racial separation (as will be seen in chapter 6, "Eras of Convergence"). During the period from which this chapter's documents come, though, Malcolm was totally committed to African American separatism.

MARTIN LUTHER KING JR.

The Ethical Demands for Integration
1963

This speech surely ranks among King's most eloquent explanations of the philosophy and values behind his and his compatriots' efforts to achieve racial integration.

A number of King's most characteristic tenets are illustrated in this document, including his beliefs that

— *all human beings have sacred intrinsic worth;*
— *segregation is a violation of people's humanity;*
— *all humanity is interrelated;*
— *the* means *of social struggle must be morally congruent with its ends; and*
— *inward transformation of the heart, as well as outward reform of institutions, is necessary for building true community.*

The problem of race and color prejudice remains America's greatest moral dilemma. When one considers the impact it has upon our nation, internally and externally, its resolution might well determine our destiny. History has thrust upon our generation an indescribably important task—to complete a process of democratization which our nation has too long developed too slowly, but which is our most powerful weapon for world respect and emulation. How we deal with this crucial situation will determine our moral health as individuals, our cultural health as a region, our political health as a nation, and our prestige as a leader of the free world. The shape of the world today does not afford us the luxury of an anemic democracy. The price that America must pay for the continued oppression of the Negro is the price of its own destruction. The hour is late; the clock of destiny is ticking out; we must act now before it is too late.

Religion and Labor (May 1963): 1, 3–4, 7–8; reprinted in James M. Washington, ed., *A Testament of Hope: The Essential Writings and Speeches of Martin Luther King Jr.* (San Francisco: HarperCollins, 1986), 117–25.

"Fanatical Death Throes"

Happily, we have made some meaningful strides in breaking down the barriers of racial segregation. Ever since 1954, when the Supreme Court examined the legal body of segregation and pronounced it constitutionally dead, the system has been on the wane. Even the devout diehards who used to cry "never," are now saying "later." Much of the tumult and the shouting interspersed with tirades against "race-mixing," "mongrelization of the races," and "outside agitators" represent the fanatical death throes of a dying system. As minimal as may be the "across-the-board" statistics, desegregation is in process. The bells of history are definitely tolling for segregation. I am convinced that in less than ten years desegregation will be a reality throughout the South.

Desegregation Not Enough

However, when the *desegregation* process is one hundred percent complete, the human relations dilemma of our nation will still be monumental unless we launch now the parallel thrust of the *integration* process. Although the terms desegregation and integration are often used interchangeably, there is a great deal of difference between the two. In the context of what our national community needs, *desegregation* alone is empty and shallow. We must always be aware of the fact that our ultimate goal is integration, and that desegregation is only a first step on the road to the good society. Perhaps this is the point at which we should define our terms.

Integration the Ultimate Goal

The word *desegregation* represents a system that is prohibitive; it denies the Negro equal access to schools, parks, restaurants, libraries and the like. *Desegregation* is eliminative and negative, for it simply removes these legal and social prohibitions. Integration is creative, and is therefore more profound and far-reaching than desegregation. Integration is the positive acceptance of desegregation and the welcomed participation of Negroes into the total range of human activities. Integration is genuine intergroup, interpersonal doing. Desegregation then, rightly, is only a short-range goal. Integration is the ultimate goal of our national community. Thus, as America pursues the important task of respecting the "letter of the law," i.e., compliance with desegregation decisions, she must be equally concerned with the "spirit of the law," i.e., commitment to the democratic dream of integration.

We do not have to look very far to see the pernicious effects of a desegregated society that is not integrated. It leads to "physical proximity without spiritual affinity." It gives us a society where men are physically desegregated and spiritually segregated, where elbows are together and hearts are apart. It gives us special togetherness and spiritual apartness. It leaves us with a stagnant equality of sameness rather than a constructive equality of oneness.

Therefore, our topic leads us to an analysis of the "oughtness" of integration. On the basis of what is right, why is integration an *end* and desegration only a *means*? In the context of justice, freedom, morality and religion, what are the basic ethical demands of integration?

The Worth of Persons

There must be a recognition of the sacredness of human personality. Deeply rooted in our political and religious heritage is the conviction that every man is an heir to a legacy of dignity and worth. Our Hebraic-Christian tradition refers to this inherent dignity of man in the Biblical term *the image of God*. This innate worth referred to in the phrase the image of God is universally shared in equal portions by all men. There is no graded scale of essential worth; there is no divine right of one race which differs from the divine right of another. Every human being has etched in his personality the indelible stamp of the Creator.

This idea of the dignity and worth of human personality is expressed eloquently and unequivocally in the Declaration of Independence. "All men," it says, "are created equal. They are endowed by their Creator with certain inalienable rights, among these are life, liberty and the pursuit of happiness." Never has a sociopolitical document proclaimed more profoundly and eloquently the sacredness of human personality.

Frederick Douglass stated the same truth in his lecture on the Constitution of the United States. He says: "Its language is, 'We the people'; not we the white people, not even we the citizens, not we the privileged class, not we the high, not we the low, but we the people ... we the human inhabitants; and if Negroes are people they are included in the benefits for which the Constitution of America was ordained and established."

Segregation stands diametrically opposed to the principle of the sacredness of human personality. It debases personality. Immanuel Kant said in one formulation of the *Categorical Imperative* that "all men must be treated as *ends* and never as mere *means*." The tragedy of segregation is that it treats men as means rather than ends, and thereby reduces them to things rather than persons. To use the words of Martin Buber, segregation substitutes an "I-it" relationship for the "I-thou" relationship. The colloquialism of the southern landed gentry that referred to slaves and/or Negro labor as "hands" betrays the "thing" quality assigned to Negroes under the system. Herein lies the root of paternalism that persists even today. The traditional southerner is fond of "his Negro" as he is of a pet or a finely-tooled fire arm. "It" serves a purpose or gets a job done. The only concern is performance, not well-being.

But man is not a thing. He must be dealt with, not as an "animated tool," but as a person sacred in himself. To do otherwise is to depersonalize the potential person and desecrate what he is. So long as the Negro is treated as a means to an end, so long as he is seen as anything less than a person of sacred worth, the image of God is abused in him and consequently and proportionately lost by those who inflict the abuse. Only by establishing a truly integrated society can we return to the Negro the quality of "thouness" which is his due because of the nature of his being.

Life Demands Freedom

A second ethical demand of integration is a recognition of the fact that a denial of freedom to an individual is a denial of life itself. The very character of the life of man demands freedom. . . .

. . . The essence of man is found in freedom. This is what Paul Tillich[1] means when he declares, "Man is man because he is free," or what Tolstoy implies when he says, "I cannot conceive of a man not being free unless he is dead."

What Is Freedom?

What is freedom? It is, first, the capacity to deliberate or weigh alternatives. "Shall I be a teacher or a lawyer?" "Shall I vote for this candidate

---

[1] Paul Tillich (1886–1965) was one of the major Protestant theologians of the twentieth century; Leo Tolstoy (1828–1910) was one of Russia's greatest novelists and an influential moral philosopher.

or the other candidate?" "Shall I be a Democrat, Republican or Socialist?" Second, freedom expresses itself in decision. The word decision like the word incision involves the image of cutting. Incision means to cut in, decision means to cut off. When I make a decision I cut off alternatives and make a choice. The existentialists say we must choose, that we are choosing animals; and if we do not choose we sink into thinghood and the mass mind. A third expression of freedom is responsibility. This is the obligation of the person to respond if he is questioned about his decisions. No one else can respond for him. He alone must respond, for his acts are determined by the centered totality of his being.

From this analysis we can clearly see the evilness of segregation. It cuts off one's capacity to deliberate, decide and respond.

The absence of freedom is the imposition of restraint on my deliberation as to what I shall do, where I shall live, how much I shall earn, the kind of tasks I shall pursue. I am robbed of the basic quality of man-ness. When I cannot choose what I shall do or where I shall live or how I shall survive, it means in fact that someone or some system has already made these a priori decisions for me, and I am reduced to an animal. I do not live; I merely exist. The only resemblances I have to real life are the motor responses and functions that are akin to humankind. I cannot adequately assume responsibility as a person because I have been made a party to a decision in which I played no part in making.

Now to be sure, this is hyperbole in some degree but only to underscore what actually happens when a man is robbed of his freedom. The very nature of his life is altered and his being cannot make the full circle of personhood because that which is basic to the character of life itself has been diminished.

"Social Leprosy"

This is why segregation has wreaked havoc with the Negro. It is sometimes difficult to determine which are the deepest—the physical wounds or the psychological wounds. Only a Negro can understand the social leprosy that segregation inflicts upon him. The suppressed fears and resentments, and the expressed anxieties and sensitivities make each day of life a turmoil. Every confrontation with the restrictions imposed is another emotional battle in a never-ending war. He is shackled in his waking moments to tiptoe stance, never quite knowing what to expect next and in his subconscious he wrestles with this added demon.

Is there any argument to support the withdrawing of life-quality from groups because of the color of their skin, or the texture of their hair or any external characteristic which has nothing at all to do with life-quality? Certainly not on the grounds of morality, justice or religion. Nothing can be more diabolical than a deliberate attempt to destroy in any man his will to be a man and to withhold from him that something that constitutes his true reserve. Desegregation then is not enough for it only travels a part of the distance. It vouchsafes the lack of restriction against one's freedom but it does not prohibit the blocking of his total capacity. Only integration can do this, for it unchains the spirit and the mind and provides for the highest degree of life-quality freedom. I may do well in a *desegregated* society but I can never know what my total capacity is until I live in an *integrated* society. I cannot be free until I have had the opportunity to fulfill my total capacity untrammeled by an artificial hindrance or barrier.

Integration demands that we recognize that a denial of freedom is a denial of life itself.

The Unity of Humanity

A third ethical demand of integration is a recognition of the solidarity of the human family. Integration seems almost inevitably desirable and practical because basically we are all one. Paul's declaration that God "hath made of one blood" all nations of the world is more anthropological fact than religious poetry. The physical differences between the races are insignificant when compared to the physical identities. The world's foremost anthropologists all agree that there is no basic difference in the racial groups of our world. Most deny the actual existence of what we have known as "race." There are four major blood types and all four are found in every racial group. There are no superior and inferior races.

The next truth is evidential in the history of mankind. Not only are all men alike (generically speaking), but man is by nature a societal creature. Aside from the strength and weakness found in *Homo sapiens*, man has been working from the beginning at the great adventure of "community." ... the mutually cooperative and voluntary venture of man to assume a semblance of responsibility for his brother....

The universe is so structured that things do not quite work out rightly if men are not diligent in their concern for others. The self cannot be self without other selves. I cannot reach fulfillment without thou. Social psychologists tell us that we cannot truly be persons unless we interact with other persons. All life is interrelated. All men are caught in an inescapable network of mutuality, tied in a single garment of destiny....

God and Human Worth

Now let me hasten to say that while all of the three aforementioned points are basic, they represent Christianity's minimal declaration of human unity. In the final analysis, says the Christian ethic, every man must be respected because God loves him. The worth of an individual does not lie in the measure of his intellect, his racial origin, or his social position. Human worth lies in relatedness to God. An individual has value because he has value to God. Whenever this is recognized, "whiteness" and "blackness" pass away as determinants in a relationship and "son" and "brother" are substituted.

For me, this is a welcome conference. In the last few years we have had to face admittedly some very sharp changes in our customs and mores in the South. They have been difficult changes, not only to whites, but also at times to Negroes.

". . . Because It Is Right!"

Nevertheless, as difficult as the changes may be, it is change produced by that which is right. Yet it is this simple truth that has escaped the focus of the nation's and the South's attention. It is sad that the moral dimension of integration has not been sounded by the leaders of government and the nation. They staunchly supported the principle of the Court's decision but their rationale fell short of being prophetic. They sounded the note that has become the verse, chorus and refrain of the so-called calm and reasonable moderates—*we must obey the law!* The temper of acceptance might be far different if only our leaders would say publicly to the nation—"We must obey the mandate of the Court *because it is right!"*

This conference places the issue of national morality squarely before us. Desegregation is not enough; integration alone is consonant with our national purpose.

Let me hasten to say that despite the tremendous difficulties that integration imposes, nonetheless, work toward its implementation is not to be abandoned for the sake of approximating the more accessible goal of desegregation. Further a word of caution might be said to those who would argue that desegregation should be abandoned and all of our energies invested in the integration process. It is not an "either-or," it is a "both-and," undertaking. Desegregation is the necessary step in the right direction if we are to achieve integration. Desegregation will not change attitudes but it will provide the contact and confrontation necessary by which integration is made possible and attainable.

Desegregation Is "Enforceable" but Integration Is Not

I can summarize all that I have been saying by affirming that the demands of desegregation are enforceable demands while the demands of integration fall within the scope of unenforceable demands.

Some time ago Dr. Harry Emerson Fosdick[2] made an impressive distinction between enforceable and unenforceable obligations. The former are regulated by the codes of society and the vigorous implementation of law-enforcement agencies. Breaking these obligations, spelled out on thousands of pages in law books, has filled numerous prisons. But unenforceable obligations are beyond the reach of the laws of society. They concern inner attitudes, genuine person-to-person relations, and expressions of compassion which law books cannot regulate and jails cannot rectify. Such obligations are met by one's commitment to an inner law, written on the heart. Man-made laws assure justice, but a higher law produces love. No code of conduct ever compelled a father to love his children or a husband to show affection to his wife. The law court may force him to provide bread for the family, but it cannot make him provide the bread of love. A good father is obedient to the unenforceable.

Law Can Help

Let us never succumb to the temptation of believing that legislation and judicial decrees play only minor roles in solving this problem. Morality cannot be legislated, but behavior can be regulated. Judicial decrees may not change the heart, but they can restrain the heartless The law cannot make an employer love an employee, but it can prevent

---

[2]Harry Emerson Fosdick (1878–1969) was a popular Protestant preacher and writer in the first half of the twentieth century.

him from refusing to hire me because of the color of my skin. The habits, if not the hearts of people, have been and are being altered everyday by legislative acts, judicial decisions and executive orders. Let us not be misled by those who argue that segregation cannot be ended by the force of law.

But acknowledging this, we must admit that the ultimate solution to the race problem lies in the willingness of men to obey the unenforceable. Court orders and federal enforcement agencies are of inestimable value in achieving desegregation, but desegregation is only a partial, though necessary step toward the final goal which we seek to realize, genuine intergroup and interpersonal living. Desegregation will break down the legal barriers and bring men together physically, but something must touch the hearts and souls of men so that they will come together spiritually because it is natural and right. A vigorous enforcement of civil rights laws will bring an end to segregated public facilities which are barriers to a truly desegregated society, but it cannot bring an end to fears, prejudice, pride, and irrationality, which are the barriers to a truly integrated society. Those dark and demonic responses will be removed only as men are possessed by the invisible, inner law which etches on their hearts the conviction that all men are brothers and that love is mankind's most potent weapon for personal and social transformation. True integration will be achieved by true neighbors who are willingly obedient to unenforceable obligations.

The Discipline of Nonviolence

I cannot conclude without saying that integration places certain ethical demands upon those who have been on the oppressed end of the old order. Perhaps this is why it is my personal conviction that the most potent instrument the Negro community can use to gain total emancipation in America is that of nonviolent resistance. The evidence of the last few years supports my faith that through the use of nonviolence much can be done to raise the Negro to a sense of self-respect and human dignity. The Gandhian concept of noninjury parallels the Hebraic-Christian teaching of the sacredness of every human being.

In the context of the Negro's thrust for the full exercise of constitutional privilege, nonviolence has introduced the additive that has helped the Negro stand taller. When a library is declared to be desegregated, the presence and practice of nonviolence allows him to seek the use of the facilities without fear and apprehension. More than this, it has instilled in him the verve to challenge segregation and discrimination in whatever form it exists. Nonviolence in so many ways has given the Negro a new sense of "somebodyness." The impact of the nonviolent discipline has done a great deal toward creating in the mind of the Negro a new image of himself. It has literally exalted the person of the Negro in the South in the face of daily confrontations that scream at him that he is inferior or less than because of the accident of his birth.

How Nonviolence Helps

Nonviolence helps the individuals to adhere to proper means and proper goals. The nonviolent technique is double-barreled; not only has the Negro developed a new image of himself employing its practices, but it has also thwarted the growth of bitterness. In a very large measure, nonviolence has helped to diminish long-repressed feelings of anger and frustration. In the course of respecting the discipline of the nonviolent way, the Negro has learned that he must respect the adversary who inflicts the system upon him and he develops the capacity to hate segregation but to love the segregationist. He learns in the midst of his determined efforts to destroy the system that has shackled him so long, that a commitment to nonviolence demands that he respect the personhood of his opponent. Thus, nonviolence exalts the personality of the *segregator* as well as the *segregated*. The common denominator of the flux of social change in the South is the growing awareness on the part of the respective opponents that mutually they confront the eternality of the basic worth of every member of the human family.

MALCOLM X

From *The Black Revolution*
1963

In *"The Black Revolution"* Malcolm forcefully advocated black separation from whites and black autonomous development. Since he was still preaching the fundamental Nation of Islam gospel, much of his rationale

---

Speech delivered at Abyssinian Baptist Church, New York City, June 1963, as reprinted in Imam Benjamin Karim, ed., *The End of White World Supremacy: Four Speeches by Malcolm X* (New York: Seaver Books, 1971), 67–74.

for separation was predicated on the Nation's belief in white society's imminent destruction.

In this speech to a predominantly black Christian audience in New York City's Abyssinian Baptist Church, Malcolm vigorously defended the positions of Mr. Muhammad and the Nation. The speech contains examples of Malcolm's skill at using the Bible to support NOI doctrines. That his talk brought frequent outbursts of applause and laughter from a predominantly Christian audience highlights his amazing ability, even while still delivering the undiluted NOI message, to connect with blacks of different views and backgrounds.

Since the black masses here in America are now in open revolt against the American system of segregation, will these same black masses turn toward integration or will they turn toward complete separation? Will these awakened black masses demand integration into the white society that enslaved them or will they demand complete separation from that cruel white society that has enslaved them? Will the exploited and oppressed black masses seek integration with their white exploiters and white oppressors or will these awakened black masses truly revolt and separate themselves completely from this wicked race that has enslaved us?

These are just some quick questions that I think will provoke some thoughts in your minds and my mind. How can the so-called Negroes who call themselves enlightened leaders expect the poor black sheep to integrate into a society of bloodthirsty white wolves, white wolves who have already been sucking on our blood for over four hundred years here in America? Or will these black sheep also revolt against the "false shepherd," the handpicked Uncle Tom Negro leader, and seek complete separation so that we can escape from the den of the wolves rather than be integrated with wolves in this wolves' den? And since we are in church and most of us here profess to believe in God, there is another question: When the "good shepherd" comes will he integrate his long-lost sheep with white wolves? According to the Bible when God comes he won't even let his sheep integrate with goats. And if his sheep can't be safely integrated with goats they certainly aren't safe integrated with wolves. The Honorable Elijah Muhammad teaches us that no people on earth fit the Bible's symbolic picture about the Lost Sheep more so than America's twenty million so-called Negroes and there has never in history been a more vicious and bloodthirsty wolf than the American white man. He teaches us that for four hundred years America has been nothing but a wolves' den for twenty million so-called Negroes, twenty million second-class citizens, and this black revolution that is developing against the white wolf today is developing because The Honorable Elijah Muhammad, a godsent shepherd, has opened the eyes of our people. And the black masses can now see that we have all been here in this white doghouse long, too long. The black masses don't want segregation nor do we want integration. What we want is complete separation. In short, we don't want to be segregated by the white man, we don't want to be integrated with the white man, we want to be separated from the white man. And now our religious leader and teacher, The Honorable Elijah Muhammad, teaches us that this is the only intelligent and lasting solution to the present race problem.... The Muslim followers of The Honorable Elijah Muhammad actually reject hypocritical promises of integration....

The Honorable Elijah Muhammad teaches us that the symbolic stories in all religious scriptures paint a prophetic picture of today. He says that the Egyptian House of Bondage was only a prophetic picture of America. Mighty Babylon was only a prophetic picture of America. The wicked cities of Sodom and Gomorrah painted only a prophetic picture of America. No one here in this church tonight can deny that America is the mightiest government on earth today, the mightiest, the richest, and the wickedest. And no one in this church tonight dare deny that America's wealth and power stemmed from 310 years of slave labor contributed from the American so-called Negro.

The Honorable Elijah Muhammad teaches us that these same so-called American Negroes are God's long-lost people who are symbolically described in the Bible as the Lost Sheep or the Lost Tribe of Israel. We who are Muslims believe in God, we believe in his scriptures, we believe in prophecy. Nowhere in the scriptures did God ever integrate his enslaved people with their slave masters. God always separates his oppressed people from their oppressor and then destroys the oppressor. God has never deviated from his divine pattern in the past and The Honorable Elijah Muhammad says that God will not deviate from that divine pattern today. Just as God destroyed the enslavers in the past, God is going to destroy this wicked white enslaver of our people here in America.

God wants us to separate ourselves from this wicked white race here in America because this American House of Bondage is number one on God's list for divine destruction today. I repeat: This American House of Bondage is number one on God's list for divine destruction today. He warns us to remember Noah never taught integration, Noah taught separation; Moses never taught integration, Moses taught separation. The innocent must always be given a chance to separate themselves from the guilty before the guilty are executed. No one is more innocent than the poor, blind, American so-called Negro who has been led astray by blind Negro leaders, and no one on earth is more guilty than the blue-eyed white man who has used his control and influence over the Negro leader to lead the rest of our people astray....

... The Honorable Elijah Muhammad says a desegregated theater, a desegregated lunch counter won't solve our problem. Better jobs won't solve our problems. An integrated cup of coffee isn't sufficient pay for four hundred years of slave labor. He also says that a better job, a better job in the white man's factory, or a better job in the white man's business, or a better job in the white man's industry or economy is, at best, only a temporary solution. He says that the only lasting and permanent solution is complete separation on some land that we can call our own. Therefore, The Honorable Elijah Muhammad says that this problem can be solved and solved forever just by sending our people back to our own homeland or back to our own people, but that this government should provide the transportation plus everything else we need to get started again in our own country. This government should give us everything we need in the form of machinery, material, and finance—enough to last for twenty to twenty-five years until we can become an independent people and an independent nation in our own land....

And in my conclusion I repeat: We want no part of integration with this wicked race that enslaved us. We want complete separation from this wicked race of devils.

Independence, Not Separation

1964

This document is from an interview with Malcolm on March 19, 1964, less than two weeks after he announced that he was leaving Elijah Muhammad's Nation of Islam and then announced formation of his own

Excerpt from "Interview with Malcolm X" by A. B. Spellman in *Monthly Review* (May 1964); reprinted in George Breitman, ed., *By Any Means Necessary: Speeches, Interviews, and a Letter by Malcolm X* (New York: Pathfinder Press, 1970), 5–10.

rival organization, Muslim Mosque, Inc. Although Malcolm had not yet rejected the goal of racial separation, his language about it was changing. America's destruction by Allah, for example, no longer appears in his reasons. He even began resisting the word "separation" to describe his program for African American progress. He clarified his program and philosophy of black nationalism, explaining that it meant African Americans' independent development and control over their own institutions and destiny.

... *Spellman:* How religious is the Muslim Mosque, Inc.? Will it be more politically oriented?

Malcolm: The Muslim Mosque, Inc., will have as its religious base the religion of Islam, which will be designed to propagate the moral reformation necessary to up the level of the so-called Negro community by eliminating the vices and the other evils that destroy the moral fiber of the community—this is the religious base. But the political philosophy of the Muslim Mosque will be black nationalism, the economic philosophy will be black nationalism, and the social philosophy will be black nationalism. And by political philosophy I mean we still believe in the Honorable Elijah Muhammad's solution as complete separation. The 22 million so-called Negroes should be separated completely from America and should be permitted to go back home to our African homeland, which is a long-range program. So the short-range program is that we must eat while we're still here, we must have a place to sleep, we must have clothes to wear, we must have better jobs, we must have better education. So that although our long-range political philosophy is to migrate back to our African homeland, our short-range program must involve that which is necessary to enable us to live a better life while we are still here. We must be in complete control of the politics of the so-called Negro community; we must gain complete control over the politicians in the so-called Negro community, so that no outsider will have any voice in the so-called Negro community. We'll do it ourselves.

... *Spellman:* What is the program for achieving your goals of separation?

Malcolm: A better word to use than separation is independence. This word separation is misused. The thirteen colonies separated from England but they called it the Declaration of Independence; they don't call it the Declaration of Separation, they call it the Declaration of Independence. When you're independent of someone you can separate from them. If you can't separate from them it means you're not independent of them. So, your question was what?

Spellman: What is your program for achieving your goals of independence?

Malcolm: When the black man in this country awakens, becomes intellectually mature and able to think for himself, you will then see that the only way he will become independent and recognized as a human being on the basis of equality with all other human beings, he has to have what they have and he has to be doing for himself what others are doing for themselves. So the first step is to awaken him to this, and that is where the religion of Islam makes him morally more able to rise above the evils and the vices of an immoral society. And the political, economic, and social philosophy of black nationalism instills within him the racial dignity and the incentive and the confidence that he needs to stand on his own feet and take a stand for himself. . . .

3

Means of Struggle: Nonviolent Resistance versus "By Any Means Necessary"

We know . . . that freedom is never voluntarily given by the oppressor; it must be demanded by the oppressed. Frankly, I have yet to engage in a direct-action campaign that was "well timed" in the view of those who have not suffered . . . from . . . segregation.
— Martin Luther King

Violence as a way of achieving racial justice is both impractical and immoral. It is impractical because it is a descending spiral ending in destruction for all. . . . Violence is immoral because it thrives on hatred rather than love. It destroys community and makes brotherhood impossible. . . . Violence ends by defeating itself. It creates bitterness in the survivors and brutality in the destroyers.
— Martin Luther King

There's no such thing as a nonviolent revolution. . . . Revolution is bloody, revolution is hostile, revolution . . . overturns and destroys everything that gets in its way. — Malcolm X

The time for you and me to allow ourselves to be brutalized nonviolently is passé. *Be nonviolent only with those who are nonviolent to you.*
— Malcolm X

Throughout his career as America's preeminent civil rights leader, King often defended the use of mass directive action and civil disobedience against charges by many whites that it unduly provoked racial conflict, disturbed the peace, and promoted disrespect for law and order; by the later sixties, ironically, he had to justify his method as well before much of black opinion. King steadfastly championed nonviolent direct action as the most potent way to confront evil and make lasting social progress.

Malcolm just as consistently insisted on African Americans' fundamental right to defend and free themselves by all means, including, if need be, violence. Malcolm thought it suicidal for blacks to disarm themselves by forswearing use of physical force against a foe who showed no such compunction. It was undeniably just, he held, and probably necessary to "fight fire with fire" and use revolutionary force to attain blacks' freedom. Even when entertaining the possibility in his post-NOI phase that physical force *might* finally prove unnecessary, Malcolm still believed that asserting African Americans' right to self-defense and keeping the threat of retributive violence alive was strategically necessary to get a positive response from whites.

MARTIN LUTHER KING JR.

Letter from Birmingham Jail
1963

While imprisoned during a campaign in Birmingham, Alabama, for desegregation, King was disturbed to read a statement in a local newspaper by eight white clergy who criticized his work and ideas as wrong and unwise. His letter in response, stating why and how he and the other protesters did what they did, which he wrote surreptitiously in jail and smuggled out in bits, is one of King's most powerful and widely published statements.

April 16, 1963
MY DEAR FELLOW CLERGYMEN:
While confined here in the Birmingham city jail, I came across your recent statement calling my present activities "unwise and untimely." Seldom do I pause to answer criticism of my work and ideas. If I sought to answer all the criticisms that cross my desk, my secretaries would have little time for anything other than such correspondence in

---

Composed while King was in jail during the 1963 desegregation campaign in Birmingham, Alabama, the letter was originally published as a pamphlet by the American Friends Committee. It was subsequently published, in slightly revised form, by King in *Why We Can't Wait* (New York: Harper & Row, 1963, 1964), 76–95; text here is from the latter source.

the course of the day, and I would have no time for constructive work. But since I feel that you are men of genuine good will and that your criticisms are sincerely set forth, I want to try to answer your statement in what I hope will be patient and reasonable terms.

I think I should indicate why I am here in Birmingham, since you have been influenced by the view which argues against "outsiders coming in." I have the honor of serving as president of the Southern Christian Leadership Conference, an organization operating in every southern state, with headquarters in Atlanta, Georgia. We have some eighty-five affiliated organizations across the South, and one of them is the Alabama Christian Movement for Human Rights. Frequently we share staff, educational, and financial resources with our affiliates. Several months ago the affiliate here in Birmingham asked us to be on call to engage in a nonviolent direct-action program if such were deemed necessary. We readily consented, and when the hour came we lived up to our promise. So I, along with several members of my staff, am here because I was invited here. I am here because I have organizational ties here.

But more basically, I am in Birmingham because injustice is here. Just as the prophets of the eighth century B.C. left their villages and carried their "thus saith the Lord" far beyond the boundaries of their home towns, and just as the Apostle Paul left his village of Tarsus[1] and carried the gospel of Jesus Christ to the far corners of the Greco-Roman world, so am I compelled to carry the gospel of freedom beyond my own home town. Like Paul, I must constantly respond to the Macedonian call for aid.[2]

Moreover, I am cognizant of the interrelatedness of all communities and states. I cannot sit idly by in Atlanta and not be concerned about what happens in Birmingham. Injustice anywhere is a threat to justice everywhere. We are caught in an inescapable network of mutuality, tied in a single garment of destiny. Whatever affects one directly, affects all indirectly. Never again can we afford to live with the narrow, provincial, "outside agitator" idea. Anyone who lives inside the United States can never be considered an outsider anywhere within its bounds.

You deplore the demonstrations taking place in Birmingham. But your statement, I am sorry to say, fails to express a similar concern for the conditions that brought about the demonstrations. I am sure that

---

[1]Tarsus, in current-day Turkey, was the birthplace of Saint Paul.
[2]*Macedonian call:* Paul frequently responded to pleas for help and visited early Christians in Philippi, a city in Macedonia, or northern Greece.

none of you would want to rest content with the superficial kind of social analysis that deals merely with effects and does not grapple with underlying causes. It is unfortunate that demonstrations are taking place in Birmingham, but it is even more unfortunate that the city's white power structure left the Negro community with no alternative.

In any nonviolent campaign there are four basic steps: collection of the facts to determine whether injustices exist; negotiation; self-purification; and direct action. We have gone through all these steps in Birmingham. There can be no gainsaying the fact that racial injustice engulfs this community. Birmingham is probably the most thoroughly segregated city in the United States. Its ugly record of brutality is widely known. Negroes have experienced grossly unjust treatment in the courts. There have been more unsolved bombings of Negro homes and churches in Birmingham than in any other city in the nation. These are the hard brutal facts of the case. On the basis of these conditions, Negro leaders sought to negotiate with the city fathers. But the latter consistently refused to engage in good-faith negotiation.

Then, last September, came the opportunity to talk with leaders of Birmingham's economic community. In the course of the negotiations, certain promises were made by the merchants—for example, to remove the stores' humiliating racial signs. On the basis of these promises, the Reverend Fred Shuttlesworth and the leaders of the Alabama Christian Movement for Human Rights agreed to a moratorium on all demonstrations. As the weeks and months went by, we realized that we were the victims of a broken promise. A few signs, briefly removed, returned; the others remained.

As in so many past experiences, our hopes had been blasted, and the shadow of deep disappointment settled upon us. We had no alternative except to prepare for direct action, whereby we would present our very bodies as a means of laying our case before the conscience of the local and the national community. Mindful of the difficulties involved, we decided to undertake a process of self-purification. We began a series of workshops on nonviolence, and we repeatedly asked ourselves: "Are you able to accept blows without retaliating?" "Are you able to endure the ordeal of jail?" We decided to schedule our direct-action program for the Easter season, realizing that except for Christmas, this is the main shopping period of the year. Knowing that a strong economic-withdrawal program would be the by-product of direct action, we felt that this would be the best time to bring pressure to bear on the merchants for the needed change.

Then it occurred to us that Birmingham's mayoral election was coming up in March, and we speedily decided to postpone action until after election day. When we discovered that the Commissioner of Public Safety, Eugene "Bull" Connor,[3] had piled up enough votes to be in the run-off, we decided again to postpone action until the day after the run-off so that the demonstrations could not be used to cloud the issues. Like many others, we waited to see Mr. Connor defeated, and to this end we endured postponement after postponement. Having aided in this community need, we felt that our direct-action program could be delayed no longer.

You may well ask, "Why direct action? Why sit-ins, marches, and so forth? Isn't negotiation a better path?" You are quite right in calling for negotiation. Indeed, this is the very purpose of direct action. Nonviolent direct action seeks to create such a crisis and foster such a tension that a community which has constantly refused to negotiate is forced to confront the issue. It seeks so to dramatize the issue that it can no longer be ignored. My citing the creation of tension as part of the work of the nonviolent resister may sound rather shocking. But I must confess that I am not afraid of the word "tension." I have earnestly opposed violent tension, but there is a type of constructive, nonviolent tension which is necessary for growth. Just as Socrates[4] felt that it was necessary to create a tension in the mind so that individuals could rise from the bondage of myths and half truths to the unfettered realm of creative analysis and objective appraisal, so must we see the need for nonviolent gadflies to create the kind of tension in society that will help men rise from the dark depths of prejudice and racism to the majestic heights of understanding and brotherhood.

The purpose of our direct-action program is to create a situation so crisis-packed that it will inevitably open the door to negotiation. I therefore concur with you in your call for negotiation. Too long has our beloved Southland been bogged down in a tragic effort to live in monologue rather than dialogue.

One of the basic points in your statement is that the action that I and my associates have taken in Birmingham is untimely. Some have asked: "Why didn't you give the new city administration time to act?"

---

[3]King and the SCLC wished to do nothing that might assist the political rise of Birmingham police commissioner Eugene "Bull" Connor, a hard-core segregationist with a quick temper, who personified racist police brutality in the South.

[4]Socrates, greatest of the ancient Greek philosophers, practiced the Socratic method, a question-answer technique to lead a person toward deeper thinking. He was executed for his own civil disobedience and his "unhealthy" effect on others in society.

The only answer that I can give to this query is that the new Birmingham administration must be prodded about as much as the outgoing one, before it will act. We are sadly mistaken if we feel that the election of Albert Boutwell as mayor will bring the millennium[5] to Birmingham. While Mr. Boutwell is a much more gentle person than Mr. Connor, they are both segregationists, dedicated to maintenance of the status quo. I have hoped that Mr. Boutwell will be reasonable enough to see the futility of massive resistance to desegregation. But he will not see this without pressure from devotees of civil rights. My friends, I must say to you that we have not made a single gain in civil rights without determined legal and nonviolent pressure. Lamentably, it is an historical fact that privileged groups seldom give up their privileges voluntarily. Individuals may see the moral light and voluntarily give up their unjust posture; but, as Reinhold Niebuhr[6] has reminded us, groups tend to be more immoral than individuals.

We know through painful experience that freedom is never voluntarily given by the oppressor; it must be demanded by the oppressed. Frankly, I have yet to engage in a direct-action campaign that was "well timed" in the view of those who have not suffered unduly from the disease of segregation. For years now I have heard the word "Wait!" It rings in the ear of every Negro with piercing familiarity. This "Wait" has almost always meant "Never." We must come to see, with one of our distinguished jurists, that "justice too long delayed is justice denied."[7]

We have waited for more than 340 years for our constitutional and God-given rights. The nations of Asia and Africa are moving with jet-like speed toward gaining political independence, but we still creep at horse-and-buggy pace toward gaining a cup of coffee at a lunch counter. Perhaps it is easy for those who have never felt the stinging darts of segregation to say, "Wait." But when you have seen vicious mobs lynch your mothers and fathers at will and drown your sisters and brothers at whim; when you have seen hate-filled policemen curse, kick, and even kill your black brothers and sisters; when you see the vast majority of your twenty million Negro brothers smothering in an airtight cage of poverty in the midst of an affluent society;

---

[5]*Millennium:* Christian belief in a thousand-year reign of peace and justice following the Second Coming of Christ.

[6]*Reinhold Niebuhr:* Early-twentieth-century founder of the Social Gospel and one of King's favorite theologians; King refers to Niebuhr's thesis in *Moral Man, Immoral Society* (1932).

[7]Supreme Court Chief Justice Earl Warren said this in 1954.

when you suddenly find your tongue twisted and your speech stammering as you seek to explain to your six-year-old daughter why she can't go to the public amusement park that has just been advertised on television, and see tears welling up in her eyes when she is told that Funtown is closed to colored children, and see ominous clouds of inferiority beginning to form in her little mental sky, and see her beginning to distort her personality by developing an unconscious bitterness toward white people; when you have to concoct an answer for a five-year-old son who is asking, "Daddy, why do white people treat colored people so mean?"; when you take a cross-country drive and find it necessary to sleep night after night in the uncomfortable corners of your automobile because no motel will accept you; when you are humiliated day in and day out by nagging signs reading "white" and "colored"; when your first name becomes "nigger," your middle name becomes "boy" (however old you are) and your last name becomes "John," and your wife and mother are never given the respected title "Mrs."; when you are harried by day and haunted by night by the fact that you are a Negro, living constantly at tiptoe stance, never quite knowing what to expect next, and are plagued with inner fears and outer resentments; when you are forever fighting a degenerating sense of "nobodiness"—then you will understand why we find it difficult to wait. There comes a time when the cup of endurance runs over, and men are no longer willing to be plunged into the abyss of despair. I hope, sirs, you can understand our legitimate and unavoidable impatience.

    You express a great deal of anxiety over our willingness to break laws. This is certainly a legitimate concern. Since we so diligently urge people to obey the Supreme Court's decision of 1954 outlawing segregation in the public schools, at first glance it may seem rather paradoxical for us consciously to break laws. One may well ask: "How can you advocate breaking some laws and obeying others?" The answer lies in the fact that there are two types of laws: just and unjust. I would be the first to advocate obeying just laws. One has not only a legal but a moral responsibility to obey just laws. Conversely, one has a moral responsibility to disobey unjust laws. I would agree with St. Augustine[8] that "an unjust law is no law at all."

    Now, what is the difference between the two? How does one determine whether a law is just or unjust? A just law is a manmade code that squares with the moral law or the law of God. An unjust law is a

---

[8] *St. Augustine:* Early church father and philosopher.

code that is out of harmony with the moral law. To put it in the terms of St. Thomas Aquinas:[9] An unjust law is a human law that is not rooted in eternal law and natural law. Any law that uplifts human personality is just. Any law that degrades human personality is unjust. All segregation statutes are unjust because segregation distorts the soul and damages the personality. It gives the segregator a false sense of superiority and the segregated a false sense of inferiority. Segregation, to use the terminology of the Jewish philosopher Martin Buber,[10] substitutes an "I-it" relationship for an "I-thou" relationship and ends up relegating persons to the status of things. Hence segregation is not only politically, economically, and sociologically unsound, it is morally wrong and sinful. Paul Tillich[11] has said that sin is separation. Is not segregation an existential expression of man's tragic separation, his awful estrangement, his terrible sinfulness? Thus it is that I can urge men to obey the 1954 decision of the Supreme Court, for it is morally right; and I can urge them to disobey segregation ordinances, for they are morally wrong.

Let us consider a more concrete example of just and unjust laws. An unjust law is a code that a numerical or power majority group compels a minority group to obey but does not make binding on itself. This is *difference* made legal. By the same token, a just law is a code that a majority compels a minority to follow and that it is willing to follow itself. This is *sameness* made legal.

Let me give another explanation. A law is unjust if it is inflicted on a minority that, as a result of being denied the right to vote, had no part in enacting or devising the law. Who can say that the legislature of Alabama which set up that state's segregation laws was democratically elected? Throughout Alabama all sorts of devious methods are used to prevent Negroes from becoming registered voters, and there are some counties in which, even though Negroes constitute a majority of the population, not a single Negro is registered. Can any law enacted under such circumstances be considered democratically structured?

Sometimes a law is just on its face and unjust in its application. For instance, I have been arrested on a charge of parading without a permit. Now, there is nothing wrong in having an ordinance which requires a permit for a parade. But such an ordinance becomes unjust when it is used to maintain segregation and to deny citizens the First Amendment privilege of peaceful assembly and protest.

[9] *St. Thomas Aquinas:* Major thirteenth-century church figure and philosopher.
[10] *Martin Buber:* Jewish theologian, wrote *I and Thou* (1929).
[11] *Paul Tillich:* Leading twentieth-century Protestant theologian.

I hope you are able to see the distinction I am trying to point out. In no sense do I advocate evading or defying the law, as would the rabid segregationist. That would lead to anarchy. One who breaks an unjust law must do so openly, lovingly, and with a willingness to accept the penalty. I submit that an individual who breaks a law that conscience tells him is unjust, and who willingly accepts the penalty of imprisonment in order to arouse the conscience of the community over its injustice, is in reality expressing the highest respect for law.

Of course, there is nothing new about this kind of civil disobedience. It was evidenced subliminally in the refusal of Shadrach, Meshach, and Abednego to obey the laws of Nebuchadnezzar,[12] on the ground that a higher moral law was at stake. It was practiced superbly by the early Christians, who were willing to face hungry lions and the excruciating pain of chopping blocks rather than submit to certain unjust laws of the Roman Empire. To a degree, academic freedom is a reality today because Socrates practiced civil disobedience. In our own nation, the Boston Tea Party represented a massive act of civil disobedience.

We should never forget that everything Adolf Hitler did in Germany was "legal" and everything the Hungarian freedom fighters[13] did in Hungary was "illegal." It was "illegal" to aid and comfort a Jew in Hitler's Germany. Even so, I am sure that, had I lived in Germany at the time, I would have aided and comforted my Jewish brothers. If today I lived in a Communist country where certain principles dear to the Christian faith are suppressed, I would openly advocate disobeying that country's antireligious laws.

I must make two honest confessions to you, my Christian and Jewish brothers. First, I must confess that over the past few years I have been gravely disappointed with the white moderate. I have almost reached the regrettable conclusion that the Negro's great stumbling block in his stride toward freedom is not the White Citizen's Counciler or the Ku Klux Klanner,[14] but the white moderate, who is more devoted to "order" than to justice; who prefers a negative peace which is the absence of tension to a positive peace which is the presence of justice; who constantly says, "I agree with you in the goal you seek, but I

---

[12]*Nebuchadnezzar:* Babylonian ruler. According to book of Daniel, he ordered the Jews Shadrach, Meshach, and Abednego, on pain of death, to worship an idol, but they refused.

[13]Hungarians rose up in a failed attempt to end Soviet rule in their country in 1956.

[14]White Citizens Councils were groups dedicated to maintaining segregation that sprang up across the South following the Supreme Court's ruling in the 1954 *Brown* decision; the Ku Klux Klan is a white supremacist terrorist group.

cannot agree with your methods of direct action"; who paternalistically believes he can set the timetable for another man's freedom; who lives by a mythical concept of time and who constantly advises the Negro to wait for a "more convenient season." Shallow understanding from people of good will is more frustrating than absolute misunderstanding from people of ill will. Lukewarm acceptance is much more bewildering than outright rejection.

I had hoped that the white moderate would understand that law and order exist for the purpose of establishing justice and that when they fail in this purpose they become the dangerously structured dams that block the flow of social progress. I had hoped that the moderate would understand that the present tension in the South is a necessary phase of the transition from an obnoxious negative peace, in which the Negro passively accepted his unjust plight, to a substantive and positive peace, in which all men will respect the dignity and worth of human personality. Actually, we who engage in nonviolent direct action are not the creators of tension. We merely bring to the surface the hidden tension that is already alive. We bring it out in the open, where it can be seen and dealt with. Like a boil that can never be cured so long as it is covered up but must be opened with all its ugliness to the natural medicines of air and light, injustice must be exposed, with all the tension its exposure creates, to the light of human conscience and the air of national opinion, before it can be cured.

In your statement you assert that our actions, even though peaceful, must be condemned because they precipitate violence. But is this a logical assertion? Isn't this like condemning a robbed man because his possession of money precipitated the evil act of robbery? Isn't this like condemning Socrates because his unswerving commitment to truth and his philosophical inquiries precipitated the act by the misguided populace in which they made him drink hemlock? Isn't this like condemning Jesus because his unique God-consciousness and never-ceasing devotion to God's will precipitated the evil act of crucifixion? We must come to see that, as the federal courts have consistently affirmed, it is wrong to urge an individual to cease his efforts to gain his basic constitutional rights because the quest may precipitate violence. Society must protect the robbed and punish the robber.

I had also hoped that the white moderate would reject the myth concerning time in relation to the struggle for freedom. I have just received a letter from a white brother in Texas. He writes: "All Christians know that the colored people will receive equal rights eventually, but it is possible that you are in too great a religious hurry. It has taken Christianity almost two thousand years to accomplish what it has. The teachings of Christ take time to come to earth." Such an attitude stems from a tragic misconception of time, from the strangely irrational notion that there is something in the very flow of time that will inevitably cure all ills. Actually, time itself is neutral; it can be used either destructively or constructively. More and more I feel that the people of ill will have used time much more effectively than have the people of good will. We will have to repent in this generation not merely for the hateful words and actions of the bad people, but for the appalling silence of the good people. Human progress never rolls in on wheels of inevitability; it comes through the tireless efforts of men willing to be co-workers with God, and without this hard work, time itself becomes an ally of the forces of social stagnation. We must use time creatively, in the knowledge that the time is always ripe to do right. Now is the time to make real the promise of democracy and transform our pending national elegy into a creative psalm of brotherhood. Now is the time to lift our national policy from the quicksand of racial injustice to the solid rock of human dignity.

You speak of our activity in Birmingham as extreme. At first I was rather disappointed that fellow clergymen would see my nonviolent efforts as those of an extremist. I began thinking about the fact that I stand in the middle of two opposing forces in the Negro community. One is a force of complacency, made up in part of Negroes who, as a result of long years of oppression, are so drained of self-respect and a sense of "somebodiness" that they have adjusted to segregation; and in part of a few middle-class Negroes who, because of a degree of academic and economic security and because in some ways they profit by segregation, have become insensitive to the problems of the masses. The other force is one of bitterness and hatred, and it comes perilously close to advocating violence. It is expressed in the various black nationalist groups that are springing up across the nation, the largest and best known being Elijah Muhammad's Muslim movement. Nourished by the Negro's frustration over the continued existence of racial discrimination, this movement is made up of people who have lost faith in America, who have absolutely repudiated Christianity, and who have concluded that the white man is an incorrigible "devil."

I have tried to stand between these two forces, saying that we need emulate neither the "do-nothingism" of the complacent nor the hatred and despair of the black nationalist. For there is the more excellent way of love and nonviolent protest. I am grateful to God that, through the influence of the Negro church, the way of nonviolence became an integral part of our struggle.

If this philosophy had not emerged, by now many streets of the South would, I am convinced, be flowing with blood. And I am further convinced that if our white brothers dismiss as "rabble-rousers" and "outside agitators" those of us who employ nonviolent direct action, and if they refuse to support our nonviolent efforts, millions of Negroes will, out of frustration and despair, seek solace and security in black nationalist ideologies—a development that would inevitably lead to a frightening racial nightmare.

Oppressed people cannot remain oppressed forever. The yearning for freedom eventually manifests itself, and that is what has happened to the American Negro. Something within has reminded him of his birthright of freedom, and something without has reminded him that it can be gained. Consciously or unconsciously, he has been caught up by the *Zeitgeist*,[15] and with his black brothers of Africa and his brown and yellow brothers of Asia, South America, and the Caribbean, the United States Negro is moving with a sense of great urgency toward the promised land of racial justice. If one recognizes this vital urge that has engulfed the Negro community, one should readily understand why public demonstrations are taking place. The Negro has many pent-up resentments and latent frustrations, and he must release them. So let him march; let him make prayer pilgrimages to the city hall; let him go on freedom rides[16]—and try to understand why he must do so. If his repressed emotions are not released in nonviolent ways, they will seek expression through violence; this is not a threat but a fact of history. So I have not said to my people, "Get rid of your discontent." Rather, I have tried to say that this normal and healthy discontent can be channeled into the creative outlet of nonviolent direct action. And now this approach is being termed extremist.

But though I was initially disappointed at being categorized as an extremist, as I continued to think about the matter I gradually gained a measure of satisfaction from the label. Was not Jesus an extremist for love: "Love your enemies, bless them that curse you, do good to them that hate you, and pray for them which despitefully use you, and

---

[15]*Zeitgeist:* German philosophical term for the general intellectual, moral, and cultural spirit of an age.

[16]*Freedom rides:* Rides of whites and blacks, organized in 1961, to test if southern buses and bus terminals were racially desegregated, as federal court decisions had required; the buses and facilities were not, and the freedom riders were met with violence in the South.

persecute you." Was not Amos an extremist for justice: "Let justice roll down like waters and righteousness like an everflowing stream." Was not Paul an extremist for the Christian gospel: "I bear in my body the marks of the Lord Jesus." Was not Martin Luther an extremist: "Here I stand; I cannot do otherwise, so help me God." And John Bunyan: "I will stay in jail to the end of my days before I make a butchery of my conscience." And Abraham Lincoln: "This nation cannot survive half slave and half free." And Thomas Jefferson: "We hold these truths to be self-evident, that all men are created equal . . ."[17] So the question is not whether we will be extremists, but what kind of extremists we will be. Will we be extremists for hate or for love? Will we be extremists for the preservation of injustice or for the extension of justice? In that dramatic scene on Calvary's hill three men were crucified. We must never forget that all three were crucified for the same crime—the crime of extremism. Two were extremists for immorality, and thus fell below their environment. The other, Jesus Christ, was an extremist for love, truth, and goodness, and thereby rose above his environment. Perhaps the South, the nation, and the world are in dire need of creative extremists.

I had hoped that the white moderate would see this need. Perhaps I was too optimistic; perhaps I expected too much. I suppose I should have realized that few members of the oppressor race can understand the deep groans and passionate yearnings of the oppressed race, and still fewer have the vision to see that injustice must be rooted out by strong, persistent, and determined action. I am thankful, however, that some of our white brothers in the South have grasped the meaning of this social revolution and committed themselves to it. They are still all too few in quantity, but they are big in quality. Some—such as Ralph McGill, Lillian Smith, Harry Golden, James McBride Dabbs, Ann Braden, and Sarah Patton Boyle—have written about our struggle[18] in eloquent and prophetic terms. Others have marched with us down nameless streets of the South. They have

---

[17] Amos, biblical prophet; the apostle Paul; Martin Luther, initiator of the Protestant Reformation; John Bunyan, popular English preacher and writer who was imprisoned for preaching the Christian gospel according to his views; Abraham Lincoln, U.S. president and emancipator of American slaves; Thomas Jefferson, U.S. president and author of the Declaration of Independence.

[18] Prominent white southern liberals and moderates who favored racial reform and many of the Civil Rights movement's goals, such as desegregation and universal voting rights. Journalist Ralph McGill was among the best-known white proponents of a "New South."

languished in filthy, roach-infested jails, suffering the abuse and brutality of policemen who view them as "dirty nigger-lovers." Unlike so many of their moderate brothers and sisters, they have recognized the urgency of the moment and sensed the need for powerful "action" antidotes to combat the disease of segregation.

Let me take note of my other major disappointment. I have been so greatly disappointed with the white church and its leadership. Of course, there are some notable exceptions. I am not unmindful of the fact that each of you has taken some significant stands on this issue. I commend you, Reverend Stallings, for your Christian stand on this past Sunday, in welcoming Negroes to your worship service on a non-segregated basis. I commend the Catholic leaders of this state for integrating Spring Hill College several years ago.

But despite these notable exceptions, I must honestly reiterate that I have been disappointed with the church. I do not say this as one of those negative critics who can always find something wrong with the church. I say this as a minister of the gospel, who loves the church; who was nurtured in its bosom; who has been sustained by its spiritual blessings and who will remain true to it as long as the cord of life shall lengthen.

When I was suddenly catapulted into the leadership of the bus protest in Montgomery, Alabama, a few years ago, I felt we would be supported by the white church. I felt that the white ministers, priests, and rabbis of the South would be among our strongest allies. Instead, some have been outright opponents, refusing to understand the freedom movement and misrepresenting its leaders; all too many others have been more cautious than courageous and have remained silent behind the anesthetizing security of stained-glass windows.

In spite of my shattered dreams, I came to Birmingham with the hope that the white religious leadership of this community would see the justice of our cause and, with deep moral concern, would serve as the channel through which our just grievances could reach the power structure. I had hoped that each of you would understand. But again I have been disappointed....

There was a time when the church was very powerful—in the time when the early Christians rejoiced at being deemed worthy to suffer for what they believed. In those days the church was not merely a thermometer that recorded the ideas and principles of popular opinion; it was a thermostat that transformed the mores of society. Whenever the early Christians entered a town, the people in power became disturbed and immediately sought to convict the Christians for being "disturbers of the peace" and "outside agitators." But the Christians pressed on, in the conviction that they were "a colony of heaven," called to obey God rather than man. Small in number, they were big in commitment. They were too God-intoxicated to be "astronomically intimidated." By their effort and example they brought an end to such ancient evils as infanticide and gladiatorial contests.

Things are different now. So often the contemporary church is a weak, ineffectual voice with an uncertain sound. So often it is an archdefender of the status quo. Far from being disturbed by the presence of the church, the powerful structure of the average community is consoled by the church's silent—and often even vocal—sanction of things as they are.

But the judgment of God is upon the church as never before. If today's church does not recapture the sacrificial spirit of the early church, it will lose its authenticity, forfeit the loyalty of millions, and be dismissed as an irrelevant social club with no meaning for the twentieth century. Every day I meet young people whose disappointment with the church has turned into outright disgust.

Perhaps I have once again been too optimistic. Is organized religion too inextricably bound to the status quo to save our nation and the world? Perhaps I must turn my faith to the inner spiritual church, the church within the church, as the true *ekklesia*[19] and the hope of the world. But again I am thankful to God that some noble souls from the ranks of organized religion have broken loose from the paralyzing chains of conformity and joined us as active partners in the struggle for freedom. They have left their secure congregations and walked the streets of Albany, Georgia, with us. They have gone down the highways of the South on torturous rides for freedom. Yes, they have gone to jail with us. Some have been dismissed from their churches, have lost the support of their bishops and fellow ministers. But they have acted in the faith that right defeated is stronger than evil triumphant. Their witness has been the spiritual salt that has preserved the true meaning of the gospel in these troubled times. They have carved a tunnel of hope through the dark mountain of disappointment.

I hope the church as a whole will meet the challenge of this decisive hour. But even if the church does not come to the aid of justice, I have no despair about the future. I have no fear about the outcome of our struggle in Birmingham, even if our motives are at present

---

[19] *ekklesia*: Greek word used in the Christian New Testament for the true church, or community of all saved individuals.

misunderstood. We will reach the goal of freedom in Birmingham and all over the nation, because the goal of America is freedom. Abused and scorned though we may be, our destiny is tied up with America's destiny. Before the pilgrims landed at Plymouth, we were here. Before the pen of Jefferson etched the majestic words of the Declaration of Independence across the pages of history, we were here. For more than two centuries our forebears labored in this country without wages; they made cotton king; they built the homes of their masters while suffering gross injustice and shameful humiliation—and yet out of a bottomless vitality they continued to thrive and develop. If the inexpressible cruelties of slavery could not stop us, the opposition we now face will surely fail. We will win our freedom because the sacred heritage of our nation and the eternal will of God are embodied in our echoing demands.

Before closing I feel impelled to mention one other point in your statement that has troubled me profoundly. You warmly commended the Birmingham police force for keeping "order" and "preventing violence." I doubt that you would have so warmly commended the police force if you had seen its dogs sinking their teeth into unarmed, nonviolent Negroes. I doubt that you would so quickly commend the policemen if you were to observe their ugly and inhumane treatment of Negroes here in the city jail; if you were to watch them push and curse old Negro women and young Negro girls; if you were to see them slap and kick old Negro men and young boys; if you were to observe them, as they did on two occasions, refuse to give us food because we wanted to sing our grace together. I cannot join you in your praise of the Birmingham police department.

It is true that the police have exercised a degree of discipline in handling the demonstrators. In this sense they have conducted themselves rather "nonviolently" in public. But for what purpose? To preserve the evil system of segregation. Over the past few years I have consistently preached that nonviolence demands that the means we use must be as pure as the ends we seek. I have tried to make clear that it is wrong to use immoral means to attain moral ends. But now I must affirm that it is just as wrong, or perhaps even more so, to use moral means to preserve immoral ends. Perhaps Mr. Connor and his policemen have been rather nonviolent in public, as was Chief Pritchett in Albany, Georgia, but they have used the moral means of nonviolence to maintain the immoral end of racial injustice. As T. S. Eliot[20]

---

[20] *T. S. Eliot:* One of the twentieth century's greatest poets.

has said, "The last temptation is the greatest treason: To do the right deed for the wrong reason."

I wish you had commended the Negro sit-inners and demonstrators of Birmingham for their sublime courage, their willingness to suffer, and their amazing discipline in the midst of great provocation. One day the South will recognize its real heroes. They will be the James Merediths,[21] with the noble sense of purpose that enables them to face jeering and hostile mobs, and with the agonizing loneliness that characterizes the life of the pioneer. They will be old, oppressed, battered Negro women, symbolized in a seventy-two-year-old woman in Montgomery, Alabama, who rose up with a sense of dignity and with her people decided not to ride segregated buses, and who responded with ungrammatical profundity to one who inquired about her weariness: "My feets is tired, but my soul is at rest." They will be the young high school and college students, the young ministers of the gospel and a host of their elders, courageously and nonviolently sitting in at lunch counters and willingly going to jail for conscience' sake. One day the South will know that when these disinherited children of God sat down at lunch counters, they were in reality standing up for what is best in the American dream and for the most sacred values in our Judaeo-Christian heritage, thereby bringing our nation back to those great wells of democracy which were dug deep by the founding fathers in their formulation of the Constitution and the Declaration of Independence.

Never before have I written so long a letter. I'm afraid it is much too long to take your precious time. I can assure you that it would have been much shorter if I had been writing from a comfortable desk, but what else can one do when he is alone in a narrow jail cell, other than write long letters, think long thoughts, and pray long prayers?

If I have said anything in this letter that overstates the truth and indicates an unreasonable impatience, I beg you to forgive me. If I have said anything that understates the truth and indicates my having a patience that allows me to settle for anything less than brotherhood, I beg God to forgive me.

I hope this letter finds you strong in the faith. I also hope that circumstances will soon make it possible for me to meet each of you, not as an integrationist or a civil rights leader but as a fellow clergyman

---

[21]*James Meredith:* In a major confrontation between state and federal authorities in 1962, he became the first African American admitted to the University of Mississippi.

and a Christian brother. Let us all hope that the dark clouds of racial prejudice will soon pass away and the deep fog of misunderstanding will be lifted from our fear-drenched communities, and in some not too distant tomorrow the radiant stars of love and brotherhood will shine over our great nation with all their scintillating beauty.

Yours in the cause of
Peace and Brotherhood,
MARTIN LUTHER KING JR.

From *Nonviolence: The Only Road to Freedom*
1966

By the time King wrote this spirited defense of nonviolence, the method's popularity was falling fast among African Americans. In light of deadly racist violence against nonviolent workers in the South and tremendous urban riots, nonviolence seemed outdated and came under unprecedented questioning, even in civil rights circles. In fact, the movement had never unanimously embraced King's commitment to nonviolence as a total way of life and inviolable principle. Many activists were willing to use peaceful protest only as a tactical tool that could be dropped if it became ineffective. Stokely Carmichael (later Kwame Ture) and his Student Nonviolent Coordinating Committee (SNCC) comrades made national headlines in 1966 by adopting the charged slogan "Black Power" to describe the goals of the black movement. Fundamentally, this phrase conveyed African Americans' determination to run their freedom struggle independently of whites as well as black people's right and need to defend themselves against violence.

Responding to mounting criticisms of his and his Southern Christian Leadership Conference's tactics, King increasingly had to defend the wisdom and efficacy of nonviolence within the Civil Rights movement. In this magazine article, King pointed to the dramatic gains of recent years, such as the national Civil Rights and Voting Rights acts, which resulted

---

Ebony 21 (Oct. 1966): 27–30; reprinted in James M. Washington, ed., *A Testament of Hope: The Essential Writings and Speeches of Martin Luther King Jr.* (San Francisco: HarperCollins, 1986), 54–61.

from nonviolent movements. He then proceeded to give his trademark critique of violence as an instrument of constructive social change. While energetically defending nonviolence, the essay also shows King's growing accommodation to the rising appeal of black nationalist ideas. He did not question every individual's right to defend himself against assault; rather, he asked people voluntarily to set aside that right to participate in a public demonstration for the purpose of publicizing and eradicating a social evil. King also endorsed Black Power's stress on African Americans organizing themselves to develop and wield independent power. He further acknowledged that using power, and not relying solely on moral appeal, would be necessary to compel a satisfactory white response to black demands for justice.

Important shifts in King and the SCLC's program are also apparent, particularly increased concentration on urban slum conditions and economic issues, rather than just on civil rights. At this time, one year after Malcolm X's assassination, King echoed Malcolm about the need to move beyond demanding only blacks' constitutional rights to more broadly seeking people's full human, including economic, rights.

The year 1966 brought with it the first public challenge to the philosophy and strategy of nonviolence from within the ranks of the civil rights movement. Resolutions of self-defense and Black Power sounded forth from our friends and brothers. At the same time riots erupted in several major cities. Inevitably a link was made between the two phenomena though movement leadership continued to deny any implications of violence in the concept of Black Power.

The nation's press heralded these incidents as an end of the Negro's reliance on nonviolence as a means of achieving freedom. Articles appeared on "The Plot to get Whitey," and, "Must Negroes fight back?" and one had the impression that a serious movement was underway to lead the Negro to freedom through the use of violence.

Indeed, there was much talk of violence. It was the same talk we have heard on the fringes of the nonviolent movement for the past ten years. It was the talk of fearful men, saying that they would not join the nonviolent movement because they would not remain nonviolent if attacked. Now the climate had shifted so that it was even more popular to talk of violence, but in spite of the talk of violence there emerged no action in this direction....

I have talked with many persons in the ghettos of the North who argue eloquently for the use of violence. But I observed none of them in the mobs that rioted in Chicago. I have heard the street-corner preachers in Harlem and in Chicago's Washington Park, but in spite of the bitterness preached and the hatred espoused, none of them has ever been able to start a riot.... Violence as a strategy for social change in America is nonexistent. All the sound and fury seems but the posturing of cowards whose bold talk produces no action and signifies nothing.

I am convinced that for practical as well as moral reasons, nonviolence offers the only road to freedom for my people. In violent warfare, one must be prepared to face ruthlessly the fact that there will be casualties by the thousands. In Vietnam, the United States has evidently decided that it is willing to slaughter millions, sacrifice some two hundred thousand men and twenty billion dollars a year to secure the freedom of some fourteen million Vietnamese.[1] This is to fight a war on Asian soil, where Asians are in the majority. Anyone leading a violent conflict must be willing to make a similar assessment regarding the possible casualties to a minority population confronting a well-armed, wealthy majority with a fanatical right wing that is capable of exterminating the entire black population and which would not hesitate such an attempt if the survival of white Western materialism were at stake.

Arguments that the American Negro is a part of a world which is two-thirds colored and that there will come a day when the oppressed people of color will rise together to throw off the yoke of white oppression are at least fifty years away from being relevant. There is no colored nation, including China, which now shows even the potential of leading a revolution of color in any international proportion....

The hard cold facts of racial life in the world today indicate that the hope of the people of color in the world may well rest on the American Negro and his ability to reform the structures of racist imperialism from within and thereby turn the technology and wealth of the West to the task of liberating the world from want.

This is no time for romantic illusions about freedom and empty philosophical debate. This is a time for action. What is needed is a strategy for change, a tactical program which will bring the Negro into the mainstream of American life as quickly as possible. So far, this has only been offered by the nonviolent movement.

Our record of achievement through nonviolent action is already re-

---

[1]Although U.S. involvement in Vietnam dated back through several administrations, in 1966, at the time of King's article, the Johnson administration was rapidly escalating the U.S. military role in that nation's war.

markable. The dramatic social changes which have been made across the South are unmatched in the annals of history. Montgomery, Albany, Birmingham and Selma have paved the way for untold progress. Even more remarkable is the fact that this progress occurred with a minimum of human sacrifice and loss of life.

Not a single person has been killed in a nonviolent demonstration. . . .

The Question of Self-Defense

There are many people who very honestly raise the question of self-defense. This must be placed in perspective. It goes without saying that people will protect their homes. This is a right guaranteed by the Constitution and respected even in the worst areas of the South. But the mere protection of one's home and person against assault by lawless night riders does not provide any positive approach to the fears and conditions which produce violence. . . .

In a nonviolent demonstration, self-defense must be approached from quite another perspective. One must remember that the cause of the demonstration is some exploitation or form of oppression that has made it necessary for men of courage and good will to demonstrate against the evil. For example, a demonstration against the evil of de facto school segregation is based on the awareness that a child's mind is crippled daily by inadequate educational opportunity. The demonstrator agrees that it is better for him to suffer publicly for a short time to end the crippling evil of school segregation than to have generation after generation of children suffer in ignorance. . . .

It is always amusing to me when a Negro man says that he can't demonstrate with us because if someone hit him he would fight back. Here is a man whose children are being plagued by rats and roaches, whose wife is robbed daily at overpriced ghetto food stores, who himself is working for about two-thirds the pay of a white person doing a similar job and with similar skills, and in spite of all this daily suffering it takes someone spitting on him or calling him a nigger to make him want to fight.

Conditions are such for Negroes in America that all Negroes ought to be fighting aggressively. It is as ridiculous for a Negro to raise the question of self-defense in relation to nonviolence as it is for a soldier on the battlefield to say he is not going to take any risks. He is there because he believes that the freedom of his country is worth the risk of his life. The same is true of the nonviolent demonstrator. He sees the misery of his people so clearly that he volunteers to suffer in their behalf and put an end to their plight. . . .

When my home was bombed in 1955 in Montgomery, many men wanted to retaliate, to place an armed guard on my home. But the issue there was not my life, but whether Negroes would achieve first-class treatment on the city's buses. Had we become distracted by the question of my safety we would have lost the moral offensive and sunk to the level of our oppressors.

I must continue by faith or it is too great a burden to bear and violence, even in self-defense, creates more problems than it solves. Only a refusal to hate or kill can put an end to the chain of violence in the world and lead us toward a community where men can live together without fear. Our goal is to create a beloved community and this will require a qualitative change in our souls as well as a quantitative change in our lives.

Strategy for Change

The American racial revolution has been a revolution to "get in" rather than to overthrow. We want a share in the American economy, the housing market, the educational system and the social opportunities. This goal itself indicates that a social change in America must be nonviolent.

If one is in search of a better job, it does not help to burn down the factory. If one needs more adequate education, shooting the principal will not help, or if housing is the goal, only building and construction will produce that end. To destroy anything, person or property, can't bring us closer to the goal that we seek.

The nonviolent strategy has been to dramatize the evils of our society in such a way that pressure is brought to bear against those evils by the forces of good will in the community and change is produced....

So far, we have had the Constitution backing most of the demands for change, and this has made our work easier, since we could be sure that the federal courts would usually back up our demonstrations legally. Now we are approaching areas where the voice of the Constitution is not clear. We have left the realm of constitutional rights and we are entering the area of human rights.

The Constitution assured the right to vote, but there is no such assurance of the right to adequate housing, or the right to an adequate income. And yet, in a nation which has a gross national product of 750 billion dollars a year, it is morally right to insist that every person has a decent house, an adequate education and enough money to provide basic necessities for one's family. Achievement of these goals will be a lot more difficult and require much more discipline, understanding, organization and sacrifice....

The past three years have demonstrated the power of a committed, morally sound minority to lead the nation. It was the coalition molded through the Birmingham movement which allied the forces of the churches, labor and the academic communities of the nation behind the liberal issues of our time. All of the liberal legislation of the past session of Congress can be credited to this coalition. Even the presence of a vital peace movement and the campus protest against the war in Vietnam can be traced back to the nonviolent action movement led by the Negro.... Negroes put the country on the move against the enemies of poverty, slums and inadequate education.

Techniques of the Future

When Negroes marched, so did the nation. The power of the nonviolent march is indeed a mystery. It is always surprising that a few hundred Negroes marching can produce such a reaction across the nation. When marches are carefully organized around well-defined issues, they represent the power which Victor Hugo phrased as the most powerful force in the world, "an idea whose time has come." Marching feet announce that time has come for a given idea. When the idea is a sound one, the cause a just one, and the demonstration a righteous one, change will be forthcoming. But if any of these conditions are not present, the power for change is missing also....

Marches must continue in the future, and they must be the kind of marches that bring about the desired result....

Our experience is that marches must continue over a period of thirty to forty-five days to produce any meaningful results. They must also be of sufficient size to produce some inconvenience to the forces in power or they go unnoticed. In other words, they must demand the attention of the press, for it is the press which interprets the issue to the community at large and thereby sets in motion the machinery for change.

Along with the march as a weapon for change in our nonviolent arsenal must be listed the boycott. Basic to the philosophy of nonviolence is the refusal to cooperate with evil. There is nothing quite so effective as a refusal to cooperate economically with the forces and institutions which perpetuate evil in our communities....

... This is nonviolence at its peak of power, when it cuts into the profit margin of a business in order to bring about a more just distribution of jobs and opportunities for Negro wage earners and consumers....

More and more, the civil rights movement will become engaged in the task of organizing people into permanent groups to protect their own interests and to produce change in their behalf. . . .

In the future we will be called upon to organize the unemployed, to unionize the businesses within the ghetto, to bring tenants together into collective bargaining units and establish cooperatives for purposes of building viable financial institutions within the ghetto that can be controlled by Negroes themselves.

There is no easy way to create a world where men and women can live together, where each has his own job and house and where all children receive as much education as their minds can absorb. But if such a world is created in our lifetime, it will be done in the United States by Negroes and white people of good will. It will be accomplished by persons who have the courage to put an end to suffering by willingly suffering themselves rather than inflict suffering upon others. It will be done by rejecting the racism, materialism and violence that has characterized Western civilization and especially by working toward a world of brotherhood, cooperation and peace.

MALCOLM X

From *The Afro-American's Right to Self-Defense*
1964

About three months after breaking with the NOI, Malcolm spoke at the founding rally of the Organization of Afro-American Unity (OAAU), which replaced the short-lived Muslim Mosque, Inc., as the chief vehicle for Malcolm's independent phase.[1] Among other things, the OAAU charter declared African Americans' natural human and U.S. constitutional

---

[1] Speaking at the OAAU's opening rally, Malcolm alternately read from the organization's founding charter and spontaneously elaborated on it. The text appearing in quotation marks signals when he is reading directly from the charter.

Excerpt from speech at Founding Rally of the Organization of Afro-American Unity given in the Audubon Ballroom, New York City, 28 June 1964; reprinted in George Breitman, ed., *By Any Means Necessary: Speeches, Interviews, and a Letter by Malcolm X* (New York: Pathfinder Press, 1970), 40–42.

right to self-defense. Although Malcolm cautioned against using violence indiscriminately or unnecessarily, he steadfastly declared that when blacks were the recipients of violence, they should respond in kind.

"Persuaded that the Charter of the United Nations, the Universal Declaration of Human Rights, the Constitution of the United States and the Bill of Rights are the principles in which we believe and that these documents if put into practice represent the essence of mankind's hopes and good intentions;

"Desirous that all Afro-American people and organizations should henceforth unite so that the welfare and well-being of our people will be assured;

"We are resolved to reinforce the common bond of purpose between our people by submerging all of our differences and establishing a nonsectarian, constructive program for human rights;

"We hereby present this charter. . . .

"II—Self Defense.

"Since self-preservation is the first law of nature, we assert the Afro-American's right to self-defense.

"The Constitution of the United States of America clearly affirms the right of every American citizen to bear arms. And as Americans, we will not give up a single right guaranteed under the Constitution. The history of unpunished violence against our people clearly indicates that we must be prepared to defend ourselves or we will continue to be a defenseless people at the mercy of a ruthless and violent racist mob.

"We assert that in those areas where the government is either unable or unwilling to protect the lives and property of our people, that our people are within our rights to protect themselves by whatever means necessary." I repeat, because to me this is the most important thing you need to know. I already know it. "We assert that in those areas where the government is either unable or unwilling to protect the lives and property of our people, that our people are within our rights to protect themselves by whatever means necessary."

This is the thing you need to spread the word about among our people wherever you go. Never let them be brainwashed into thinking that whenever they take steps to see that they're in a position to defend themselves that they're being unlawful. The only time you're being unlawful is when you break the law. It's lawful to have something to defend yourself. Why, I heard President Johnson either today or yesterday, I guess it was today, talking about how quick this country would go to war to defend itself. Why, what kind of a fool do you look like, living in a country that will go to war at the drop of a hat to defend itself, and here you've got to stand up in the face of vicious police dogs and blue-eyed crackers[2] waiting for somebody to tell you what to do to defend yourself!

Those days are over, they're gone, that's yesterday. The time for you and me to allow ourselves to be brutalized nonviolently is *passé*. Be nonviolent only with those who are nonviolent to you. And when you can bring me a nonviolent racist, bring me a nonviolent segregationist, then I'll get nonviolent. But don't teach me to be nonviolent until you teach some of those crackers to be nonviolent. You've never seen a nonviolent cracker. It's hard for a racist to be nonviolent. It's hard for anyone intelligent to be nonviolent. Everything in the universe does something when you start playing with his life, except the American Negro. He lays down and says, "Beat me, daddy."

So it says here: "A man with a rifle or a club can only be stopped by a person who defends himself with a rifle or a club." That's equality. If you have a dog, I must have a dog. If you have a rifle, I must have a rifle. If you have a club, I must have a club. This is equality. If the United States government doesn't want you and me to get rifles, then take the rifles away from those racists. If they don't want you and me to use clubs, take the clubs away from the racists. If they don't want you and me to get violent, then stop the racists from being violent. Don't teach us nonviolence while those crackers are violent. Those days are over.

"Tactics based solely on morality can only succeed when you are dealing with people who are moral or a system that is moral. A man or system which oppresses a man because of his color is not moral. It is the duty of every Afro-American person and every Afro-American community throughout this country to protect its people against mass murderers, against bombers, against lynchers, against floggers, against brutalizers and against exploiters."

---

[2]*Cracker:* Derogatory slang term, similar to "redneck," for a white person, especially a prejudiced, rural, poorly educated southern one.

From *On Revolution*
1963

This statement of Malcolm's teaching on revolution comes from Malcolm's important 1963 speech "Message to the Grassroots." In it, Malcolm distinguished between what he characteristically called the "Black Revolution" and the "Negro Revolution." Malcolm endorsed the first as a real black nationalist revolution. He had only contempt for the "Negro [nonviolent Civil Rights] Revolution."

He often raised the theme of fighting for land in his NOI days, since the chief concession that the group asked of whites, as reparation for slavery, was separate territory for African Americans. After leaving the NOI, Malcolm revised his initial position that real revolutions were invariably bloody and over land.

I would like to make a few comments concerning the difference between the black revolution and the Negro revolution. Are they both the same? And if they're not, what is the difference? What is the difference between a black revolution and a Negro revolution? First, what is a revolution? Sometimes I'm inclined to believe that many of our people are using this word "revolution" loosely, without taking careful consideration of what this word actually means, and what its historic characteristics are. . . .

Look at the American Revolution in 1776. That revolution was for what? For land. Why did they want land? Independence. How was it carried out? Bloodshed. Number one, it was based on land, the basis of independence. And the only way they could get it was bloodshed. The French Revolution—what was it based on? The landless against the landlord. What was it for? Land. How did they get it? Bloodshed. Was no love lost, was no compromise, was no negotiation. I'm telling you —you don't know what a revolution is. Because when you find out what it is, you'll get back in the alley, you'll get out of the way.

Excerpt from "Message to the Grassroots," speech given during the Northern Negro Grass Roots Leadership Conference at King Solomon Baptist Church, Detroit, Mich., 10 Nov. 1963; recorded by the Afro-American Broadcasting Co.; reprinted in George Breitman, ed., *Malcolm X Speaks: Selected Speeches and Statements* (New York: Grove Press, 1982), 6–10.

The Russian Revolution—what was it based on? Land; the landless against the landlord. How did they bring it about? Bloodshed. You haven't got a revolution that doesn't involve bloodshed. And you're afraid to bleed. I said, you're afraid to bleed.

As long as the white man sent you to Korea, you bled. He sent you to Germany, you bled. He sent you to the South Pacific to fight the Japanese, you bled. You bleed for white people, but when it comes to seeing your own churches being bombed and little black girls murdered, you haven't got any blood. You bleed when the white man says bleed; you bite when the white man says bite; and you bark when the white man says bark. I hate to say this about us, but it's true. How are you going to be nonviolent in Mississippi, as violent as you were in Korea? How can you justify being nonviolent in Mississippi and Alabama, when your churches are being bombed, and your little girls are being murdered[1] . . . ?

If violence is wrong in America, violence is wrong abroad. If it is wrong to be violent defending black women and black children and black babies and black men, then it is wrong for America to draft us and make us violent abroad in defense of her. And if it is right for America to draft us, and teach us how to be violent in defense of her, then it is right for you and me to do whatever is necessary to defend our own people right here in this country.

The Chinese Revolution—they wanted land. They threw the British out, along with the Uncle Tom Chinese. Yes, they did. They set a good example. . . .

. . . There's been a revolution, a black revolution, going on in Africa. In Kenya, the Mau Mau[2] were revolutionary. . . . They believed in scorched earth, they knocked everything aside that got in their way, and their revolution also was based on land, a desire for land. . . .

So I cite these various revolutions, brothers and sisters, to show you that you don't have a peaceful revolution. You don't have a turn-the-other-cheek revolution. There's no such thing as a nonviolent revolution. The only kind of revolution that is nonviolent is the Negro revolution. The only revolution in which the goal is loving your enemy

---

[1]Malcolm refers to white supremacists' bombing of a black church in Birmingham, Alabama, on September 15, 1963. Four young African American girls were murdered in the blast, which occurred just a few weeks after the March on Washington. Earlier in the same paragraph, Malcolm refers to U.S. military engagements in the Korean War (1950–53) and Second World War (1941–45).

[2]*Mau Mau:* Anti-European African guerrillas during the 1950s who fought against British colonial rule in Kenya.

is the Negro revolution. It's the only revolution in which the goal is a desegregated lunch counter, a desegregated theater, a desegregated park, and a desegregated public toilet; you can sit down next to white folks—on the toilet. That's no revolution. Revolution is based on land. Land is the basis of all independence. Land is the basis of freedom, justice, and equality.

The white man knows what a revolution is. He knows that the black revolution is world-wide in scope and in nature.... You don't know what a revolution is. If you did, you wouldn't use that word.

Revolution is bloody, revolution is hostile, revolution knows no compromise, revolution overturns and destroys everything that gets in its way. And you, sitting around here like a knot on the wall, saying, "I'm going to love these folks no matter how much they hate me." No, you need a revolution. Whoever heard of a revolution where they lock arms... singing "We Shall Overcome"? You don't do that in a revolution. You don't do any singing, you're too busy swinging. It's based on land. A revolutionary wants land so he can set up his own nation, an independent nation. These Negroes aren't asking for any nation— they're trying to crawl back on the plantation.

When you want a nation, that's called nationalism. When the white man became involved in a revolution in this country against England, what was it for? He wanted this land so he could set up another white nation. That's white nationalism. The American Revolution was white nationalism. The French Revolution was white nationalism.... All the revolutions that are going on in Asia and Africa today are based on what?—black nationalism. A revolutionary is a black nationalist. He wants a nation.... If you're afraid of black nationalism, you're afraid of revolution. And if you love revolution, you love black nationalism.

4

On America: Dream or Nightmare?

I... have a dream... that one day this nation will rise up and live out the true meaning of its creed... that all men are created equal.
— Martin Luther King

To Redeem the Soul of America — SCLC Motto

No, I'm not an American.... I'm not... speaking to you as an American, or a patriot,... or flag-waver.... I see America through the eyes of the victim. I don't see any American dream; I see an American nightmare.
— Malcolm X

White America must now pay for her sins.... White America is doomed!
— Malcolm X

Throughout his public career, King proclaimed America's ideals and his optimism about their achievement. King's patriotic style was socially challenging. He characteristically deplored the nation's racism as betraying its ideals. Ever loving his country and its traditions, King challenged the nation to embody more fully its professed devotion to freedom and equality.

King voiced a sharply critical but also accepting attitude toward white Americans. He regularly upbraided them for violating their own best political and religious traditions by denying African Americans' equal citizenship rights. King often spoke in the stern tones of a biblical prophet chastising the straying chosen people. Yet, as he often said, there could be no great disappointment where there was no great love. Once having rebuked whites for their prejudicial actions, King always forgave them their faults, seeking to channel the energy of whites' released guilt into resolve to take the immediate steps that—King ever maintained—would bring about America's final destiny.

As a Nation of Islam minister, Malcolm embraced the organization's teachings about the nature and origin of whites as inherently evil and oppressive. Even as a Nation zealot, though, Malcolm's words resonated with many non-NOI blacks, since he always insisted that *objective* analysis of the facts also showed whites' evil nature. Even later when acknowledging that individual whites could be sincere in desiring justice for African Americans, he still held that the facts demonstrated the undeniable *collective* evil of white society.

Malcolm was at his most electric when fearlessly denouncing whites for their evil deeds against African Americans. Presenting such facts as whites' enslavement, rape, and lynching of blacks, Malcolm made a compelling moral case against white America's past and present record. One writer called Malcolm chief witness for the prosecution when it came to finding the white race guilty of horrible crimes. Many non-NOI blacks, including many civil rights activists who disagreed with him about virtually everything else, basically agreed with his diagnosis of white racist evil.

It was not just what Malcolm said that was so striking, moreover, but *how* he said it. His seething anger addressing whites was almost palpable; he spoke with passionate intensity in both voice and body language, often thrusting a challenging finger, as he denounced whites for their crimes.

MARTIN LUTHER KING JR.

I Have a Dream

1963

King's most famous and widely quoted speech was made while standing in front of the Lincoln Memorial on August 28, 1963, at the March on Washington for Jobs and Freedom. The march was called to galvanize

The Negro History Bulletin 31 (May 1968): 10–15; reprinted in James M. Washington, ed., *A Testament of Hope: The Essential Writings and Speeches of Martin Luther King Jr.* (San Francisco: HarperCollins, 1986), 217–20.

support for the Kennedy administration's newly introduced major civil rights bill, which would become the 1964 Civil Rights Act, ending legal racial segregation and discrimination. The speech is a prime example of King's critical brand of patriotism. True patriots, he ever held, must courageously protest present denials of liberty and fight to bring the nation's reality into line with its guiding principles. The speech's closing peroration, the famous "I have a dream" refrain, memorably declares King's faith in America's future.

I am happy to join with you today in what will go down in history as the greatest demonstration for freedom in the history of our nation.

Fivescore years ago, a great American, in whose symbolic shadow we stand today, signed the Emancipation Proclamation. This momentous decree came as a great beacon light of hope to millions of Negro slaves who had been seared in the flames of withering injustice. It came as a joyous daybreak to end the long night of their captivity.

But one hundred years later, the Negro still is not free; one hundred years later, the life of the Negro is still sadly crippled by the manacles of segregation and the chains of discrimination; one hundred years later, the Negro lives on a lonely island of poverty in the midst of a vast ocean of material prosperity; one hundred years later, the Negro is still languished in the corners of American society and finds himself in exile in his own land.

So we've come here today to dramatize a shameful condition. In a sense we've come to our nation's capital to cash a check. When the architects of our republic wrote the magnificent words of the Constitution and the Declaration of Independence, they were signing a promissory note to which every American was to fall heir. This note was the promise that all men, yes, black men as well as white men, would be guaranteed the unalienable rights of life, liberty, and the pursuit of happiness.

It is obvious today that America has defaulted on this promissory note in so far as her citizens of color are concerned. Instead of honoring this sacred obligation, America has given the Negro people a bad check; a check which has come back marked "insufficient funds." We refuse to believe that there are insufficient funds in the great vaults of opportunity of this nation. And so we've come to cash this check, a check that will give us upon demand the riches of freedom and the security of justice.

We have also come to this hallowed spot to remind America of the fierce urgency of now. This is no time to engage in the luxury of cooling off or to take the tranquilizing drug of gradualism. Now is the time to make real the promises of democracy; now is the time to rise from the dark and desolate valley of segregation to the sunlit path of racial justice; now is the time to lift our nation from the quicksands of racial injustice to the solid rock of brotherhood; now is the time to make justice a reality for all God's children. It would be fatal for the nation to overlook the urgency of the moment. This sweltering summer of the Negro's legimate discontent will not pass until there is an invigorating autumn of freedom and equality.

Nineteen sixty-three is not an end, but a beginning. And those who hope that the Negro needed to blow off steam and will now be content, will have a rude awakening if the nation returns to business as usual.

There will be neither rest nor tranquility in America until the Negro is granted his citizenship rights. The whirlwinds of revolt will continue to shake the foundations of our nation until the bright day of justice emerges.

But there is something that I must say to my people who stand on the warm threshold which leads into the palace of justice. In the process of gaining our rightful place we must not be guilty of wrongful deeds.

Let us not seek to satisfy our thirst for freedom by drinking from the cup of bitterness and hatred. We must forever conduct our struggle on the high plane of dignity and discipline. We must not allow our creative protest to degenerate into physical violence. Again and again we must rise to the majestic heights of meeting physical force with soul force.

The marvelous new militancy which has engulfed the Negro community must not lead us to a distrust of all white people, for many of our white brothers, as evidenced by their presence here today, have come to realize that their destiny is tied up with our destiny and they have come to realize that their freedom is inextricably bound to our freedom. This offense we share mounted to storm the battlements of injustice must be carried forth by a biracial army. We cannot walk alone.

And as we walk, we must make the pledge that we shall always march ahead. We cannot turn back. There are those who are asking the devotees of civil rights, "When will you be satisfied?" We can never be satisfied as long as the Negro is the victim of the unspeakable horrors of police brutality.

We can never be satisfied as long as our bodies, heavy with fatigue of travel, cannot gain lodging in the motels of the highways and the hotels of the cities. We cannot be satisfied as long as the Negro's basic mobility is from a smaller ghetto to a larger one.

We can never be satisfied as long as our children are stripped of their selfhood and robbed of their dignity by signs stating "for whites only." We cannot be satisfied as long as a Negro in Mississippi cannot vote and a Negro in New York believes he has nothing for which to vote. No, we are not satisfied, and we will not be satisfied until justice rolls down like waters and righteousness like a mighty stream.

I am not unmindful that some of you have come here out of excessive trials and tribulation. Some of you have come fresh from narrow jail cells. Some of you have come from areas where your quest for freedom left you battered by the storms of persecution and staggered by the winds of police brutality. You have been the veterans of creative suffering. Continue to work with the faith that unearned suffering is redemptive.

Go back to Mississippi; go back to Alabama; go back to South Carolina; go back to Georgia; go back to Louisiana; go back to the slums and ghettos of the northern cities, knowing that somehow this situation can, and will be changed. Let us not wallow in the valley of despair.

So I say to you, my friends, that even though we must face the difficulties of today and tomorrow, I still have a dream. It is a dream deeply rooted in the American dream that one day this nation will rise up and live out the true meaning of its creed—we hold these truths to be self-evident, that all men are created equal.

I have a dream that one day on the red hills of Georgia, sons of former slaves and sons of former slave-owners will be able to sit down together at the table of brotherhood.

I have a dream that one day, even the state of Mississippi, a state sweltering with the heat of injustice, sweltering with the heat of oppression, will be transformed into an oasis of freedom and justice.

I have a dream my four little children will one day live in a nation where they will not be judged by the color of their skin but by the content of their character. I have a dream today!

I have a dream that one day, down in Alabama, with its vicious racists, with its governor having his lips dripping with the words of interposition and nullification, that one day, right there in Alabama, little black boys and black girls will be able to join hands with little white boys and white girls as sisters and brothers. I have a dream today!

I have a dream that one day every valley shall be exalted, every hill and mountain shall be made low, the rough places shall be made plain, and the crooked places shall be made straight and the glory of the Lord will be revealed and all flesh shall see it together.

This is our hope. This is the faith that I go back to the South with. With this faith we will be able to hew out of the mountain of despair a stone of hope. With this faith we will be able to transform the jangling discords of our nation into a beautiful symphony of brotherhood.

With this faith we will be able to work together, to pray together, to struggle together, to go to jail together, to stand up for freedom together, knowing that we will be free one day. This will be the day when all of God's children will be able to sing with new meaning— "my country 'tis of thee; sweet land of liberty; of thee I sing; land where my fathers died, land of the pilgrim's pride; from every mountain side, let freedom ring"—and if America is to be a great nation, this must become true.

So let freedom ring from the prodigious hilltops of New Hampshire.
Let freedom ring from the mighty mountains of New York.
Let freedom ring from the heightening Alleghenies of Pennsylvania.
Let freedom ring from the snow-capped Rockies of Colorado.
Let freedom ring from the curvaceous slopes of California.
But not only that.
Let freedom ring from Stone Mountain of Georgia.
Let freedom ring from Lookout Mountain of Tennessee.
Let freedom ring from every hill and molehill of Mississippi, from every mountainside, let freedom ring.

And when we allow freedom to ring, when we let it ring from every village and hamlet, from every state and city, we will be able to speed up that day when all of God's children—black men and white men, Jews and Gentiles, Catholics and Protestants—will be able to join hands and to sing in the words of the old Negro spiritual, "Free at last, free at last; thank God Almighty, we are free at last."

MALCOLM X

Every white man in America, when he looks into a black man's eyes, should fall to his knees and say "I'm sorry, I'm sorry—my kind has committed history's greatest crime against your kind; will you give me the chance to atone?" But do you . . . expect any white man to do that? No, *you* know *better! And why won't he do it? Because he can't do it. The white man was* created *a devil, to bring chaos upon this earth.*

—Malcolm X

The White Man Is a Devil: Statements on Whites
1965

"The White Man Is a Devil" consists of excerpts from the Autobiography that expressed Malcolm's attitude toward whites and white America in his period as a Nation zealot.

[Malcolm recalled his first basic talk as a new Nation of Islam minister.]

The Rapist Slavemaster

"... my *beautiful,* black brothers and sisters! And when we say 'black,' we mean everything not white, brothers and sisters! Because *look* at your skins! We're all black to the white man, but we're a thousand and one different colors. Turn around, *look* at each other! What shade of black African polluted by devil white man are you? You see me—well, in the streets they used to call me Detroit Red. Yes! Yes, that raping, red-headed devil was my *grandfather*! That close, yes! My *mother's* father! She didn't like to speak of it, can you blame her? She said she never laid eyes on him! She was *glad* for that! I'm *glad* for her! If I could drain away *his* blood that pollutes *my* body, and pollutes *my* complexion, I'd do it! Because I hate every drop of the rapist's blood that's in me!

"And it's not just me, it's *all* of us! During slavery, *think* of it, it was a *rare* one of our black grandmothers, our great-grandmothers and our great-great-grandmothers who escaped the white rapist slavemaster. That rapist slavemaster who emasculated the black man ... with threats, with fear ... until even today the black man lives with fear of the white man in his heart! Lives even today still under the heel of the white man!

"*Think* of it—think of that black slave man filled with fear and dread, hearing the screams of his wife, his mother, his daughter being *taken*—in the barn, the kitchen, in the bushes! *Think* of it, my dear brothers and sisters! *Think* of hearing wives, mothers, daughters, being *raped*! And you were too filled with *fear* of the rapist to do anything about it! And his vicious, animal attacks' offspring, this white man named things like 'mu-

The Autobiography of Malcolm X, 205–6, 245, 271–73, 276–77, 292.

latto' and 'quadroon' and 'octoroon' and all those other things that he has called us—you and me—when he is not calling us *'nigger'*!

"Turn around and look at each other, brothers and sisters, and *think* of this! You and me, polluted all these colors—and this devil has the arrogance and the gall to think we, his victims, should *love* him!"

I would become so choked up that sometimes I would walk in the streets until late into the night. Sometimes I would speak to no one for hours, thinking to myself about what the white man had done to our poor people here in America. . . .

[In this text, Malcolm described his attitude toward the whites whom he met and debated in his many press, radio, and television appearances as NOI spokesperson.]

Devil-in-the-Flesh

. . . "Mr. Malcolm X, why do you teach black supremacy, and hate?" A red flag waved for me, something chemical happened inside me, every time I heard that. When we Muslims had talked about "the devil white man" he had been relatively abstract, someone we Muslims rarely actually came into contact with, but now here was that devil-in-the-flesh on the phone—with all of his calculating, cold-eyed, self-righteous tricks and nerve and gall. The voices questioning me became to me as breathing, living devils.

And I tried to pour on pure fire in return. "The white man so guilty of white supremacy can't hide *his* guilt by trying to accuse The Honorable Elijah Muhammad of teaching black supremacy and hate! All Mr. Muhammad is doing is trying to uplift the black man's mentality and the black man's social and economic condition in this country.

"The guilty, two-faced white man can't decide *what* he wants. Our slave foreparents would have been put to death for advocating so-called 'integration' with the white man. Now when Mr. Muhammad speaks of 'separation,' the white man calls us 'hate-teachers' and 'fascists'!

"The white man doesn't *want* the blacks! He doesn't *want* the blacks that are a parasite upon him! He doesn't *want* this black man whose presence and condition in this country expose the white man to the world for what he is! So why do you attack Mr. Muhammad?"

I'd have *scathing* in my voice; I *felt* it.

"For the white man to ask the black man if he hates him is just like the rapist asking the *raped,* or the wolf asking the *sheep,* 'Do you hate me?' The white man is in no moral *position* to accuse anyone else of hate! . . ."

[Even while still a Nation fundamentalist, Malcolm sometimes for persuasive purposes stressed the collective, rather than individual, nature of white evil. Later, even after he had renounced the Nation's doctrine of innate white devilry, he still asserted that collectively *white society, judged by its objective current and historical record, was demonstrably evil.]*

The Collective White Man's Record

... An amazing percentage of the white letter-writers agreed entirely with Mr. Muhammad's analysis of the problem—but not with his solution. One odd ambivalence was how some letters, otherwise all but championing Mr. Muhammad, would recoil at the expression "white devils." I tried to explain this in subsequent speeches:

"Unless we call one white man, by name, a 'devil,' we are not speaking of any *individual* white man. We are speaking of the *collective* white man's *historical* record. We are speaking of the collective white man's cruelties, and evils, and greeds, that have seen him *act* like a devil toward the non-white man. Any intelligent, honest, objective person cannot fail to realize that this white man's slave trade, and his subsequent devilish actions are directly *responsible* for not only the *presence* of this black man in America, but also for the *condition* in which we find this black man here. You cannot find *one* black man, I do not care who he is, who has not been personally damaged in some way by the devilish acts of the collective white man!" ...

This white man—give him his due—has an extraordinary intelligence, an extraordinary cleverness.... You can hardly name a scientific problem he can't solve. Here he is now solving the problems of sending men exploring into outer space—and returning them safely to earth.

But in the arena of dealing with human beings, the white man's working intelligence is hobbled. His intelligence will fail him altogether if the humans happen to be non-white. The white man's emotions superseded his intelligence. He will commit against non-whites the most incredible spontaneous emotional acts, so psyche-deep is his "white superiority" complex.

Where was the A-bomb dropped ... "to save American lives"? Can the white man be so naive as to think the clear import of this *ever* will be lost upon the non-white two-thirds of the earth's population? ...

Historically, the non-white complexion has evoked and exposed the "devil" in the very nature of the white man. ...

[Malcolm refused to make any substantial distinction between white southern segregationist conservatives and northern pro-civil rights liberals. Both were black people's enemies, he always taught; liberals were just more sly and deceptive.]

Pull Off That White Liberal's Halo

... The Deep South white press generally blacked me out. But they front-paged what I felt about Northern white and black Freedom Riders going *South* to "demonstrate." I called it "ridiculous"; their own Northern ghettoes, right at home, had enough rats and roaches to kill to keep all of the Freedom Riders busy. I said that ultra-liberal New York had more integration problems than Mississippi. If the Northern Freedom Riders wanted more to do, they could work on the roots of such ghetto evils as the little children out in the streets at midnight, with apartment keys on strings around their necks to let themselves in, and their mothers and fathers drunk, drug addicts, thieves, prostitutes. Or the Northern Freedom Riders could light some fires under Northern city halls, unions, and major industries to give more jobs to Negroes to remove so many of them from the relief and welfare rolls, which created laziness, and which deteriorated the ghettoes into steadily worse places for humans to live. It was all—it *is* all—the absolute truth; but what did I want to *say* it for? Snakes couldn't have turned on me faster than the liberal.

Yes, I will pull off that liberal's halo that he spends such efforts cultivating! The North's liberals have been for so long pointing accusing fingers at the South and getting away with it that they have fits when they are exposed as the world's worst hypocrites.

I believe my own life *mirrors* this hypocrisy. I know nothing about the South. I am a creation of the Northern white man and of his hypocritical attitude toward the Negro.

The white Southerner was always given his due by Mr. Muhammad. The white Southerner, you can say one thing—he is honest. He bares his teeth to the black man; he tells the black man, to his face, that Southern whites never will accept phony "integration." The Southern white goes further, to tell the black man that he means to fight him every inch of the way—against even the so-called "tokenism." The advantage of this is the Southern black man never has been under any illusions about the opposition he is dealing with.

... But the Northern white man, he grins with his teeth, and his mouth has always been full of tricks and lies of "equality" and "integration." When one day all over America, a black hand touched the white man's shoulder, and the white man turned, and there stood the Negro saying "Me, too..." why, that Northern liberal shrank from that black man with as much guilt and dread as any Southern white man.

Actually, America's most dangerous and threatening black man is the one who has been kept sealed up by the Northerner in the black ghettoes—the Northern white power structure's system to keep talking democracy while keeping the black man out of sight somewhere, around the corner.

The word "integration" was invented by a Northern liberal. The word has no real meaning.... The truth is that "integration" is an *image,* it's a foxy Northern liberal's smokescreen that confuses the true wants of the American black man....

[This excerpt tells of a white college student who so strongly reacted to Malcolm's speech at her college that she flew to Harlem to ask Malcolm how she, a white, could make amends for the past and things better for blacks. Malcolm's response indicates his early categorical rejection of any aid or goodwill from whites. Later, near the end of his life (see chapter 6), Malcolm regretted the answer he gave the young woman here.]

"What Can I *Do*?" . . . I Told Her, "Nothing."

... I never will forget one little blonde co-ed after I had spoken at her New England college. She must have caught the next plane behind that one I took to New York. She found the Muslim restaurant in Harlem. I just happened to be there when she came in....

Anyway, I'd never seen anyone I ever spoke before more affected than this little white college girl. She demanded, right up in my face, "Don't you believe there are any *good* white people?" I didn't want to hurt her feelings. I told her, "People's *deeds* I believe in, Miss—not their words."

"What can I *do*?" she exclaimed. I told her, "Nothing." She burst out crying, and ran out....

From *God's Judgment of White America*
1963

This document is one of Malcolm's classic fiery denunciations, as spokesperson for the Nation of Islam, of white America and the Western world. Here Minister Malcolm relied heavily on NOI prophecy about the coming end of white world dominance and restoration of original black rule. He also stressed the NOI programmatic goal of acquiring land.

The speech is famous for the statement Malcolm made during questions and answers afterward that President John F. Kennedy's recent assassination was a case of "the chickens coming home to roost," which America greatly deserved. Elijah Muhammad's suspension of Malcolm, ostensibly for this remark, began the process that led to Malcolm's eventual departure from the Nation.

The Honorable Elijah Muhammad teaches us that as it was the evil sin of slavery that caused the downfall and destruction of ancient Egypt and Babylon, and of ancient Greece, as well as ancient Rome....

So we of this present generation are also witnessing how the enslavement of millions of black people in this country is now bringing White America to her hour of judgment, to her downfall as a respected nation.... It is only a matter of time before White America too will be utterly destroyed by her own sins, and all traces of her former glory will be removed from this planet forever.

The Honorable Elijah Muhammad teaches us that as it was divine will in the case of the destruction of the slave empires of the ancient and modern past, America's *judgment* and *destruction* will also be brought about by divine will and divine power. Just as ancient nations paid for their sins against humanity, White America must now pay for her sins against twenty-two million "Negroes."...

... We believe that we are living in the time of "prophecy fulfillment," the time predicted by the ancient prophets of God, when this one God would use his one religion to establish one world here on earth—the world of Islam, or Muslim world... which only means: a

---

Speech delivered at Manhattan Center, New York City, 4 Dec. 1963; reprinted in Imam Benjamin Karim, ed., *The End of White World Supremacy: Four Speeches by Malcolm X* (New York: Seaver Books, 1971), 121–32.

world of universal brotherhood that will be based upon the principles of truth, freedom, justice, equality, righteousness, and peace.

But before God can set up his new world, the Muslim world, or world of Islam, which will be established on the principles of truth, peace, and brotherhood, God himself must first destroy this evil Western world, the white world ... a wicked world, ruled by a race of devils, that preaches falsehood, practices slavery, and thrives on indecency and immorality.

You and I are living in that great Doomsday, the final hour, when the ancient prophets predicted that God himself would appear in person, in the flesh, and with divine power He would bring about the judgment and destruction of this present evil world.

The hour of judgment and doom is upon White America for the evil seeds of slavery and hypocrisy she has sown; and God himself has declared that no one shall escape the doom of this Western world, except those who accept Allah as God, Islam as his only religion, and The Honorable Elijah Muhammad as his Messenger to the twenty-two million ex-slaves here in America, twenty-two million "Negroes" who are referred to in the symbolism of the Scriptures as the Lost Sheep, the Lost Tribes, or the Lost People of God.

White America is doomed! God has declared that The Honorable Elijah Muhammad is your only means of escape. When you reject The Honorable Elijah Muhammad, when you refuse to hear his message or heed his warning, you are closing your only door of escape. When you cut yourself off from him, you cut yourself off from your only way out of the divine disaster that is fast approaching White America....

... When God prepared to turn his wrath upon the Egyptians, that House of Bondage, or Land of Slavery, God raised his servant Moses as a warner to the cruel slave master, Pharaoh.

Moses' message to the slave master was simple and clear: "Let my people go ... Let them no longer be *segregated* by you; stop trying to deceive them with false promises of *integration* with you; let them *separate* themselves from you. Let them go with me to a place wherein the God of our forefathers has prepared a land for us ... a land in which we can serve our own God, practice righteousness; and live in peace among our own kind."

And Moses warned Pharaoh: "If you will not let them *separate* from you and go with me, then our God will destroy you and your entire slave empire from the face of this earth."

Pharaoh's wealth and power made him too proud to listen to the little inarticulate ex-slave named Moses. He ridiculed Moses' lack of eloquence. White America's attitude today is the same toward The Honorable Elijah Muhammad. They ridicule him because of his lack of education and his cotton-field origin in Georgia. White America chooses to listen to the Negro civil rights leaders, the Big Six.[1] Six puppets who have been trained by the whites in white institutions and then placed over our people by these same whites as "spokesmen" for our people. These handpicked "spokesmen" do nothing but parrot for the whites exactly what they know the whites want to hear.

Pharaoh used this same strategy to oppose Moses. Pharaoh also set up puppet-magicians to parrot his lies and to deceive the Hebrew slaves into thinking that Moses was a hate-teacher, an extremist, who was advocating violence and racial supremacy simply because Moses was trying to restore unto his people their own lost culture, their lost identity, their lost racial dignity ... the same as The Honorable Elijah Muhammad is trying to do among the twenty-two million "Negro" slaves here in this modern House of Bondage today.

By opposing Moses, Pharaoh was actually opposing Moses' God; thus that same God (Jehovah) was forced to drown Pharaoh in the Red Sea, destroy his slave empire, and remove the Egyptian influence from the face of this earth.

History is repeating itself today. America now faces the same fate at the hands of Almighty God. That same divine handwriting is now on the walls of this modern American House of Bondage....

The Honorable Elijah Muhammad's mission as Messenger is to remind America that God has not forgotten America's crimes against his Long-Lost people, who have spent four hundred miserable years in this Land of Bondage. His mission is to warn America of the divine destruction that will soon rain down upon her from the very skies above her.

His mission is to warn America to repent, and to atone for her sins against God's people ... or face complete destruction and permanent removal from the face of this earth ... and removal not only as a nation but *removal even as a race!* ...

The time is past when the white world can exercise unilateral authority and control over the dark world. The independence and power of the dark world is on the increase; the dark world is rising in wealth, power, prestige, and influence. It is the rise of the dark world that is causing the fall of the white world.

---

[1] Besides King of SCLC, this group included such major civil rights leaders as Roy Wilkins of the NAACP, James Farmer of CORE, Whitney Young of the Urban League, and labor leader A. Philip Randolph.

As the white man loses his power to oppress and exploit the dark world, the white man's own wealth (power or "world") decreases. His world is on its way down; it is on its way out ... and it is the will and power of God himself that is bringing an end to the white world.

You and I were born at this turning point in history; we are witnessing the fulfillment of prophecy. Our present generation is witnessing the end of colonialism, Europeanism, Westernism, or "White-ism" ... the end of white supremacy, the end of the evil white man's unjust rule....

Justice only means that the wicked slave master must reap the fruit (or harvest) of the evil seeds of slavery he has planted. This is justice! Other slave empires received justice, and now White America must receive justice....

White America is doomed! Death and devastating destruction hang at this very moment in the skies over America. But why must her divine execution take place? Is it too late for her to avoid this catastrophe?

All the prophets of the past listed America as number one among the guilty nations that would be too proud, and too blind, to repent and atone when God's last Messenger is raised in her midst to warn her. America's last chance, her last warning, is coming from the lips of The Honorable Elijah Muhammad today. Accept him and be saved; reject him and be damned!

It is written that White America will reject him; it is also written that White America will be damned and doomed ... and the prophets who make these prophecies are never wrong in their divine predictions.

5
Critiques of Rival Racial Programs and Philosophies

> *Most of the Negroes you see running around ... talking about "love everybody" ... don't have any love whatsoever for their own kind. ... White people follow King. White people pay King. ... King is the best weapon that the white man, who wants to brutalize Negroes, has ever gotten in this country.* —Malcolm X
>
> *Black Power is a cry of disappointment born from the wounds of despair. ... But revolution ... cannot long be [so] sustained. ... The Negro cannot entrust his destiny to a philosophy nourished solely on despair [for] today's despair is a poor chisel to carve out tomorrow's justice.* —Martin Luther King

Throughout his career King criticized two groups in the African American community: the many conservative, apolitical clergy and comfortable middle-class individuals who stayed out of the civil rights struggle and those groups, such as the Nation of Islam, who King said resisted oppression with hatred and violence. Both were, he held, immoral and incapable of removing the evil of white supremacy. King always championed nonviolent protest as, morally and practically, "a more excellent way."

Malcolm harshly criticized middle-class blacks, whom he regarded as self hating, white-loving traitors. He showed contempt for what he called "black bourgeoisie" and "integration-mad Negroes" and anger at their race desertion. Malcolm detested persons in the overlapping categories of Christian, bourgeois, nonviolent, and pro–civil rights African American. He saw such selfish, deluded black leaders as puppets of their white masters and enemies of the black masses' fight for freedom.

The Nation of Islam particularly denounced Christians, as Christianity was their main religious rival among African Americans and,

NOI members believed, the main agent of blacks' brainwashing and control by whites. King himself, as a middle-class professional, outspoken Christian, and prominent symbol of the integrationist Civil Rights movement was a frequent target for Malcolm's scorn.

MARTIN LUTHER KING JR.

Three Responses of Oppressed Groups
1958

In his book Stride toward Freedom: The Montgomery Story, *King identified three opposing ways by which, he claimed, members of oppressed groups respond to oppression: by acquiescing to it; by violently resisting it; or by resisting it through disciplined, loving nonviolence. Passive acquiescence indicated lack of courage and self-respect and perpetuated injustice. Violence, while at least resisting evil, was nevertheless "both impractical and immoral."*

It is telling that, although King criticized both passivity and violent resistance as responses to social injustice, he considered the latter less immoral than the former, since the worst possible response was failing to resist oppression. King used his trademark dialectical method of reconciling opposites to present nonviolence as a higher synthesis that "seeks to reconcile the truths of two opposites—acquiescence and violence—while avoiding the extremes and immoralities of both."

... Oppressed people deal with their oppression in three characteristic ways. One way is acquiescence: the oppressed resign themselves to their doom. They tacitly adjust themselves to oppression, and thereby become conditioned to it. In every movement toward freedom some of the oppressed prefer to remain oppressed. Almost twenty-eight hundred years ago Moses set out to lead the children of Israel from the slavery of Egypt to the freedom of the promised land. He soon discovered that

---

From *Stride toward Freedom: The Montgomery Story;* reprinted in James M. Washington, ed., *A Testament of Hope: The Essential Writings and Speeches of Martin Luther King Jr.* (San Francisco: HarperCollins, 1986), 481–83.

slaves do not always welcome their deliverers. They become accustomed to being slaves. They would rather bear those ills they have, as Shakespeare pointed out, than flee to others that they know not of. They prefer the "fleshpots of Egypt" to the ordeals of emancipation.[1]

There is such a thing as the freedom from exhaustion. Some people are so worn down by the yoke of oppression that they give up. A few years ago in the slum areas of Atlanta, a Negro guitarist used to sing almost daily: "Ben down so long that down don't bother me." This is the type of negative freedom and resignation that often engulfs the life of the oppressed.

But this is not the way out. To accept passively an unjust system is to cooperate with that system; thereby the oppressed become as evil as the oppressor. Noncooperation with evil is as much a moral obligation as is cooperation with good. The oppressed must never allow the conscience of the oppressor to slumber. Religion reminds every man that he is his brother's keeper. To accept injustice or segregation passively is to say to the oppressor that his actions are morally right. It is a way of allowing his conscience to fall asleep. At this moment the oppressed fails to be his brother's keeper. So acquiescence—while often the easier way—is not the moral way. It is the way of the coward. The Negro cannot win the respect of his oppressor by acquiescing; he merely increases the oppressor's arrogance and contempt. Acquiescence is interpreted as proof of the Negro's inferiority. The Negro cannot win the respect of the white people of the South or the peoples of the world if he is willing to sell the future of his children for his personal and immediate comfort and safety.

A second way that oppressed people sometimes deal with oppression is to resort to physical violence and corroding hatred. Violence often brings about momentary results. Nations have frequently won their independence in battle. But in spite of temporary victories, violence never brings permanent peace. It solves no social problem; it merely creates new and more complicated ones.

Violence as a way of achieving racial justice is both impractical and immoral. It is impractical because it is a descending spiral ending in destruction for all. The old law of an eye for an eye leaves everybody blind. It is immoral because it seeks to humiliate the opponent rather than win his understanding; it seeks to annihilate rather than to convert. Violence is immoral because it thrives on hatred rather than

---

[1]The phrase "fleshpots of Egypt" refers to when the recently freed Israelites nostalgically recalled having had ample food as slaves.

love. It destroys community and makes brotherhood impossible. It leaves society in monologue rather than dialogue. Violence ends by defeating itself. It creates bitterness in the survivors and brutality in the destroyers. A voice echoes through time saying to every potential Peter, "Put up your sword."[2] History is cluttered with the wreckage of nations that failed to follow this command.

If the American Negro and other victims of oppression succumb to the temptation of using violence in the struggle for freedom, future generations will be the recipients of a desolate night of bitterness, and our chief legacy to them will be an endless reign of meaningless chaos. Violence is not the way.

The third way open to oppressed people in their quest for freedom is the way of nonviolent resistance. Like the synthesis in Hegelian philosophy, the principle of nonviolent resistance seeks to reconcile the truths of two opposites—acquiescence and violence—while avoiding the extremes and immoralities of both. The nonviolent resister agrees with the person who acquiesces that one should not be physically aggressive toward his opponent but he balances the equation by agreeing with the person of violence that evil must be resisted. He avoids the nonresistance of the former and the violent resistance of the latter. With nonviolent resistance, no individual or group need submit to any wrong, nor need anyone resort to violence in order to right a wrong.

It seems to me that this is the method that must guide the actions of the Negro in the present crisis in race relations. Through nonviolent resistance the Negro will be able to rise to the noble height of opposing the unjust system while loving the perpetrators of the system. The Negro must work passionately and unrelentingly for full stature as a citizen, but he must not use inferior methods to gain it. He must never come to terms with falsehood, malice, hate, or destruction....

By nonviolent resistance, the Negro can also enlist all men of good will in his struggle for equality. The problem is not a purely racial one, with Negroes set against whites. In the end, it is not a struggle between people at all, but a tension between justice and injustice. Nonviolent resistance is not aimed against oppressors but against oppression. Under its banner consciences, not racial groups, are enlisted.

If the Negro is to achieve the goal of integration, he must organize himself into a militant and nonviolent mass movement. All three ele-

---

[2]Jesus rebuked his disciple Peter for attempting to defend him from arrest by the authorities.

ments are indispensable. The movement for equality and justice can only be a success if it has both a mass and militant character; the barriers to be overcome require both. Nonviolence is an imperative in order to bring about ultimate community. . . .

On Black Nationalists and Malcolm X
1965

King generally avoided discussing Malcolm and the Nation in public. Rather than directly answering their intemperate charges against him and the nonviolent Civil Rights movement, he mostly chose to ignore them, limiting himself to occasional brief comments. In Alex Haley's interview with him for Playboy *magazine, King said about as much as he ever publicly did on the subject.*

In this excerpt from the interview, King deplored the NOI and minimized its influence among African Americans; at the same time, he strategically used it to show what might result if white Americans failed to heed blacks' legitimate, nonviolently expressed demands. Even as he distanced himself from radical black nationalists, however, King endorsed the nationalistic stress on a shared identity between Africans and Americans of African descent. King's keen international interests and anti-imperialism were common bonds between him and many nationalists, including Malcolm.

King: . . . The Negro revolution is a genuine revolution, born from the same womb that produces all massive social upheavals—the womb of intolerable conditions and unendurable situations.

Playboy: Is it destined to be a violent revolution?

King: God willing, no. But white Americans must be made to understand the basic motives underlying Negro demonstrations. Many

---

Excerpt from interview of Martin Luther King Jr., by Alex Haley, *Playboy* (Jan. 1965): 117ff.; reprinted in James M. Washington, ed., *A Testament of Hope: The Essential Writings and Speeches of Martin Luther King Jr.* (San Francisco: HarperCollins, 1986), 363–65.

pent-up resentments and latent frustrations are boiling inside the Negro, and he must release them. It is not a threat but a fact of history that if an oppressed people's pent-up emotions are not nonviolently released, they will be violently released. So let the Negro march. Let him make pilgrimages to city hall. Let him go on freedom rides. And above all, make an effort to understand why he must do this. For if his frustration and despair are allowed to continue piling up, millions of Negroes will seek solace and security in black-nationalist ideologies. And this, inevitably, would lead to a frightening racial nightmare.

Playboy: Among whites, the best-known and most feared of these militantly racist Negro sects is the Black Muslims. What is your estimation of its power and influence among the Negro masses?

King: Except in a few metropolitan ghettos, my experience has been that few Negroes have any interest at all in this organization, much less give any allegiance to its pessimistic doctrines. The Black Muslims are a quasi-religious, sociopolitical movement that has appealed to some Negroes who formerly were Christians. For the first time, the Negro was presented with a choice of a religion other than Christianity. What this appeal actually represented was an indictment of Christian failures to live up to Christianity's precepts; for there is nothing in Christianity, nor in the Bible, that justifies racial segregation. But when the Negroes' genuine fighting spirit rose during 1963, the appeal of the Muslims began to diminish.

Playboy: One of the basic precepts of black nationalism has been the attempt to engender a sense of communion between the American Negro and his African "brother," a sense of identity between the emergence of black Africa and the Negro's struggle for freedom in America. Do you feel that this is a constructive effort?

King: Yes, I do, in many ways. There is a distinct, significant and inevitable correlation. The Negro across America, looking at his television set, sees black statesmen voting in the United Nations on vital world issues, knowing that in many of America's cities, he himself is not yet permitted to place his ballot. The Negro hears of black kings and potentates ruling in palaces, while he remains ghettoized in urban slums. It is only natural that Negroes would react to this extreme irony. Consciously or unconsciously, the American Negro has been caught up by the black *Zeitgeist*. He feels a deepening sense of identification with his black African brothers, and with his brown and yellow brothers of Asia, South America and the

Caribbean. With them he is moving with a sense of increasing urgency toward the promised land of racial justice.

Playboy: Do you feel that the African nations, in turn, should involve themselves more actively in American Negro affairs?

King: I do indeed. The world is now so small in terms of geographic proximity and mutual problems that no nation should stand idly by and watch another's plight. I think that in every possible instance Africans should use the influence of their governments to make it clear that the struggle of their brothers in the U.S. is part of a worldwide struggle. In short, injustice anywhere is a threat to justice everywhere, for we are tied together in a garment of mutuality. What happens in Johannesburg affects Birmingham, however indirectly.[1] We are descendants of the Africans. Our heritage is Africa. We should never seek to break the ties, nor should the Africans.

Playboy: One of the most articulate champions of black Afro-American brotherhood has been Malcolm X, the former Black Muslim leader who recently renounced his racist past and converted to orthodox Mohammedanism. What is your opinion of him and his career?

King: I met Malcolm X once in Washington, but circumstances didn't enable me to talk with him for more than a minute.[2] He is very articulate, as you say, but I totally disagree with many of his political and philosophical views—at least insofar as I understand where he now stands. I don't want to seem to sound self-righteous, or absolutist, or that I think I have the only truth, the only way. Maybe he *does* have some of the answers. I don't know how he feels now, but I know that I have often wished that he would talk less of violence, because violence is not going to solve our problem. And in his litany of articulating the despair of the Negro without offering any positive, creative alternative, I feel that Malcolm has done himself and our people a great disservice. Fiery, demagogic oratory in the black ghettos, urging Negroes to arm themselves and prepare to engage in violence, as he has done, can reap nothing but grief.

Playboy: For them or for whites?

King: For everyone, but mostly for them. Even the extremist leaders who preach revolution are invariably unwilling to lead what they

---

[1]Johannesburg, South Africa, and Birmingham, Alabama, were two of the most racially segregated cities in the world during the post–World War II decades.

[2]King and Malcolm's meeting in the U.S. Capitol building on March 26, 1964 (see front cover photograph).

know would certainly end in bloody, chaotic and total defeat; for in the event of a violent revolution, we would be sorely outnumbered. And when it was all over, the Negro would face the same unchanged conditions, the same squalor and deprivation—the only difference being that his bitterness would be even more intense, his disenchantment even more abject. Thus, in purely practical as well as moral terms, the American Negro has no rational alternative to nonviolence.

Playboy: You categorically reject violence as a tactical technique for social change. Can it not be argued, however, that violence, historically, has effected massive and sometimes constructive social change in some countries?

King: I'd be the first to say that some historical victories have been won by violence; the U.S. Revolution is certainly one of the foremost. But the Negro revolution is seeking integration, not independence. Those fighting for independence have the purpose to *drive out* the oppressors. But here in America, we've got to live together. We've got to find a way to reconcile ourselves to living in community, one group with the other....

The Nightmare of Violence: Regarding the Death of Malcolm X
1965

King released the following statement within days of Malcolm X's assassination; ironically, it was the fullest public statement King ever made on Malcolm. In it and similar statements from around that time, King used Malcolm's bloody end as a metaphor for the endemic, escalating violence in American life. While reiterating his still profound disagreement with Malcolm, King wrote of him with genuine respect and sympathy: He noted that "Malcolm was still turning and growing" intellectually and politically at his untimely end, and that his murder "deprives the world of a potentially great leader." King's remarkable analysis of the tragic

"People to People: The Nightmare of Violence," 26 Feb. 1965, 1–3, King Center Archives, Atlanta.

sociological roots of Malcolm X's life and ministry is as insightful as any offered by Malcolm biographers. Ultimately Malcolm was, in King's view, "a victim of the despair that inevitably derives from the conditions of oppression, poverty, and injustice which engulf the masses of our race."

The present ghastly nightmare of violence and counter-violence is one of the most tragic blots to occur on the pages of the Negro's history in this country. In many ways, however, it is typical of the displacement of aggressions which has occurred throughout the frustrated circumstances of our existence.

How often the frustrations of second-class citizenship and humiliating status lead us into blind outrage against each other and the real cause and source of our dilemma ignored? It is sadly ironic that those who so clearly pointed to the white world as the seed of evil should now spend their energies in their own destruction.

Malcolm X came to the fore as a public figure partially as a result of a TV documentary entitled, "The Hate that Hate Produced."[1] That title points clearly to the nature of Malcolm's life and death.

Malcolm X was clearly a product of the hate and violence invested in the Negro's blighted existence in this nation. He, like so many of our number, was a victim of the despair that inevitably derives from the conditions of oppression, poverty, and injustice which engulf the masses of our race. But in his youth, there was no hope, no preaching, teaching or movements of non-violence. He was too young for the Garvey Movement, too poor to be a Communist—for the Communists geared their work to Negro intellectuals and labor without realizing that the masses of Negroes were unrelated to either—and yet he possessed a native intelligence and drive which demanded an outlet and means of expression. He turned first to the underworld, but this did not fulfill the quest for meaning which grips young minds. It is a testimony to Malcolm's personal depth and integrity that he could not become an underworld czar, but turned again and again to religion for meaning and destiny. Malcolm was still turning and growing at the time of his brutal and meaningless assassination.

In his recent visit to Selma, he spoke at length to my wife Coretta about his personal struggles and expressed an interest in working

---

[1] "The Hate That Hate Produced" was a five-part televised report by Mike Wallace that aired on WTNA-TV Channel 13 in New York on July 13–17, 1959.

more closely with the non-violent movement but he was not yet able to renounce violence and overcome the bitterness which life had invested in him. There were also indications of an interest in politics as a way of dealing with the problems of the Negro. All of these were signs of a man of passion and zeal seeking for a program through which he could channel his talents.

But history would not have it so. A man who lived under the torment of knowledge of the rape of his Grandmother and murder of his father and under the conditions of the present social order, does not readily accept that social order or seek to integrate into it. And so Malcolm was forced to live and die in it as an outsider, a victim of the violence that spawned him, and with which he courted through his brief but promising life.

The American Negro cannot afford to destroy its leadership any more than the Congo can. Men of talent are too scarce to be destroyed by envy, greed and tribal rivalry before they reach their full maturity. Like the murder of Lumumba,[2] the murder of Malcolm X deprives the world of a potentially great leader. I could not agree with either of these men, but I could see in them a capacity for leadership which I could respect, and which was only beginning to mature in judgment and statesmanship.

Surely the young men of Harlem and Negro communities throughout the nation ought to be ready to seek another way. Let us learn that violence and hate only breed violence and hate, and that Jesus' word still goes out to every potential Peter, "Put up thy sword." Certainly we will continue to disagree, but we must disagree without becoming violently disagreeable. We will still suffer the temptation to bitterness, but we must learn that hate is too great a burden to bear for a people moving on toward their date with destiny.

---

[2]Pro-independence leader and prime minister of Congo Patrice Lumumba was killed during intra-black political conflict in early 1961.

MALCOLM X

Black Bodies with White Heads!

1965

In this selection, Malcolm gave his opinions about the professional, pro-integration African Americans with whom he verbally sparred on hundreds of media panels, talk shows, and other forums.

... Today's Uncle Tom doesn't wear a handkerchief on his head. This modern, twentieth-century Uncle Thomas now often wears a top hat. He's usually well-dressed and well-educated.... The twentieth-century Uncle Thomas sometimes speaks with a Yale or Harvard accent. Sometimes he is known as Professor, Doctor, Judge, and Reverend, even Right Reverend Doctor. This twentieth-century Uncle Thomas is a *professional* Negro ... by that I mean his profession is being a Negro for the white man.

Never before in America had these hand-picked so-called "leaders" been publicly blasted in this way....

"Black bodies with white heads!" I called them what they were....

It was hot, hot copy, both in the white and the black press. *Life, Look, Newsweek* and *Time* reported us....[1]

Before very long, radio and television people began asking me to defend our Nation of Islam in panel discussions and debates. I was to be confronted by hand-picked scholars, both whites and some of those Ph.D. "house" and "yard" Negroes who had been attacking us....

I'd walk into those studios. The devils and black Ph.D. puppets would be acting so friendly and "integrated" with each other—laughing and calling each other by first names, and all that; it was such a big lie it made me sick in my stomach....

... Why, sometimes I've felt I ought to jump down off that stand and get *physical* with some of those brainwashed white man's tools, parrots, puppets...

---

[1] Some of the leading news and entertainment magazines of the era.

The Autobiography of Malcolm X, 247–49, 290.

One particular university's "token-integrated" black Ph.D. associate professor I never will forget; he got me so mad I couldn't see straight. As badly as our 22 millions of educationally deprived black people need the help of any brains he has, there he was looking like some fly in the buttermilk among white "colleagues"—and he was trying to *eat me up!* He was ranting about what a "divisive demagogue" and what a "reverse racist" I was. I was racking my head, to spear that fool; finally I held up my hand, and he stopped. "Do you know what white racists call black Ph.D.'s?" He said something like, "I believe that I happen not to be aware of that"—you know, one of these ultra-proper-talking Negroes. And I laid the word down on him, loud: *"Nigger!"* . . .

From *Message to the Grassroots*
1963

This statement by Malcolm is a lengthy excerpt from one of his most important speeches, "Message to the Grassroots." In it, he juxtaposed two of his best-known rhetorical riffs, "house Negroes versus field Negroes" and "the farce on Washington."

To understand this, you have to go back to . . . the house Negro and the field Negro back during slavery. There were two kinds of slaves, the house Negro and the field Negro. The house Negroes—they lived in the house with master, they dressed pretty good, they ate good because they ate his food—what he left. They lived in the attic or the basement, but still they lived near the master; and they loved the master more than the master loved himself. They would give their life to save the master's house—quicker than the master would. If the master said, "We got a good house here," the house Negro would say, "Yeah, we got a good house here." Whenever the master said "we," he said "we." That's how you can tell a house Negro.

"Message to the Grassroots," 10 Nov. 1963, Detroit Mich.; reprinted in George Breitman, ed., *Malcolm X Speaks: Selected Speeches and Statements* (New York: Grove Press, 1982), 10–13, 13–17.

If the master's house caught on fire, the house Negro would fight harder to put the blaze out than the master would. If the master got sick, the house Negro would say, "What's the matter, boss, *we* sick?" *We* sick! He identified himself with his master, more than his master identified with himself. And if you came to the house Negro and said, "Let's run away, let's escape, let's separate," the house Negro would look at you and say, "Man, you crazy. What you mean, separate? Where is there a better house than this? Where can I wear better clothes than this? Where can I eat better food than this?" That was that house Negro. In those days he was called a "house nigger." And that's what we call them today, because we've still got some house niggers running around here.

This modern house Negro loves his master. He wants to live near him. He'll pay three times as much as the house is worth just to live near his master, and then brag about "I'm the only Negro out here." "I'm the only one on my job." "I'm the only one in this school." You're nothing but a house Negro. And if someone comes to you right now and says, "Let's separate," you say the same thing that the house Negro said on the plantation. "What you mean, separate? From America, this good white man? . . ."

On that same plantation, there was the field Negro. The field Negroes—those were the masses. There were always more Negroes in the field than there were Negroes in the house. The Negro in the field caught hell. He ate leftovers. In the house they ate high up on the hog. The Negro in the field didn't get anything but what was left of the insides of the hog. They call it "chitt'lings" nowadays. In those days they called them what they were—guts. That's what you were—gut-eaters. And some of you are still gut-eaters.

The field Negro was beaten from morning to night; he lived in a shack, in a hut; he wore old, castoff clothes. He hated his master. I say he hated his master. He was intelligent. That house Negro loved his master, but that field Negro—remember, they were in the majority, and they hated the master. When the house caught on fire, he didn't try to put it out; that field Negro prayed for a wind, for a breeze. When the master got sick, the field Negro prayed that he'd die. If someone came to the field Negro and said, "Let's separate, let's run," he didn't say "Where we going?" He'd say, "Any place is better than here." You've got field Negroes in America today. I'm a field Negro. The masses are the field Negroes. When they see this man's house on fire, you don't hear the little Negroes talking about "*our* government is in trouble." They say, "*The* government is in trouble." Imagine a Negro: "*Our* government"! I even heard one say "*our* astronauts." They won't even let him near the plant—and "*our* astronauts"! "*Our* Navy"—that's a Negro that is out of his mind, a Negro that is out of his mind.

Just as the slavemaster of that day used Tom, the house Negro, to keep the field Negroes in check, the same old slavemaster today has Negroes who are nothing but modern Uncle Toms, twentieth-century Uncle Toms, to keep you and me in check, to keep us under control, keep us passive and peaceful and nonviolent. That's Tom making you nonviolent. It's like when you go to the dentist, and the man's going to take your tooth. You're going to fight him when he starts pulling. So he squirts some stuff in your jaw called novocaine, to make you think they're not doing anything to you. So you sit there and because you've got all that novocaine in your jaw, you suffer—peacefully. Blood running all down your jaw, and you don't know what's happening. Because someone has taught you to suffer—peacefully.

The white man does the same thing to you in the street, when he wants to put knots on your head and take advantage of you and not have to be afraid of your fighting back. To keep you from fighting back, he gets these old religious Uncle Toms to teach you and me, just like novocaine, to suffer peacefully. Don't stop suffering—just suffer peacefully. . . .

This is the way it is with the white man in America. He's a wolf—and you're sheep. Any time a shepherd, a pastor, teaches you and me not to run from the white man and, at the same time, teaches us not to fight the white man, he's a traitor to you and me. Don't lay down a life all by itself. No, preserve your life, it's the best thing you've got. And if you've got to give it up, let it be even-steven.

The slavemaster took Tom and dressed him well, fed him well and even gave him a little education—a *little* education; gave him a long coat and a top hat and made all the other slaves look up to him. Then he used Tom to control them. The same strategy that was used in those days is used today, by the same white man. He takes a Negro, a so-called Negro, and makes him prominent, builds him up, publicizes him, makes him a celebrity. And then he becomes a spokesman for Negroes—and a Negro leader.

I would like to mention just one other thing quickly, and that is the method that the white man uses, how the white man uses the "big guns," or Negro leaders, against the Negro revolution. They are not a part of the Negro revolution. They are used against the Negro revolution.

When Martin Luther King failed to desegregate Albany, Georgia, the civil-rights struggle in America reached its low point.[1] King became bankrupt almost, as a leader. The Southern Christian Leadership Conference was in financial trouble; and it was in trouble, period, with the people when they failed to desegregate Albany, Georgia. Other Negro civil-rights leaders of so-called national stature became fallen idols. As they became fallen idols, began to lose their prestige and influence, local Negro leaders began to stir up the masses. In Cambridge, Maryland, Gloria Richardson; in Danville, Virginia, and other parts of the country, local leaders began to stir up our people at the grass-roots level. This was never done by these Negroes of national stature.[2] They control you, but they have never incited you or excited you. They control you, they contain you, they have kept you on the plantation.

As soon as King failed in Birmingham, Negroes took to the streets. King went out to California to a big rally and raised I don't know how many thousands of dollars. He came to Detroit and had a march and raised some more thousands of dollars. And recall, right after that Roy Wilkins attacked King. He accused King and CORE [Congress Of Racial Equality] of starting trouble everywhere and then making the NAACP [National Association for the Advancement of Colored People] get them out of jail and spend a lot of money; they accused King and CORE of raising all the money and not paying it back. This happened; I've got it in documented evidence in the newspaper. Roy started attacking King, and King started attacking Roy, and Farmer started attacking both of them. And as these Negroes of national stature began to attack each other, they began to lose their control of the Negro masses.

The Negroes were out there in the streets. They were talking about how they were going to march on Washington. Right at that time Birmingham had exploded, and the Negroes in Birmingham—remember, they also exploded. They began to stab the crackers in the back and bust them up 'side their head—yes, they did. That's when Kennedy sent in the troops, down in Birmingham. After that, Kennedy got on the television and said "this is a moral issue." That's when he said he was going to put out a civil rights bill. And when he mentioned

---

[1] King and the SCLC's campaign to desegregate Albany, Georgia, during 1961–62 failed because of black internal disunity and lack of visible police repression to induce media attention and public pressure.

[2] Much the same national black leadership group that in "God's Judgment of White America" Malcolm calls the "Big Six." In this group were King, NAACP President Roy Wilkins, James Farmer of CORE, Whitney Young of the Urban League, and labor leader A. Philip Randolph.

civil-rights bill and the Southern crackers started talking about how they were going to boycott or filibuster it, then the Negroes started talking—about what?[3] That they were going to march on Washington, march on the Senate, march on the White House, march on the Congress, and tie it up, bring it to a halt, not let the government proceed. They even said they were going out to the airport and lay down on the runway and not let any airplanes land. I'm telling you what they said. That was revolution. That was revolution. That was the black revolution.

It was the grass roots out there in the street. It scared the white man to death, scared the white power structure in Washington, D.C., to death; I was there. When they found out that this black steamroller was going to come down on the capital, they called in Wilkins, they called in Randolph, they called in these national Negro leaders that you respect and told them, "Call it off." Kennedy said, "Look, you all are letting this thing go too far." And Old Tom said, "Boss, I can't stop it, because I didn't start it." I'm telling you what they said. They said, "I'm not even in it, much less at the head of it." They said, "These Negroes are doing things on their own. They're running ahead of us." And that old shrewd fox, he said, "If you all aren't in it, I'll put you in it. I'll put you at the head of it. I'll endorse it. I'll welcome it. I'll help it. I'll join it." ...

Once they formed it, with the white man over it, he promised them and gave them $800,000 to split up among the Big Six; and told them that after the march was over they'd give them $700,000 more. A million and a half dollars—split up between leaders that you have been following, going to jail for, crying crocodile tears for. And they're nothing but Frank James and Jesse James and the what-do-you-call-'em brothers.[4]

As soon as they got the setup organized, the white man made available to them top public-relations experts; opened the news media across the country at their disposal, which then began to project these Big Six as the leaders of the march. Originally they weren't even in the march. You were talking this march talk on Hastings Street, you were talking march talk on Lenox Avenue, and on Fillmore Street, and on Central Avenue, and 32nd Street and 63rd Street. That's where the

---

[3] Senate opponents of the Johnson civil rights bill used a parliamentary procedure by which any senator may, by speaking on the floor, delay a vote on a bill indefinitely. It takes sixty of the one hundred total U.S. senators' votes to end a filibuster.

[4] Legendary American outlaw gangs.

march talk was being talked. But the white man put the Big Six at the head of it; made them the march. They became the march. They took it over. And the first move they made after they took it over, they invited Walter Reuther,[5] a white man; they invited a priest, a rabbi, and an old white preacher, yes, an old white preacher....

It's just like when you've got some coffee that's too black, which means it's too strong. What do you do? You integrate it with cream, you make it weak. But if you pour too much cream in it, you won't even know you ever had coffee. It used to be hot, it becomes cool. It used to be strong, it becomes weak. It used to wake you up, now it puts you to sleep. This is what they did with the march on Washington. They joined it. They didn't integrate it, they infiltrated it. They joined it, became a part of it, took it over. And as they took it over, it lost its militancy. It ceased to be angry, it ceased to be hot, it ceased to be uncompromising. Why, it even ceased to be a march. It became a picnic, a circus. Nothing but a circus, with clowns and all. You had one right here in Detroit—I saw it on television—with clowns leading it, white clowns and black clowns. I know you don't like what I'm saying, but I'm going to tell you anyway. Because I can prove what I'm saying. If you think I'm telling you wrong, you bring me Martin Luther King and A. Philip Randolph and James Farmer and those other three, and see if they'll deny it over a microphone.

No, it was a sellout. It was a takeover.... They controlled it so tight, they told those Negroes what time to hit town, how to come, where to stop, what signs to carry, what song to sing, what speech they could make, and what speech they couldn't make; and then told them to get out of town by sundown. And every one of those Toms was out of town by sundown. Now I know you don't like my saying this. But I can back it up. It was a circus, a performance that beat anything Hollywood could ever do, the performance of the year. Reuther and those other three devils should get an Academy Award for the best actors because they acted like they really loved Negroes and fooled a whole lot of Negroes. And the six Negro leaders should get an award too, for the best supporting cast.

[5] Walter P. Reuther, a prominent U.S. labor leader, then vice president of the AFL-CIO.

King Is the White Man's Best Weapon
1963

In an interview with Kenneth B. Clark, Malcolm trenchantly criticized King's leadership, charging that white people supported and financed him, that King controlled blacks for whites, and that King's insistence on nonviolence disarmed blacks before racist violence and oppression.

Malcolm X: ... The Muslims who follow the Honorable Elijah Muhammad don't advocate violence, but Mister Muhammad does teach us that any human being who is intelligent has the right to defend himself.... Mr. Muhammad teaches us to love each other, and when I say love each other—love our own kind. This is all black people need to be taught in this country because the only ones whom we don't love are our own kind. Most of the Negroes you see running around here talking about "love everybody"—they don't have any love whatsoever for their own kind. When they say, "Love everybody," what they are doing is setting up a situation for us to love white people. This is what their philosophy is. Or when they say, "Suffer peacefully," they mean suffer peacefully at the hands of the white man, because the same non-violent Negroes are the advocators of non-violence. If a Negro attacks one of them, they'll fight that Negro all over Harlem. It's only when the white man attacks them that they believe in non-violence, all of them.

Clark: Mister X, is this a criticism of the Reverend Martin Luther King?

Malcolm X: You don't have to criticize Reverend Martin Luther King. His actions criticize him.

Clark: What do you mean by this?

Malcolm X: Any Negro who teaches other Negroes to turn the other cheek is disarming that Negro. Any Negro who teaches Negroes to turn the other cheek in the face of attack is disarming that Negro of his God-given right, of his moral right, of his natural right, of his intelligent right to defend himself. Everything in nature can defend

---

Televised interview with Malcolm X by Kenneth B. Clark, June 1963, New York City, reprinted in Kenneth B. Clark, ed., *King, Malcolm, Baldwin: Three Interviews* (Middletown, Conn.: Wesleyan University Press, 1985), 41–43.

itself, and is right in defending itself except the American Negro. And men like King—their job is to go among Negroes and teach Negroes "Don't fight back." He doesn't tell them, "Don't fight each other." "Don't fight the white man" is what he's saying in essence, because the followers of Martin Luther King will cut each other from head to foot, but they will not do anything to defend themselves against the attacks of the white man. But King's philosophy falls upon the ears of only a small minority. The majority or masses of black people in this country are more inclined in the direction of the Honorable Elijah Muhammad than Martin Luther King.

Clark: Is it not a fact though—

Malcolm X: <u>White</u> people follow King. <u>White</u> people pay King. <u>White</u> people subsidize King. <u>White</u> people support King. But the masses of black people don't support Martin Luther King. King is the best weapon that the white man, who wants to brutalize Negroes, has ever gotten in this country, because he is setting up a situation where, when the white man wants to attack Negroes, they can't defend themselves, because King has put this foolish philosophy out—you're not supposed to fight or you're not supposed to defend yourself.

Clark: But Mister X, is it not a fact that Reverend King's movement was successful in Montgomery—

Malcolm X: You can't tell me that you have had success—excuse me, sir.

Clark: Was it not a success in Birmingham?

Malcolm X: No, no. What kind of success did they get in Birmingham? A chance to sit at a lunch counter and drink some coffee with a cracker—that's success? A chance to—thousands of little children went to jail; they didn't get out, they were bonded out by King.[1] They had to *pay* their way out of jail. That's not any kind of advancement or success. . . .

---

[1] Refers to King and the SCLC's tactic of having schoolchildren demonstrate during the 1963 Birmingham desegregation campaign. Many children were arrested. King was criticized for this daring escalation tactic during the demonstrations, including here by Malcolm.

6
Eras of Convergence

*The goal has always been the same, with the approaches to it as different as mine and Dr. Martin Luther King's non-violent marching....
And in the racial climate of this country today, it is anybody's guess which of the "extremes" in approach to the black man's problems might personally meet a fatal catastrophe first—"non-violent" Dr. King, or so-called "violent" me.* —Malcolm X

For years I labored with the idea of reforming the existing institutions, a little here, a little there. Now I feel differently. I think you've got to go for a reconstruction of the entire society, a total revolution of values. —Martin Luther King

I've done a lot of traveling and, I think overall, travel does broaden one's soul... That's probably the most important [part] of what's happened to me during the past five or six months. —Malcolm X

That was a bad scene [his old NOI life].... The sickness and madness... I'm glad to be free of them. It's time for martyrs now. And if I'm to be one, it will be in the cause of brotherhood. That's the only thing that can save this country. —Malcolm X

Truly America is much, much sicker than I realized when I began.
—Martin Luther King

During the last part of each man's public career—circa 1966–68 for King, and 1964–65 for Malcolm—the leaders moved so rapidly toward goals and rhetoric more associated with the other that they closed much of their once yawning gap in programs and ideologies. That each was moving toward the other just before his murder leaves historians wondering whether their paths might ever have converged. Given King's unshakable commitment to nonviolent means of social struggle and Malcolm's continuing critique of unconditional reliance on it, and Malcolm's nationalistic focus on black people and King's persistently multiethnic approach, it seems unlikely that the two would ever have agreed on every major issue or question of strategy concerning the African American freedom movement. So it remains a tantalizing, but unanswerable, question what their future relations and roles in the movement might have been had they not shared their tragic fates as martyrs.

MARTIN LUTHER KING JR.

By 1966, King had become deeply disturbed by the rapidly deteriorating state of national affairs, particularly with the explosion of urban riots and war in Vietnam. There were also polarizing public opinion trends of Black Power militancy on the one hand and, on the other, a "white backlash" against further racial protests and support for tough "law and order" responses. Driven by a growing sense of desperation, King struck out ever more bravely and boldly to present solutions for the nation's severe multiple crises. He was never more discouraged about the prospects for national progressive reform, however, as both blacks and whites proved ever less inclined to heed his calls for peace and justice.

From mid 1965 on, with legal segregation being substantially dismantled by the Civil Rights Act and African Americans' ability to vote largely secured by the Voting Rights Act, King raised combating poverty and slum conditions to the top of his agenda. The SCLC's 1966 Chicago Campaign, therefore, focused on achieving materially better and racially open housing in America's cities. The Chicago campaign had mixed results, however, and was widely seen at the time as having failed. The Poor People's Campaign, King's last planned major protest campaign, was still being organized when he was assassinated in April 1968. For months, the SCLC had been recruiting poor people from around the country and training them in nonviolent protest techniques. King and the SCLC planned to bring this nonviolent multiracial army of the poor to the national capital to demonstrate and, if necessary, immobilize the U.S. government until it took meaningful action to improve the conditions of America's poor. Ironically, this plan was substantially what Malcolm had recommended back in 1963 as a real, meaningful black protest in contrast to that year's great march which he so witheringly ridiculed in his "farce on Washington" routine (see chapter 5).

By 1967, King had become an outspoken critic of the U.S. war in Vietnam. King increasingly considered the goals of advancing human rights and making peace to be inextricably entwined. As his critique of capitalism and of the U.S. government and its foreign policy grew more strident, his support in the government and popularity in white opinion plummeted. President Lyndon Johnson privately raged against King's "ungrateful" criticisms of his war policies, and the FBI bugged and harassed him, aiming to destroy his public effectiveness. King's optimism about whites' goodwill and reformation waned; he was deeply discouraged in his final years about the nation's will and direction.

At the same time that King's growing radicalism was hurting his influence with whites, the most militant, student-led wing of the black struggle—the wing to which Malcolm had been trying to attach himself since 1963—increasingly dismissed him (echoing Malcolm's old sentiments) as an unreliable "Uncle Tom," too prone to compromise with whites and "sell out" blacks. King was losing public esteem and influence on every side during his tumultuous final period.

From *Beyond Vietnam*
1967

King's 1967 address at New York City's Riverside Church was a major media event and the main forum he chose for addressing the nation on the Vietnam War. Although he had briefly spoken out in 1965 against U.S. military intervention in Vietnam, until this address King had kept mainly silent, calculating that opposing the war would jeopardize President Johnson's support for more domestic social and economic reforms.

In this memorable speech, King tried to lay out a reasonable, moral, and patriotic case against the war capable of persuading some elements of the U.S. government, the national media, and the middle-class African American establishment. This hope was dashed. Immediately after his address, King was blasted by the national political establishment and press for his "traitorous" remarks. Negative response to his stand against

---

Speech delivered at Riverside Church, New York City, 4 April 1967; text follows transcription of recording by Martin Luther King Jr. Papers Project staff, reprinted in Clayborne Carson and Kris Shephard, eds., *A Call to Conscience: The Landmark Speeches of Dr. Martin Luther King Jr.* (New York: Warner Books, 2001), 139–64.

the war deepened King's growing sense of urgency and pessimism by the late 1960s about the nation's will and ability to reform.

"Beyond Vietnam" contains examples of such central points of King's final public message as his increasing focus on internationalism and anti-imperialism, ending poverty, and a "Revolution of Values" in America to transform its social and economic institutions.[1]

I come to this magnificent house of worship tonight because my conscience leaves me no other choice. I join you in this meeting because I am in deepest agreement with the aims and work of the organization which has brought us together, Clergy and Laymen Concerned About Vietnam. The recent statements of your executive committee are the sentiments of my own heart, and I found myself in full accord when I read its opening lines: "A time comes when silence is betrayal." That time has come for us in relation to Vietnam. . . .

Over the past two years, as I have moved to break the betrayal of my own silences and to speak from the burnings of my own heart, as I have called for radical departures from the destruction of Vietnam, many persons have questioned me about the wisdom of my path. At the heart of their concerns, this query has often loomed large and loud: "Why are you speaking about the war, Dr. King? Why are you joining the voices of dissent?" "Peace and civil rights don't mix," they say. "Aren't you hurting the cause of your people?" they ask. And when I hear them, though I often understand the source of their concern, I am nevertheless greatly saddened, for such questions mean that the inquirers have not really known me, my commitment, or my calling. Indeed, their questions suggest that they do not know the world in which they live. In the light of such tragic misunderstanding, I deem it of signal importance to try to state clearly, and I trust concisely, why I believe that the path from Dexter Avenue Baptist Church—the church in Montgomery, Alabama, where I began my pastorate—leads clearly to this sanctuary tonight.

I come to this platform tonight to make a passionate plea to my beloved nation. . . . Tonight . . . I wish not to speak with Hanoi and the National Liberation Front, but rather to my fellow Americans.[2]

---

[1] Italicized type in parentheses, e.g., (*Amen*), indicates audience verbal response.
[2] Hanoi was the capital of communist North Vietnam. The National Liberation Front, or Vietcong, were South Vietnamese guerrilla forces who, aided by North Vietnam, fought to overthrow the U.S.-backed anti-Communist government of South Vietnam.

Since I am a preacher by calling, I suppose it is not surprising that I have seven major reasons for bringing Vietnam into the field of my moral vision. There is at the outset a very obvious and almost facile connection between the war in Vietnam and the struggle I and others have been waging in America. A few years ago there was a shining moment in that struggle. It seemed as if there was a real promise of hope for the poor, both black and white, through the poverty program. There were experiments, hopes, new beginnings. Then came the buildup in Vietnam, and I watched this program broken and eviscerated as if it were some idle political plaything of a society gone mad on war. And I knew that America would never invest the necessary funds or energies in rehabilitation of its poor so long as adventures like Vietnam continued to draw men and skills and money like some demonic, destructive suction tube. So I was increasingly compelled to see the war as an enemy of the poor and to attack it as such.

Perhaps a more tragic recognition of reality took place when it became clear to me that the war was doing far more than devastating the hopes of the poor at home. It was sending their sons and their brothers and their husbands to fight and to die in extraordinarily high proportions relative to the rest of the population. We were taking the black young men who had been crippled by our society and sending them eight thousand miles away to guarantee liberties in Southeast Asia which they had not found in southwest Georgia and East Harlem. So we have been repeatedly faced with the cruel irony of watching Negro and white boys on TV screens as they kill and die together for a nation that has been unable to seat them together in the same schools. So we watch them in brutal solidarity burning the huts of a poor village, but we realize that they would hardly live on the same block in Chicago. I could not be silent in the face of such cruel manipulation of the poor.

My third reason moves to an even deeper level of awareness, for it grows out of my experience in the ghettos of the North over the last three years, especially the last three summers. As I have walked among the desperate, rejected, and angry young men, I have told them that Molotov cocktails and rifles would not solve their problems. I have tried to offer them my deepest compassion while maintaining my conviction that social change comes most meaningfully through nonviolent action. But they asked, and rightly so, "What about Vietnam?" They asked if our own nation wasn't using massive doses of violence to solve its problems, to bring about the changes it wanted. Their questions hit home, and I knew that I could never again raise my voice against the violence of the oppressed in the ghettos without having first spoken clearly to the greatest purveyor of violence in the world today: my own government. For the sake of those boys, for the sake of this government, for the sake of the hundreds of thousands trembling under our violence, I cannot be silent.

For those who ask the question, "Aren't you a civil rights leader?" and thereby mean to exclude me from the movement for peace, I have this further answer. In 1957, when a group of us formed the Southern Christian Leadership Conference, we chose as our motto: "To save the soul of America." We were convinced that we could not limit our vision to certain rights for black people, but instead affirmed the conviction that America would never be free or saved from itself until the descendants of its slaves were loosed completely from the shackles they still wear. In a way we were agreeing with Langston Hughes, that black bard of Harlem, who had written earlier:

> O, yes, I say it plain,
> America never was America to me,
> And yet I swear this oath—
> America will be![3]

Now it should be incandescently clear that no one who has any concern for the integrity and life of America today can ignore the present war. If America's soul becomes totally poisoned, part of the autopsy must read "Vietnam." It can never be saved so long as it destroys the deepest hopes of men the world over. So it is that those of us who are yet determined that "America will be" are led down the path of protest and dissent, working for the health of our land.

As if the weight of such a commitment to the life and health of America were not enough, another burden of responsibility was placed upon me in [1964]. And I cannot forget that the Nobel Peace Prize was also a commission, a commission to work harder than I had ever worked before for the brotherhood of man. This is a calling that takes me beyond national allegiances.

But even if it were not present, I would yet have to live with the meaning of my commitment to the ministry of Jesus Christ. To me, the relationship of this ministry to the making of peace is so obvious that I sometimes marvel at those who ask me why I am speaking against the war. Could it be that they do not know that the Good News

---

[3] Langston Hughes, *The Dream Keeper* (New York: Alfred A. Knopf, 1946), 7.

was meant for all men—for communist and capitalist, for their children and ours, for black and for white, for revolutionary and conservative? Have they forgotten that my ministry is in obedience to the one who loved his enemies so fully that he died for them? What then can I say to the Vietcong or to Castro or to Mao as a faithful minister of this one?[4] Can I threaten them with death or must I not share with them my life?

Finally, as I try to explain for you and for myself the road that leads from Montgomery to this place, I would have offered all that was most valid if I simply said that I must be true to my conviction that I share with all men the calling to be a son of the living God. Beyond the calling of race or nation or creed is this vocation of sonship and brotherhood. Because I believe that the Father is deeply concerned, especially for His suffering and helpless and outcast children, I come tonight to speak for them. This I believe to be the privilege and the burden of all of us who deem ourselves bound by allegiances and loyalties which are broader and deeper than nationalism and which go beyond our nation's self-defined goals and positions. We are called to speak for the weak, for the voiceless, for the victims of our nation, for those it calls "enemy," for no document from human hands can make these humans any less our brothers.

And as I ponder the madness of Vietnam and search within myself for ways to understand and respond in compassion, my mind goes constantly to the people of that peninsula. I speak now not of the soldiers of each side, not of the ideologies of the Liberation Front, not of the junta in Saigon, but simply of the people who have been living under the curse of war for almost three continuous decades now. I think of them, too, because it is clear to me that there will be no meaningful solution there until some attempt is made to know them and hear their broken cries.

They must see Americans as strange liberators. . . .[5]

The only change came from America as we increased our troop commitments in support of governments which were singularly corrupt, inept, and without popular support. All the while the people read our leaflets and received the regular promises of peace and democracy and land reform. Now they languish under our bombs and con-

---

[4]Fidel Castro and Mao Zedong were the top Communist leaders of Cuba and China, respectively.

[5]Here King went on to describe, in considerable length, the history of Vietnam's struggle for national independence, first against the Japanese, then the French imperialists, and finally the Americans.

sider us, not their fellow Vietnamese, the real enemy. They move sadly and apathetically as we herd them off the land of their fathers into concentration camps where minimal social needs are rarely met. They know they must move on or be destroyed by our bombs.

So they go, primarily women and children and the aged. They watch as we poison their water, as we kill a million acres of their crops. They must weep as the bulldozers roar through their areas preparing to destroy the precious trees. They wander into the hospitals with at least twenty casualties from American firepower for one Vietcong-inflicted injury. So far we may have killed a million of them, mostly children. They wander into the towns and see thousands of the children, homeless, without clothes, running in packs on the streets like animals. They see the children degraded by our soldiers as they beg for food. They see the children selling their sisters to our soldiers, soliciting for their mothers.

What do the peasants think as we ally ourselves with the landlords and as we refuse to put any action into our many words concerning land reform? What do they think as we test out our latest weapons on them, just as the Germans tested out new medicine and new tortures in the concentration camps of Europe? Where are the roots of the independent Vietnam we claim to be building? Is it among these voiceless ones?

We have destroyed their two most cherished institutions: the family and the village. We have destroyed their land and their crops. . . .

Now there is little left to build on, save bitterness. . . .

Somehow this madness must cease. We must stop now. <u>I speak as a child of God and brother to the suffering poor of Vietnam</u>. I speak for those whose land is being laid waste, whose homes are being destroyed, whose culture is being subverted. I speak for the poor of America who are paying the double price of smashed hopes at home, and dealt death and corruption in Vietnam. I speak as a citizen of the world, for the world as it stands aghast at the path we have taken. I speak as one who loves America, to the leaders of our own nation: The great initiative in this war is ours; the initiative to stop it must be ours. . . .

If we continue, there will be no doubt in my mind and in the mind of the world that we have no honorable intentions in Vietnam. If we do not stop our war against the people of Vietnam immediately, the world will be left with no other alternative than to see this as some horrible, clumsy, and deadly game. . . . The world now demands a maturity of America that we may not be able to achieve. It demands that we admit that we have been wrong from the beginning of our adventure in Vietnam, that we have been detrimental to the life of the Vietnamese people. The situation is one in which we must be ready to turn sharply from our present ways. In order to atone for our sins and errors in Vietnam, we should take the initiative in bringing a halt to this tragic war....[6]

... Meanwhile [*Applause*], meanwhile, we in the churches and synagogues have a continuing task while we urge our government to disengage itself from a disgraceful commitment. We must continue to raise our voices and our lives if our nation persists in its perverse ways in Vietnam. We must be prepared to match actions with words by seeking out every creative method of protest possible....

... Every man of humane convictions must decide on the protest that best suits his convictions, but we must all protest.

Now there is something seductively tempting about stopping there and sending us all off on what in some circles has become a popular crusade against the war ... but I wish to go on now to say something even more disturbing.

The war in Vietnam is but a symptom of a far deeper malady within the American spirit, and if we ignore this sobering reality [*Applause*], and if we ignore this sobering reality, we will find ourselves organizing "clergy and laymen concerned" committees for the next generation. They will be concerned about Guatemala and Peru. They will be concerned about Thailand and Cambodia. They will be concerned about Mozambique and South Africa. We will be marching for these and a dozen other names and attending rallies without end unless there is a significant and profound change in American life and policy. [*Sustained applause*] So such thoughts take us beyond Vietnam, but not beyond our calling as sons of the living God.

In 1957 a sensitive American official overseas said that it seemed to him that our nation was on the wrong side of a world revolution. During the past ten years we have seen emerge a pattern of suppression which has now justified the presence of U.S. military advisors in Venezuela. This need to maintain social stability for our investments accounts for the counterrevolutionary action of American forces in Guatemala. It tells why American helicopters are being used against

---

[6]King next listed several immediate steps that the United States should take to help bring an end to the conflict, including suspending U.S. bombing and opening peace talks involving the United States, South Vietnam, North Vietnam, the Vietcong, and the People's Republic of China.

guerrillas in Cambodia and why American napalm and Green Beret forces have already been active against rebels in Peru.[7]

It is with such activity in mind that the words of the late John F. Kennedy come back to haunt us. Five years ago he said, "Those who make peaceful revolution impossible will make violent revolution inevitable." [*Applause*] Increasingly, by choice or by accident, this is the role our nation has taken, the role of those who make peaceful revolution impossible by refusing to give up the privileges and the pleasures that come from the immense profits of overseas investments. I am convinced that if we are to get on the right side of the world revolution, we as a nation must undergo a radical revolution of values. We must rapidly begin [*Applause*], we must rapidly begin the shift from a thing-oriented society to a person-oriented society. When machines and computers, profit motives and property rights, are considered more important than people, the giant triplets of racism, extreme materialism, and militarism are incapable of being conquered.

A true revolution of values will soon cause us to question the fairness and justice of many of our past and present policies. On the one hand we are called to play the Good Samaritan on life's roadside, but that will be only an initial act. One day we must come to see that the whole Jericho Road must be transformed so that men and women will not be constantly beaten and robbed as they make their journey on life's highway. True compassion is more than flinging a coin to a beggar. It comes to see that an edifice which produces beggars needs restructuring. [*Applause*]

A true revolution of values will soon look uneasily on the glaring contrast of poverty and wealth. With righteous indignation, it will look across the seas and see individual capitalists of the West investing huge sums of money in Asia, Africa, and South America, only to take the profits out with no concern for the social betterment of the countries, and say, "This is not just." It will look at our alliance with the landed gentry of South America and say, "This is not just." The Western arrogance of feeling that it has everything to teach others and nothing to learn from them is not just.

A true revolution of values will lay hand on the world order and say of war, "This way of settling differences is not just." This business of burning human beings with napalm, of filling our nation's homes with orphans and widows, of injecting poisonous drugs of hate into the

---

[7]The Green Berets, created under President Kennedy, were an elite U.S. Army corps trained in antiguerrilla tactics.

veins of peoples normally humane, of sending men home from dark and bloody battlefields physically handicapped and psychologically deranged, cannot be reconciled with wisdom, justice, and love. A nation that continues year after year to spend more money on military defense than on programs of social uplift is approaching spiritual death. [*Sustained applause*]

America, the richest and most powerful nation in the world, can well lead the way in this revolution of values. There is nothing except a tragic death wish to prevent us from reordering our priorities so that the pursuit of peace will take precedence over the pursuit of war....

These are revolutionary times. All over the globe men are revolting against old systems of exploitation and oppression.... The shirtless and barefoot people of the land are rising up as never before.... We in the West must support these revolutions.

It is a sad fact that because of comfort, complacency, a morbid fear of communism, and our proneness to adjust to injustice, the Western nations that initiated so much of the revolutionary spirit of the modern world have now become the arch antirevolutionaries. This has driven many to feel that only Marxism has a revolutionary spirit.... Our only hope today lies in our ability to recapture the revolutionary spirit and go out into a sometimes hostile world declaring eternal hostility to poverty, racism, and militarism....

A genuine revolution of values means in the final analysis that our loyalties must become ecumenical rather than sectional. Every nation must now develop an overriding loyalty to mankind as a whole in order to preserve the best in their individual societies.

This call for a worldwide fellowship that lifts neighborly concern beyond one's tribe, race, class, and nation is in reality a call for an all-embracing and unconditional love for all mankind.... I am speaking of that force which all of the great religions have seen as the supreme unifying principle of life. Love is somehow the key that unlocks the door which leads to ultimate reality. This Hindu-Muslim-Christian-Jewish-Buddhist belief about ultimate reality is beautifully summed up in the first epistle of Saint John: "Let us love one another (*Yes*), for love is God. (*Yes*) And every one that loveth is born of God and knoweth God. He that loveth not knoweth not God, for God is love.... If we love one another, God dwelleth in us and his love is perfected in us." Let us hope that this spirit will become the order of the day.

We can no longer afford to worship the god of hate or bow before the altar of retaliation. The oceans of history are made turbulent by the ever-rising tides of hate. History is cluttered with the wreckage of nations and individuals that pursued this self-defeating path of hate.... We still have a choice today: nonviolent coexistence or violent coannihilation. We must move past indecision to action. We must find new ways to speak for peace in Vietnam and justice throughout the developing world, a world that borders on our doors....

Now let us begin. Now let us rededicate ourselves to the long and bitter, but beautiful, struggle for a new world....

We are now faced..., my friends, with the fierce urgency of now. In this unfolding conundrum of life and history, there is such a thing as being too late.... The choice is ours, and though we might prefer it otherwise, we must choose in this crucial moment of human history....

And if we will only make the right choice, we will be able to transform this pending cosmic elegy into a creative psalm of peace. If we will make the right choice, we will be able to transform the jangling discords of our world into a beautiful symphony of brotherhood. If we will but make the right choice, we will be able to speed up the day, all over America and all over the world, when justice will roll down like waters, and righteousness like a mighty stream. [*Sustained applause*]

From *Where Do We Go from Here?*

1967

The title of King's final presidential address at the 1967 annual convention of the Southern Christian Leadership Conference, which was also the title of his last book, indicates his profound concern over the nation's state. King presented, here before his closest colleagues, his best thinking about how the SCLC should proceed in the present crisis.

This speech shows King in his late, most radical phase. Near its end, King answered his own query, "Where do we go from here?" saying, "The

---

Speech delivered at the Eleventh Annual Convention of the Southern Christian Leadership Conference, Atlanta, 16 Aug. 1967; text follows transcription of recording by Martin Luther King Jr. Papers Project staff, printed in Clayborne Carson and Kris Shephard, eds., *A Call to Conscience: The Landmark Speeches of Dr. Martin Luther King Jr.* (New York: Warner Books, 2001), 171–99.

movement must address itself to the question of restructuring the whole of American society." An edifice that produces beggars, he declared, must be restructured. King's concern for the poor was paramount by this time, and his highest goal was improving their condition at home and abroad. This speech reflects King's considerable concessions to and areas of agreement with the nationalistic Black Power movement. King endorsed such nationalistic themes as African American cultural pride and building independent black power through self-organization. He still adamantly rejected racial separatism as a final solution, on the other hand, and forcefully reiterated his total, unconditional commitment to nonviolence and to the Christian love ethic.[1]

... For this, we can feel a legitimate pride.[2] But in spite of a decade of significant progress, the problem is far from solved. The deep rumbling of discontent in our cities is indicative of the fact that the plant of freedom has grown only a bud and not yet a flower. ...

With all the struggle and all the achievements, we must face the fact ... that the Negro still lives in the basement of the Great Society.[3] He is still at the bottom, despite the few who have penetrated to slightly higher levels. Even where the door has been forced partially open, mobility for the Negro is still sharply restricted. There is often no bottom at which to start, and when there is there's almost no room at the top. In consequence, Negroes are still impoverished aliens in an affluent society. ...

And so we still have a long, long way to go before we reach the promised land of freedom. Yes, we have left the dusty soils of Egypt, and we have crossed a Red Sea that had for years been hardened by a long and piercing winter of massive resistance, but before we reach the majestic shores of the Promised Land, there will still be gigantic mountains of opposition ahead and prodigious hilltops of injustice. (*That's right*) We still need some Paul Revere of conscience to alert every hamlet and every village of America that revolution is still at hand. Yes, we need a chart; we need a compass; indeed, we need

---

[1] Italicized type in parentheses, e.g., (*Amen*), indicates audience verbal response.
[2] King had just finished recounting the historic gains made through the activities of the Southern Christian Leadership Conference (SCLC) in the previous decade, such as national legislation abolishing segregation and protecting minority voting rights.
[3] "The Great Society" was a name and slogan for President Lyndon Johnson's domestic reform agenda in the mid 1960s.

some North Star to guide us into a future shrouded with impenetrable uncertainties.[4]

Now in order to answer the question, "Where do we go from here?" which is our theme, we must first honestly recognize where we are now.... Of the good things in life, the Negro has approximately one half those of whites. Of the bad things of life, he has twice those of whites. Thus, half of all Negroes live in substandard housing. And Negroes have half the income of whites. When we turn to the negative experiences of life, the Negro has a double share: There are twice as many unemployed; the rate of infant mortality among Negroes is double that of whites; and there are twice as many Negroes dying in Vietnam as whites in proportion to their size in the population. [*Applause*] . . .

Where do we go from here? First, we must massively assert our dignity and worth. We must stand up amid a system that still oppresses us and develop an unassailable and majestic sense of values. We must no longer be ashamed of being black. The job of arousing manhood within a people that have been taught for so many centuries that they are nobody is not easy.

Even semantics have conspired to make that which is black seem ugly and degrading. (*Yes*) In Roget's *Thesaurus* there are some 120 synonyms for blackness and at least sixty of them are offensive, such words as blot, soot, grim, devil, and foul. And there are some 134 synonyms for whiteness and all are favorable, expressed in such words as purity, cleanliness, chastity, and innocence. A white lie is better than a black lie. (*Yes*) The most degenerate member of a family is the "black sheep." (*Yes*) Ossie Davis[5] has suggested that maybe the English language should be reconstructed so that teachers will not be forced to teach the Negro child sixty ways to despise himself and thereby perpetuate his false sense of inferiority, and the white child 134 ways to adore himself and thereby perpetuate his false sense of superiority. [*Applause*] The tendency to ignore the Negro's contribution to American life and strip him of his personhood is as old as the earliest history books and as contemporary as the morning's newspaper.

---

[4]In this paragraph King uses three mythic metaphors for contemporary civil rights forces' search for their proper next direction: the Israolites' long journey to their Promised Land after their release from Egyptian slavery, as told in the biblical book of Exodus; the American Revolutionary War hero Paul Revere energetically alerting Americans to danger; and the North Star, or Polaris, which before the Civil War guided African American slaves fleeing from the South to free northern states and Canada.

[5]Ossie Davis, the successful African American actor, was very active in the black freedom struggle during the 1960s.

To offset this cultural homicide, the Negro must rise up with an affirmation of his own Olympian manhood. (*Yes*) Any movement for the Negro's freedom that overlooks this necessity is only waiting to be buried. (*Yes*) As long as the mind is enslaved, the body can never be free. (*Yes*) Psychological freedom, a firm sense of self-esteem, is the most powerful weapon against the long night of physical slavery. No Lincolnian Emancipation Proclamation, no Johnsonian civil rights bill can totally bring this kind of freedom. The Negro will only be free when he reaches down to the inner depths of his own being and signs with the pen and ink of assertive manhood his own emancipation proclamation. And with a spirit straining toward true self-esteem, the Negro must boldly throw off the manacles of self-abnegation and say to himself and to the world, "I am somebody. (*Oh yeah*) I am a person. I am a man with dignity and honor. (*Go ahead*) I have a rich and noble history, however painful and exploited that history has been. Yes, I was a slave through my foreparents, and now I'm not ashamed of that. I'm ashamed of the people who were so sinful to make me a slave." (*Yes sir*) Yes [*Applause*], yes, we must stand up and say, "I'm black, but I'm black and beautiful." (*Yes*) This [*Applause*], this self-affirmation is the black man's need, made compelling (*All right*) by the white man's crimes against him.

Now another basic challenge is to discover how to organize our strength into economic and political power. No one can deny that the Negro is in dire need of this kind of legitimate power. Indeed, one of the great problems that the Negro confronts is his lack of power. From the old plantations of the South to the newer ghettos of the North, the Negro has been confined to a life of voicelessness (*That's true*) and powerlessness. (*So true*) ... The plantation and the ghetto were created by those who had power, both to confine those who had no power and to perpetuate their powerlessness. Now the problem of transforming the ghetto, therefore, is a problem of power, a confrontation between the forces of power demanding change and the forces of power dedicated to the preserving of the status quo. Now, power properly understood is nothing but the ability to achieve purpose. It is the strength required to bring about social, political, and economic change. ...

Now a lot of us are preachers, and all of us have our moral convictions and concerns, and so often we have problems with power. There is nothing wrong with power if power is used correctly. ...

... What is needed is a realization that power without love is reckless and abusive, and that love without power is sentimental and anemic. (*Yes*) Power at its best (*Speak*) [*Applause*], power at its best is love (*Yes*) implementing the demands of justice, and justice at its best is love correcting everything that stands against love. (*Speak*) And this is what we must see as we move on.

Now what has happened is that we've had it wrong and mixed up in our country, and this has led Negro Americans in the past to seek their goals through love and moral suasion devoid of power, and white Americans to seek their goals through power devoid of love and conscience. It is leading a few extremists today to advocate for Negroes the same destructive and conscienceless power that they have justly abhorred in whites. It is precisely this collision of immoral power with powerless morality which constitutes the major crisis of our times.

Now we must develop . . . a program . . . that will drive the nation to a guaranteed annual income. Now early in the century this proposal would have been greeted with ridicule and denunciation as destructive of initiative and responsibility. . . . Now we realize that dislocations in the market operation of our economy and the prevalence of discrimination thrust people into idleness and bind them in constant or frequent unemployment against their will. The poor are less often dismissed, I hope, from our conscience today by being branded as inferior and incompetent. We also know that no matter how dynamically the economy develops and expands, it does not eliminate all poverty.

The problem indicates that our emphasis must be twofold: We must create full employment, or we must create incomes. People must be made consumers by one method or the other. Once they are placed in this position, we need to be concerned that the potential of the individual is not wasted. New forms of work that enhance the social good will have to be devised for those for whom traditional jobs are not available. . . .

Work of this sort could be enormously increased, and we are likely to find that the problem of housing, education, instead of preceding the elimination of poverty, will themselves be affected if poverty is first abolished. . . .

Now our country can do this . . . a guaranteed annual income could be done for about twenty billion dollars a year.[6] And I say to you today,

---

[6]Establishing a guaranteed annual income for all Americans was a concept that in 1967 and 1968 increasingly appealed to King as one of the most immediately effective ways to end poverty. An annual income would mean that those below a set minimum income level, instead of paying tax on income, would receive payment from the U.S. government until the income level needed to surmount poverty was reached.

that if our nation can spend thirty-five billion dollars a year to fight an unjust, evil war in Vietnam, and twenty billion dollars to put a man on the moon, it can spend billions of dollars to put God's children on their own two feet right here on earth. [*Applause*]

Now let me rush on to say we must reaffirm our commitment to nonviolence. And I want to stress this. This futility of violence in the struggle for racial justice has been tragically etched in all the recent Negro riots.... There is something painfully sad about a riot. One sees screaming youngsters and angry adults fighting hopelessly and aimlessly against impossible odds. (*Yeah*) Deep down within them, you perceive a desire for self-destruction, a kind of suicidal longing. (*Yes*)

Occasionally, Negroes contend that the 1965 Watts riot[7] and the other riots in various cities represented effective civil rights action. But those who express this view always end up with stumbling words when asked what concrete gains have been won as a result. At best the riots have produced a little additional anti-poverty money allotted by frightened government officials, and a few water sprinklers to cool the children of the ghettos. It is something like improving the food in the prison while the people remain securely incarcerated behind bars. (*That's right*) Nowhere have the riots won any concrete improvement such as have the organized protest demonstrations.

And when one tries to pin down advocates of violence as to what acts would be effective, the answers are blatantly illogical. Sometimes they talk of overthrowing racist state and local governments and they talk about guerrilla warfare. They fail to see that no internal revolution has ever succeeded in overthrowing a government by violence unless the government had already lost the allegiance and effective control of its armed forces. Anyone in his right mind knows that this will not happen in the United States. In a violent racial situation, the power structure has the local police, the state troopers, the National Guard, and finally, the Army to call on, all of which are predominantly white. (*Yes*) ... It is perfectly clear that a violent revolution on the part of American blacks would find no sympathy and support from the white population and very little from the majority of the Negroes themselves.

This is no time for romantic illusions and empty philosophical debates about freedom. This is a time for action. (*All right*) What is

---

[7]The Watts riot in the black section of Los Angeles began on August 11, 1965. Its violent lawlessness caused 34 deaths, 900 injuries, and 3,500 arrests.

needed is a strategy for change, a tactical program that will bring the Negro into the mainstream of American life as quickly as possible. So far, this has only been offered by the nonviolent movement....

And so I say to you today that I still stand by nonviolence. (*Yes*) And I am still convinced [*Applause*], and I'm still convinced that it is the most potent weapon available to the Negro in his struggle for justice in this country.

And the other thing is, I'm concerned about a better world. I'm concerned about justice; I'm concerned about brotherhood; I'm concerned about truth. And when one is concerned about that, he can never advocate violence. For through violence you may murder a murderer, but you can't murder murder. Through violence you may murder a liar, but you can't establish truth. Through violence you may murder a hater, but you can't murder hate through violence. (*All right, That's right*) Darkness cannot put out darkness; only light can do that. [*Applause*]

And I say to you, I have also decided to stick with love, for I know that love is ultimately the only answer to mankind's problems. And I'm going to talk about it everywhere I go. I know it isn't popular to talk about it in some circles today. And I'm not talking about emotional bosh when I talk about love; I'm talking about a strong, demanding love. For I have seen too much hate. I've seen too much hate on the faces of sheriffs in the South. (*Yeah*) I've seen hate on the faces of too many Klansmen and too many White Citizens' Councilors in the South to want to hate, myself, because every time I see it, I know that it does something to their faces and their personalities, and I say to myself that hate is too great a burden to bear.[8] (*Yes*) I have decided to love. [*Applause*] If you are seeking the highest good, I think you can find it through love....

I want to say to you as I move to my conclusion, as we talk about "Where do we go from here?" that we must honestly face the fact that the movement must address itself to the question of restructuring the whole of American society. There are forty million poor people here, and one day we must ask the question, "Why are there forty million poor people in America?" And when you begin to ask that question, you are raising a question about the economic system, about a broader

---

[8]"Klansmen" refers to members of the racist terrorist organization the Ku Klux Klan. White Citizens Councils were more "respectable" segregationist organizations that sprang up across the South following the Supreme Court's 1954 *Brown v. Board of Education* decision against segregation in public schools.

distribution of wealth. When you ask that question, you begin to question the capitalistic economy. (*Yes*) And I'm simply saying that more and more, we've got to begin to ask questions about the whole society. We are called upon to help the discouraged beggars in life's marketplace. (*Yes*) But one day we must come to see that an edifice which produces beggars needs restructuring. (*All right*) It means that questions must be raised. And you see, my friends, when you deal with this you begin to ask the question, "Who owns the oil?" (*Yes*) You begin to ask the question, "Who owns the iron ore?" (*Yes*) You begin to ask the question, "Why is it that people have to pay water bills in a world that's two-thirds water?" (*All right*) These are words that must be said. (*All right*)

Now don't think you have me in a bind today. I'm not talking about communism. What I'm talking about is far beyond communism. (*Yeah*) My inspiration didn't come from Karl Marx[9] (*Speak*).... I have to reject that.

What I'm saying to you this morning is communism forgets that life is individual. (*Yes*) Capitalism forgets that life is social. (*Yes, Go ahead*) And the kingdom of brotherhood is found neither in the thesis of communism nor the antithesis of capitalism, but in a higher synthesis. (*Speak*) [*Applause*] It is found in a higher synthesis (*Come on*) that combines the truths of both. (*Yes*) Now when I say questioning the whole society, it means ultimately coming to see that the problem of racism, the problem of economic exploitation, and the problem of war are all tied together. (*All right*) These are the triple evils that are interrelated.

And if you will let me be a preacher just a little bit. (*Speak*) One day [*Applause*], one night, a juror came to Jesus (*Yes sir*) and he wanted to know what he could do to be saved.... (*Yes*) So instead of just getting bogged down on one thing, Jesus looked at him and said, "Nicodemus, you must be born again." (*Speak*) [*Applause*][10]

In other words, "Your whole structure (*Yes*) must be changed." [*Applause*] A nation that will keep people in slavery for 244 years will "thingify" them and make them things. (*Speak*) And therefore, they will exploit them and poor people generally economically. (*Yes*) And a nation that will exploit economically will have to have foreign investments and everything else, and it will have to use its military might to protect them. All of these problems are tied together. (*Yes*) [*Applause*]

---

[9] *Karl Marx:* Nineteenth-century German political philosopher and socialist considered to be the founder of modern communism.

[10] *Nicodemus:* The name of the man who, when asking Jesus what he had to do to be saved, was told by Jesus that he had to be "born again," in John 3:1–7.

What I'm saying today is that we must go from this convention and say, "America, you must be born again!" [*Applause*]

And so I conclude by saying today that we have a task, and let us go out with a divine dissatisfaction. (*Yes*) ...

Let us be dissatisfied (*Yes*) until the tragic walls that separate the outer city of wealth and comfort from the inner city of poverty and despair shall be crushed by the battering rams of the forces of justice.

Let us be dissatisfied (*Yes*) until those who live on the outskirts of hope are brought into the metropolis of daily security.

Let us be dissatisfied (*Yes*) until slums are cast into the junk heaps of history (*Yes*), and every family will live in a decent, sanitary home.

Let us be dissatisfied (*Yes*) until the dark yesterdays of segregated schools will be transformed into bright tomorrows of quality integrated education.

Let us be dissatisfied until integration is not seen as a problem but as an opportunity to participate in the beauty of diversity.

Let us be dissatisfied (*All right*) until men and women, however black they may be, will be judged on the basis of the content of their character, not on the basis of the color of their skin. (*Yeah*) Let us be dissatisfied. [*Applause*]. ...

Let us be dissatisfied until that day when nobody will shout, "White Power!" when nobody will shout, "Black Power!" but everybody will talk about God's power and human power. [*Applause*]

And I must confess, my friends (*Yes sir*), that the road ahead will not always be smooth. (*Yes*) There will still be rocky places of frustration (*Yes*) and meandering points of bewilderment. There will be inevitable setbacks here and there. (*Yes*) And there will be those moments when the buoyancy of hope will be transformed into the fatigue of despair. (*Well*) Our dreams will sometimes be shattered and our ethereal hopes blasted. (*Yes*) We may again, with tear-drenched eyes, have to stand before the bier of some courageous civil rights worker whose life will be snuffed out by the dastardly acts of bloodthirsty mobs. (*Well*) But difficult and painful as it is, we must walk on in the days ahead with an audacious faith in the future. ...

... When our days become dreary with low-hovering clouds of despair (*Well*), and when our nights become darker than a thousand midnights (*Well*), let us remember that there is a creative force in this universe working to pull down the gigantic mountains of evil (*Well*), a power that is able to make a way out of no way (*Yes*) and transform dark yesterdays into bright tomorrows. (*Speak*)

Let us realize that the arc of the moral universe is long, but it bends toward justice. Let us realize that William Cullen Bryant is right:

"Truth, crushed to earth, will rise again." Let us go out realizing that the Bible is right: "Be not deceived. God is not mocked. (*Oh yeah*) Whatsoever a man soweth (*Yes*), that (*Yes*) shall he also reap." This is our hope for the future, and with this faith we will be able to sing in some not too distant tomorrow, with a cosmic past tense: "We have overcome! (*Yes*) We have overcome! Deep in my heart, I *did* believe (*Yes*) we would overcome." [*Applause*][11]

MALCOLM X

All of the following Malcolm documents are from 1964 or 1965, years that marked both the Civil Rights movement's peak and Malcolm's disengagement from the Nation of Islam and emergence as an independent black leader and follower of orthodox Sunni Islam.

Breaking with the NOI belief in universal white wickedness helped Malcolm better position himself to enter the surging Civil Rights movement. He announced his willingness to cooperate with all black leaders and organizations committed to acting to gain black rights and freedom. He urged a united black front and stated his desire to join in protests against segregation and for African American voting rights, including ones led by King. Accordingly, he ceased his former vitriolic denunciations of civil rights leaders and stated his continuing differences with aspects of their approach far more civilly.

In his post-NOI phase, Malcolm not only attempted to join mainstream black protest but to take it to another level. Malcolm urged traditional civil rights forces to lift the domestic struggle to a higher plane by adding to it the goal of securing African Americans' universal human rights.

Central themes of Malcolm's final, still-evolving message to blacks, America, and humanity were: African Americans' need for unity, domestically and internationally; blacks' need to demand their natural human as well as constitutional rights; and the possibility and desirability of justice and comity among all the world's people.

From both conviction and necessity, Malcolm was struggling to shed his former image as a fanatical hate monger. He was doggedly "trying to turn the corner" in his last period to a new, more

---

[11]"Truth, crushed to earth," quotation from William Cullen Bryant, "The Battlefield" (1839), stanza 9; "whatsoever a man soweth" biblical quotation from Galatians 6:7; King changes tense of the lyrics in the civil rights anthem, "We Shall Overcome."

respectable leadership position. But he felt constantly blocked by his old "hate and violence" image still held by the media, by many conservative and moderate civil rights leaders who still considered him too extreme (and perhaps still resented his former stinging attacks on them), even by some militant nationalists who found the "new" Malcolm too moderate!

Press Conference on Return from Africa
1964

Below is Malcolm's account in the Autobiography *of his press conference on returning from his pilgrimage to Mecca. Malcolm's "Letters from Mecca," relating his rejection of racist NOI dogma and newfound acceptance of the ideal of interracial brotherhood had already caused a stir among his followers and the New York media even before his return from his hajj and African travels. In his recollection of that press conference, Malcolm was proud that he not only managed in it to state his newfound belief in an interracial community under Allah—which was all the white press corps wished him to talk about—but also got in his equally important new stress on building unity among all the world's darker races and on internationalizing the struggle by, for example, charging the United States with human rights violations in the United Nations.*

... In the biggest press conference that I had ever experienced anywhere, the camera bulbs flashed, and the reporters fired questions....

I slipped in on the reporters something they hadn't been expecting. I said that the American black man needed to quit thinking what the white man had taught him –which was that the black man had no alternative except to beg for his so-called "civil rights." I said that the American black man needed to recognize that he had a strong, airtight case to take the United States before the United Nations on a formal accusation of "denial of human rights"– and that if Angola and South Africa were precedent cases, then there would be no easy way

The Autobiography of Malcolm X, 367–70.

that the U.S. could escape being censured, right on its own home ground.

Just as I had known, the press wanted to get me off that subject. I was asked about my "Letter From Mecca"—I was all set with a speech regarding that:

"I hope that once and for all my Hajj to the Holy City of Mecca has established our Muslim Mosque's authentic religious affiliation with the 750 million Muslims of the orthodox Islamic World. And I *know* once and for all that the Black Africans look upon America's 22 million blacks as long-lost *brothers*! They *love* us! They *study* our struggle for freedom! They were so *happy* to hear how we are awakening from our long sleep—after so-called 'Christian' white America had taught us to be *ashamed* of our African brothers and homeland!

"Yes—I wrote a letter from Mecca. You're asking me 'Didn't you say that now you accept white men as brothers?' Well, my answer is that in the Muslim World, I saw, I felt, and I wrote home how my thinking was broadened! Just as I wrote, I shared true, brotherly love with many white-complexioned Muslims who never gave a single thought to the race, or to the complexion, of another Muslim.

"My pilgrimage broadened my scope. It blessed me with a new insight. In two weeks in the Holy Land, I saw what I never had seen in thirty-nine years here in America. I saw all *races,* all *colors,*—blue-eyed blonds to black-skinned Africans—in *true* brotherhood! In unity! Living as one! Worshiping as one! No segregationists—no liberals; they would not have known how to interpret the meaning of those words.

"In the past, yes, I have made sweeping indictments of *all* white people. I never will be guilty of that again—as I know now that some white people *are* truly sincere, that some truly are capable of being brotherly toward a black man. The true Islam has shown me that a blanket indictment of all white people is as wrong as when whites make blanket indictments against blacks.

"Yes, I have been convinced that *some* American whites do want to help cure the rampant racism which is on the path to *destroying* this country!

"It was in the Holy World that my attitude was changed, by what I experienced there, and by what I witnessed there, in terms of brotherhood—not just brotherhood toward me, but brotherhood between all men, of all nationalities and complexions, who were there. And now that I am back in America, my attitude here concerning white people has to be governed by what my black brothers and I experience here, and what we witness here—in terms of brotherhood. The *problem* here in America is that we meet such a small minority of individual so-called 'good,' or 'brotherly' white people. Here in the United States, notwithstanding those few 'good' white people, it is the *collective* 150 million white people whom the *collective* 22 million black people have to deal with!

"Why, here in America, the seeds of racism are so deeply rooted in the white people collectively, their belief that they are 'superior' in some way is so deeply rooted, that these things are in the national white subconsciousness. Many whites are even actually unaware of their own racism, until they face some test, and then their racism emerges in one form or another.

"Listen! The white man's racism toward the black man here in America is what has got him in such trouble all over this world, with other non-white peoples.... And the non-white peoples of the world are sick of the condescending white man! That's why you've got all of this trouble in places like Viet Nam. Or right here in the Western Hemisphere.... In the West Indies, Cuba, Brazil, Venezuela, all of South America, Central America! All of those lands are full of people with African blood! On the African continent, even, the white man has maneuvered to divide the black African from the brown Arab, to divide the so-called 'Christian African' from the Muslim African. Can you imagine what can happen, what would certainly happen, if all of these African-heritage peoples ever *realize* their blood bonds, if they ever realize they all have a common goal—if they ever *unite?*"

The press was glad to get rid of me that day. I believe that the black brothers whom I had just recently left in Africa would have felt that I did the subject justice. Nearly through the night, my telephone at home kept ringing. My black brothers and sisters around New York and in some other cities were calling to congratulate me on what they had heard on the radio and television news broadcasts, and people, mostly white, were wanting to know if I would speak here or there.

The next day I was in my car driving along the freeway when at a red light another car pulled alongside. A white woman was driving and on the passenger's side, next to me, was a white man. *"Malcolm X!"* he called out—and when I looked, he stuck his hand out of his car, across at me, grinning. "Do you mind shaking hands with a white man?" Imagine that! Just as the traffic light turned green, I told him, "I don't mind shaking hands with human beings. Are you one?" ...

Sincere Whites (That Coed Again)
1964

Like the "Press Conference" document, "Sincere Whites" illustrates the impact Malcolm's hajj and international trips had on his beliefs, especially his willingness to entertain the possibility of white goodwill and of interracial harmony.

... One of the major troubles that I was having in building the organization that I wanted—an all-black organization whose ultimate objective was to help create a society in which there could exist honest white-black brotherhood—was that my earlier public image, my old so-called "Black Muslim" image, kept blocking me. I was trying to gradually reshape that image. I was trying to turn a corner, into a new regard by the public, especially Negroes; I was no less angry than I had been, but at the same time the true brotherhood I had seen in the Holy World had influenced me to recognize that anger can blind human vision. . . .

. . . I made a lot of speeches, saying: "True Islam taught me that it takes *all* of the religious, political, economic, psychological, and racial ingredients, or characteristics, to make the Human Family and the Human Society complete.

"Since I learned the *truth* in Mecca, my dearest friends have come to include *all* kinds—some Christians, Jews, Buddhists, Hindus, agnostics, and even atheists! I have friends who are called capitalists, Socialists, and Communists! Some of my friends are moderates, conservatives, extremists—some are even Uncle Toms! My friends today are black, brown, red, yellow, and *white!*" . . .

I knew, better than most Negroes, how many white people truly wanted to see American racial problems solved. I knew that many whites were as frustrated as Negroes. I'll bet I got fifty letters some days from white people. The white people in meeting audiences would throng around me, asking me, after I had addressed them somewhere, "What *can* a sincere white person do?"

The Autobiography of Malcolm X, 382–85.

When I say that here now, it makes me think about that little co-ed I told you about, the one who flew from her New England college down to New York and came up to me in the Nation of Islam's restaurant in Harlem, and I told her that there was "nothing" she could do.[1] I regret that I told her that. I wish that now I knew her name, or where I could telephone her, or write to her, and tell her what I tell white people now when they present themselves as being sincere, and ask me, one way or another, the same thing that she asked.

The first thing I tell them is that at least where my own particular Black Nationalist organization, the Organization of Afro-American Unity, is concerned, they can't *join* us. . . . Where the really sincere white people have got to do their "proving" of themselves is not among the black *victims*, but out on the battle lines of where America's racism really *is*—and that's in their own home communities; America's racism is among their own fellow whites. That's where the sincere whites who really mean to accomplish something have got to work. . . .

I tell sincere white people, "Work in conjunction with us—each of us working among our own kind." Let sincere white individuals find all other white people they can who feel as they do—and let them form their own all-white groups, to work trying to convert other white people who are thinking and acting so racist. Let sincere whites go and teach non-violence to white people!

We will completely respect our white co-workers. They will deserve every credit. We will give them every credit. We will meanwhile be working among our own kind, in our own black communities—showing and teaching black men in ways that only other black men can—that the black man has got to help himself. Working separately, the sincere white people and sincere black people actually will be working together.

In our mutual sincerity we might be able to show a road to the salvation of America's very soul. It can only be salvaged if human rights and dignity, in full, are extended to black men. Only such real, meaningful actions as those which are sincerely motivated from a deep sense of humanism and moral responsibility can get at the basic causes that produce the racial explosions in America today. . . .

---

[1]See "'What Can I *Do*?' . . . I Told Her, 'Nothing'" in chapter 4, "The White Man Is a Devil."

I'm Not a Racist
1964

In this excerpt from his speech to the Organization of Afro-American Unity (OAAU) upon his homecoming from Africa and the Middle East, Malcolm acknowledged the error of considering all whites irredeemably evil. He announced that he would now judge each person by his or her actions. Equally significant, though, was his continuing claim that white society collectively was demonstrably evil. Malcolm, to the end, never let whites escape responsibility for their crimes against people of color.

Malcolm's growing Pan-Africanism and internationalist perspective are very evident.

... But I think then the white man should know one thing—when I say white man, I'm not saying all of you, whatever you are, because some of you might be all right. And whichever one of you acts all right with me, you're all right with me, as long as you act all right. But if you don't act all right, you're not all right. All you've got to do to be all right with me is act all right. But don't come thinking you're all right just because you're white.

I think that that point has to be made because if you don't clarify it, they go out of here saying you're a racist, that you're against all white people. We're not against all white people. We're against all those that aren't right....

... It should be emphasized over and over and over by you and me that we aren't racists. One of the worst categories to let them put you in is the category of racist.

I'm not a racist. I don't judge a man because of his color. I get suspicious of a lot of them and cautious around a lot of them—from experience. Not because of their color, but because of what experience has taught me concerning their overall behavior toward us. So, please don't ever go away saying that we are against people because of their color. We are against them because of what they *do* to us and because

---

Excerpted from speech at the Homecoming Rally of the Organization of Afro-American Unity, New York City, 29 Nov. 1964; reprinted in George Breitman, ed., *By Any Means Necessary: Speeches, Interviews, and a Letter by Malcolm X* (New York: Pathfinder Press, 1970), 151–54.

of what they do to others. All they have to do to get our good will is to show their good will and stop doing all those dirty things to our people. Is that understood?

Also, within the next couple of weeks we will spell out the type of support we got on our effort to bring the United States into the United Nations and charge her with violating our human rights. You and I *must* take this government before a world forum and show the world that this government has absolutely failed in its duty toward us. It has failed from Washington, D.C., all the way in to New York City. They have failed in their duty toward you and me. They have failed to protect us, they have failed to represent us, they have failed to respect us. And since they have failed, either willingly or because of their inability, we think that they should be brought up there so the world can see them as they actually are.

Now, if this government doesn't want to have her linen washed in public, then we give her a week or two to get her house in order. And if she can't get it in order in two weeks, then get on out there with South Africa and Portugal and the rest of those criminals who have been exploiting and abusing dark-skinned people now for far too long. We're all fed up. Right? Right....

... But the point and thing that I would like to impress upon every Afro-American leader is that there is no kind of action in this country ever going to bear fruit unless that action is tied in with the overall international struggle.

You waste your time when you talk to this man, just you and him. So when you talk to him, let him know your brother is behind you, and you've got some more brothers behind that brother. That's the only way to talk to him, that's the only language he knows. Why do I say, "Make sure your brother is behind you"? Because you're going to have to fight this man, believe me, yes, *you're going to have to fight him.* You're going to have to fight him. He doesn't know any other language....

.. Once you know what language he speaks in, then you can talk to him. And if you want to know what his language is, study his history. His language is blood, his language is power, his language is brutality....

America Can Have a Bloodless Revolution
1964

Politically, Malcolm's most dramatic departures were his new emphases on building nonsectarian black solidarity in the freedom struggle, on internationalizing the movement to advocate universal human rights, and on the desirability of securing and using African Americans' existent rights under the U.S. Constitution. All these important late-Malcolm themes are demonstrated in the following two documents.

"America Can Have a Bloodless Revolution" radically revised Malcolm's NOI-day notion of what constituted meaningful change for African Americans and the means by which positive change could be accomplished (see Malcolm's "On Revolution" in chapter 3). Missing is his earlier insistence that true revolutions are necessarily bloody. Instead, here Malcolm held out the prospect that a real "black revolution" might be accomplished peacefully through African Americans' vote, which, he declared, if used intelligently and strategically, would "change the entire political structure of the country."

... So, in my conclusion, in speaking about the black revolution, America today is at a time ... where she is the first country on this earth that can actually have a bloodless revolution. In the past, revolutions have been bloody. Historically you just don't have a peaceful revolution. Revolutions are bloody, revolutions are violent, revolutions cause bloodshed and death follows in their paths. America is the only country in history in a position to bring about a revolution without violence and bloodshed. ...

Why is America in a position to bring about a bloodless revolution? Because the Negro in this country holds the balance of power, and if the Negro in this country were given what the Constitution says he is supposed to have, the added power of the Negro in this country would sweep all of the racists and the segregationists out of office. It would change the entire political structure of the country. It would wipe out the Southern segregationism that now controls America's foreign policy, as well as America's domestic policy.

"The Black Revolution," speech delivered at Palm Gardens, N.Y., 8 Apr. 1964; reprinted in George Breitman, ed., *Malcolm X Speaks: Selected Speeches and Statements* (New York: Grove Press, 1982), 56–57.

And the only way without bloodshed that this can be brought about is that the black man has to be given full use of the ballot in every one of the fifty states. But if the black man doesn't get the ballot, then you are going to be faced with another man who forgets the ballot and starts using the bullet. . . .

From *The Ballot or the Bullet*
1964

Although he made many of its points elsewhere, "The Ballot or the Bullet" was Malcolm's fullest statement of his political strategy of using African American voting power to bring positive near-term changes for them. He made a major concession to the mainstream civil rights agenda in confirming the value of obtaining and leveraging blacks' civil-political rights. The Student Nonviolent Coordinating Committee's 1964 Mississippi Freedom Summer Project focused on voter registration among Deep South blacks, while King and the SCLC's chief objective of 1965 was securing national voting rights legislation, the goal of its victorious campaign that year in Selma, Alabama. Malcolm in 1965 voiced his approval of SNCC and the SCLC's voting rights goal and offered to help protect King and nonviolent demonstrators in Selma.

In this speech Malcolm stressed his new willingness to join with all black groups in the quest for civil rights. But for all such change, he was still in many respects his usual militant self. If the government failed to enforce blacks' voting rights and to protect them from racist violence, he warned, African Americans would justifiably turn to the bullet instead. His call at speech's end for militant but peaceful black protesters to march on Washington, D.C., and refuse to stop demonstrating or leave until their demands were met foreshadowed the basic idea of King's last planned mass demonstration, the National Poor People's Campaign (except that King's protest was to be multiracial).

The speech also shows Malcolm's late emphasis on internationalizing the black freedom struggle.

"The Ballot or the Bullet," speech delivered at Cory Methodist Church, Cleveland, Ohio, 3 Apr. 1964; reprinted in George Breitman, ed., *Malcolm X Speaks: Selected Speeches and Statements* (New York: Grove Press, 1982), 24–44.

Before we try and explain what is meant by the ballot or the bullet, I would like to clarify something concerning myself. I'm still a Muslim, my religion is still Islam. That's my personal belief. Just as Adam Clayton Powell[1] is a Christian minister who heads the Abyssinian Baptist Church in New York, but at the same time takes part in the political struggles to try and bring about rights to the black people in this country; and Dr. Martin Luther King is a Christian minister down in Atlanta, Georgia, who heads another organization fighting for the civil rights of black people in this country . . . , I myself am a minister, not a Christian minister, but a Muslim minister; and I believe in action on all fronts by whatever means necessary.

Although I'm still a Muslim, I'm not here tonight to discuss my religion. I'm not here to try and change your religion. I'm not here to argue or discuss anything that we differ about, because it's time for us to submerge our differences and realize that it is best for us to first see that we have the same problem, a common problem—a problem that will make you catch hell whether you're a Baptist, or a Methodist, or a Muslim, or a nationalist. Whether you're educated or illiterate, whether you live on the boulevard or in the alley, you're going to catch hell just like I am. We're all in the same boat and we all are going to catch the same hell from the same man. He just happens to be a white man. All of us have suffered here, in this country, political oppression at the hands of the white man, economic exploitation at the hands of the white man, and social degradation at the hands of the white man.

Now in speaking like this, it doesn't mean that we're anti-white, but it does mean we're anti-exploitation, we're anti-degradation, we're anti-oppression. And if the white man doesn't want us to be anti-him, let him stop oppressing and exploiting and degrading us. Whether we are Christians or Muslims or nationalists or agnostics or atheists, we must first learn to forget our differences. If we have differences, let us differ in the closet; when we come out in front, let us not have anything to argue about until we get finished arguing with the man. . . .

If we don't do something real soon, I think you'll have to agree that we're going to be forced either to use the ballot or the bullet. It's one or the other in 1964. It isn't that time is running out—time has run out! 1964 threatens to be the most explosive year America has ever witnessed. The most explosive year. Why? It's also a political year. It's the year when all of the white politicians will be back in the so-called

---

[1] Adam Clayton Powell Jr. (1908–1972) was a black Baptist minister, civil rights leader, and controversial Democratic congressman from New York City.

Negro community jiving you and me for some votes. The year when all of the white political crooks will be right back in your and my community with their false promises, building up our hopes for a letdown, with their trickery and their treachery, with their false promises which they don't intend to keep. As they nourish these dissatisfactions, it can only lead to one thing, an explosion; and now we have the type of black man on the scene in America today—I'm sorry, Brother Lomax[2]—who just doesn't intend to turn the other cheek any longer.

Don't let anybody tell you anything about the odds are against you. If they draft you, they send you to Korea and make you face 800 million Chinese.[3] If you can be brave over there, you can be brave right here. These odds aren't as great as those odds. And if you fight here, you will at least know what you're fighting for.

I'm not a politician . . . I'm not a Democrat, I'm not a Republican, and I don't even consider myself an American. If you and I were Americans, there'd be no problem. Those Hunkies that just got off the boat, they're already Americans; Polacks are already Americans; the Italian refugees are already Americans.[4] Everything that came out of Europe, every blue-eyed thing, is already an American. And as long as you and I have been over here, we aren't Americans yet.

Well, I am one who doesn't believe in deluding myself. . . . Being born here in America doesn't make you an American. Why, if birth made you American, you wouldn't need any legislation, you wouldn't need any amendments to the Constitution, you wouldn't be faced with civil-rights fililbustering in Washington, D.C., right now.[5] They don't have to pass civil-rights legislation to make a Polack an American.

No, I'm not an American. I'm one of the 22 million black people who are the victims of Americanism. One of the 22 million black people who are the victims of democracy, nothing but disguised hypocrisy. So, I'm not standing here speaking to you as an American, or a patriot, or a flag-saluter, or a flag-waver—no, not I. I'm speaking as a victim of

---

[2]Louis E. Lomax, who represented CORE (Congress of Racial Equality) and the nonviolent civil rights view, had spoken before Malcolm at the same symposium.
[3]China's approximate population in the mid sixties was 800 million. Chinese armed forces intervened to aid North Korea against U.S. and United Nations troops in the Korean War, 1950–53.
[4]*Hunkies:* A derogatory term for U.S. immigrants and their descendants from eastern and southern Europe. *Polack:* A slur for Polish Americans.
[5]*Filibuster:* A parliamentary maneuver whereby a minority can indefinitely prevent a vote on a bill in the U.S. Senate; used by segregationist and southern senators to try to stop passage of the 1964 Civil Rights Act.

this American system. And I see America through the eyes of the victim. I don't see any American dream; I see an American nightmare.

These 22 million victims are waking up. Their eyes are coming open. They're beginning to see what they used to only look at. They're becoming politically mature. They are realizing that there are new political trends from coast to coast. As they see these new political trends, it's possible for them to see that every time there's an election the races are so close that they have to have a recount.... And the same with Kennedy and Nixon when they ran for president. It was so close they had to count all over again. Well, what does this mean? It means that when white people are evenly divided, and black people have a bloc of votes of their own, it is left up to them to determine who's going to sit in the White House and who's going to be in the dog house.

It was the black man's vote that put the present administration in Washington, D.C. Your vote, your dumb vote, your ignorant vote, your wasted vote put in an administration in Washington, D.C., that has seen fit to pass every kind of legislation imaginable, saving you until last, then filibustering on top of that. And your and my leaders have the audacity to run around clapping their hands and talk about how much progress we're making. And what a good president we have.... And these Negro leaders have the audacity to go and have some coffee in the White House with a Texan, a Southern cracker—that's all he is—and then come out and tell you and me that he's going to be better for us....

In this present administration they have in the House of Representatives 257 Democrats to only 177 Republicans. They control two-thirds of the House vote. Why can't they pass something that will help you and me? In the Senate, there are 67 senators who are of the Democratic Party. Only 33 of them are Republicans. Why, the Democrats have got the government sewed up, and you're the one who sewed it up for them. And what have they given you for it? Four years in office, and just now getting around to some civil-rights legislation. Just now, after everything else is gone, out of the way, they're going to sit down now and play with you all summer long—the same old giant con game that they call filibuster....

So it's time in 1964 to wake up. And when you see them coming up with that kind of conspiracy, let them know your eyes are open. And let them know you got something else that's wide open too. It's got to be the ballot or the bullet. The ballot or the bullet. If you're afraid to use an expression like that, you should get on out of the country, you should get back in the cotton patch, you should get back in the alley. They get all the Negro vote, and after they get it, the Negro gets nothing in return. All they did when they got to Washington was give a few big Negroes big jobs. Those big Negroes didn't need big jobs, they already had jobs. That's camouflage, that's trickery, that's treachery, window-dressing. I'm not trying to knock out the Democrats for the Republicans, we'll get to them in a minute. But it is true—you put the Democrats first and the Democrats put you last.

Look at it the way it is. What alibis do they use, since they control Congress and the Senate? What alibi do they use when you and I ask, "Well, when are you going to keep your promise?" They blame the Dixiecrats.[6] What is a Dixiecrat? A Democrat. A Dixiecrat is nothing but a Democrat in disguise. The titular head of the Democrats is also the head of the Dixiecrats, because the Dixiecrats are a part of the Democratic Party. The Democrats have never kicked the Dixiecrats out of the party. The Dixiecrats bolted themselves once, but the Democrats didn't put them out. Imagine, these lowdown Southern segregationists put the Northern Democrats down. But the Northern Democrats have never put the Dixiecrats down. No, look at that thing the way it is. They have got a con game going on, a political con game, and you and I are in the middle. It's time for you and me to wake up and start looking at it like it is, and trying to understand it like it is; and then we can deal with it like it is.

The Dixiecrats in Washington, D.C., control the key committees that run the government. The only reason the Dixiecrats control these committees is because they have seniority. The only reason they have seniority is because they come from states where Negroes can't vote. This is not even a government that's based on democracy.... Half of the people in the South can't even vote. Eastland is not even supposed to be in Washington.[7] Half of the senators and congressmen who occupy these key positions in Washington, D.C., are there illegally, are there unconstitutionally.

I was in Washington, D.C., a week ago Thursday, when they were debating whether or not they should let the bill come onto the floor.

---

[6]*Dixiecrats:* Popular name for the prosegregation "States Rights Party," a group of southern Democrats who broke with the Democratic Party in 1948 after its national convention adopted a plank favoring civil rights legislation. They ran Governor Strom Thurmond of South Carolina as their 1948 presidential candidate in the general election against Democrat Harry S Truman and Republican Thomas E. Dewey.

[7]James O. Eastland (1904–1986) was a longtime Democratic senator from Mississippi and an untiring opponent of civil rights legislation.

And in the back of the room where the Senate meets, there's a huge map of the United States, and on that map it shows the location of Negroes throughout the country. And it shows that the Southern section of the country, the states that are most heavily concentrated with Negroes, are the ones that have senators and congressmen standing up filibustering and doing all other kinds of trickery to keep the Negro from being able to vote. This is pitiful. But it's not pitiful for us any longer; ... because soon now, as the Negro awakens ... the Negro's going to develop a new tactic.

These senators and congressmen actually violate the constitutional amendments that guarantee the people of that particular state or county the right to vote. And the Constitution itself has within it the machinery to expel any representative from a state where the voting rights of the people are violated.[8] You don't even need new legislation. Any person in Congress right now, who is there from a state or a district where the voting rights of the people are violated, that particular person should be expelled from Congress. And when you expel him, you've removed one of the obstacles in the path of any real meaningful legislation in this country. In fact, when you expel them, you don't need new legislation, because they will be replaced by black representatives from counties and districts where the black man is in the majority, not in the minority.

If the black man in these Southern states had his full voting rights, the key Dixiecrats in Washington, D.C., which means the key Democrats in Washington, D.C., would lose their seats. The Democratic Party itself would lose its power. It would cease to be powerful as a party. When you see the amount of power that would be lost by the Democratic Party if it were to lose the Dixiecrat wing ... you can see where it's against the interests of the Democrats to give voting rights to Negroes in states where the Democrats have been in complete power and authority ever since the Civil War. You just can't belong to that party without analyzing it....

... That's why, in 1964, it's time now for you and me to become more politically mature and realize what the ballot is for; what we're supposed to get when we cast a ballot; and that if we don't cast a ballot, it's going to end up in a situation where we're going to have to cast a bullet. It's either a ballot or a bullet.

---

[8]Malcolm was probably referring to Section 2 of the Fourteenth Amendment to the U.S. Constitution, which authorizes reduction of the congressional representation of states that violate citizens' right to vote.

In the North, they do it a different way. They have a system that's known as gerrymandering.... It means when Negroes become too heavily concentrated in a certain area, and begin to gain too much political power, the white man comes along and changes the district lines. You may say, "Why do you keep saying white man?" Because it's the white man who does it. I haven't ever seen any Negro changing any lines. They don't let him get near the line. It's the white man who does this. And usually, it's the white man who grins at you the most, and pats you on the back, and is supposed to be your friend. He may be friendly, but he's not your friend.

So, what I'm trying to impress upon you, in essence, is this: You and I in America are faced not with a segregationist conspiracy, we're faced with a government conspiracy. Everyone who's filibustering is a senator—that's the government. Everyone who's finagling in Washington, D.C., is a congressman—that's the government. You don't have anybody putting blocks in your path but people who are a part of the government. The same government that you go abroad to fight for and die for is the government that is in a conspiracy to deprive you of your voting rights, deprive you of your economic opportunities, deprive you of decent housing, deprive you of decent education.... It is the government itself, the government of America, that is responsible for the oppression and exploitation and degradation of black people in this country. And you should drop it in their lap....

So, where do we go from here? First, we need some friends. We need some new allies. The entire civil-rights struggle needs a new interpretation, a broader interpretation. We need to look at this civil-rights thing from another angle—from the inside as well as from the outside. To those of us whose philosophy is black nationalism, the only way you can get involved in the civil-rights struggle is give it a new interpretation. That old interpretation excluded us. It kept us out. So, we're giving a new interpretation to the civil-rights struggle, an interpretation that will enable us to come into it, take part in it....

And now you're facing a situation where the young Negro's coming up. They don't want to hear that "turn-the-other-cheek" stuff, no. In Jacksonville, those were teenagers, they were throwing Molotov cocktails. Negroes have never done that before. But it shows you there's a new deal coming in. There's new thinking coming in. There's new strategy coming in. It'll be Molotov cocktails this month, hand grenades next month, and something else next month. It'll be ballots, or it'll be bullets. It'll be liberty, or it will be death....

The black nationalists, those whose philosophy is black nationalism, in bringing about this new interpretation of the entire meaning of civil rights, look upon it as meaning ... equality of opportunity. Well, we're justified in seeking civil rights, if it means equality of opportunity, because all we're doing there is trying to collect for our investment. Our mothers and fathers invested sweat and blood. Three hundred and ten years we worked in this country without a dime in return—I mean without a *dime* in return. You let the white man walk around here talking about how rich this country is, but you never stop to think how it got rich so quick. It got rich because you made it rich....

This is our investment. This is our contribution—our blood. Not only did we give of our free labor, we gave of our blood. Every time he had a call to arms, we were the first ones in uniform. We died on every battlefield the white man had. We have made a greater sacrifice than anybody who's standing up in America today. We have made a greater contribution and have collected less. Civil rights, for those of us whose philosophy is black nationalism, means: "Give it to us now. Don't wait for next year. Give it to us yesterday, and that's not fast enough."

I might stop right here to point out one thing. Whenever you're going after something that belongs to you, anyone who's depriving you of the right to have it is a criminal. Understand that. Whenever you are going after something that is yours, you are within your legal rights to lay claim to it. And anyone who puts forth any effort to deprive you of that which is yours, is breaking the law, is a criminal. And this was pointed out by the Supreme Court decision. It outlawed segregation. Which means segregation is against the law. Which means a segregationist is breaking the law. A segregationist is a criminal. You can't label him as anything other than that. And when you demonstrate against segregation, the law is on your side. The Supreme Court is on your side.

Now, who is it that opposes you in carrying out the law? The police department itself. With police dogs and clubs.... Any time you demonstrate against segregation and a man has the audacity to put a police dog on you, kill that dog, kill him, I'm telling you, kill that dog. I say it, if they put me in jail tomorrow, kill—that—dog. Then you'll put a stop to it....

If you don't take this kind of stand, your little children will grow up and look at you and think "shame." If you don't take an uncompromising stand—I don't mean go out and get violent; but at the same time you should never be nonviolent unless you run into some nonviolence. I'm nonviolent with those who are nonviolent with me. But when you drop that violence on me, then you've made me go insane, and I'm not responsible for what I do. And that's the way every Negro should get....

When we begin to get in this area, we need new friends, we need new allies. We need to expand the civil-rights struggle to a higher level—to the level of human rights. Whenever you are in a civil-rights struggle, whether you know it or not, you are confining yourself to the jurisdiction of Uncle Sam.[9] No one from the outside world can speak out in your behalf as long as your struggle is a civil-rights struggle. Civil rights comes within the domestic affairs of this country. All of our African brothers and our Asian brothers and our Latin-American brothers cannot open their mouths and interfere in the domestic affairs of the United States. And as long as it's civil rights, this comes under the jurisdiction of Uncle Sam.

But the United Nations has what's known as the charter of human rights, it has a committee that deals in human rights. You may wonder why all of the atrocities that have been committed in Africa and in Hungary and in Asia and in Latin America are brought before the UN, and the Negro problem is never brought before the UN. This is part of the conspiracy. This old, tricky, blue-eyed liberal who is supposed to be your and my friend, supposed to be in our corner, supposed to be subsidizing our struggle, and supposed to be acting in the capacity of an adviser, never tells you anything about human rights. They keep you wrapped up in civil rights....

When you expand the civil-rights struggle to the level of human rights, you can then take the case of the black man in this country before the nations in the UN. You can take it before the General Assembly. You can take Uncle Sam before a world court. But the only level you can do it on is the level of human rights. Civil rights keeps you under his restrictions, under his jurisdiction. Civil rights keeps you in his pocket. Civil rights means you're asking Uncle Sam to treat you right. Human rights are something you were born with. Human rights are your God-given rights. Human rights are the rights that are recognized by all nations of this earth. And any time any one violates your human rights, you can take them to the world court. Uncle Sam's hands are dripping with blood, dripping with the blood of the black man in this country. He's the earth's number-one hypocrite. He has the audacity—yes, he has—imagine him posing as the leader of the free world. The free world!—and you over here singing "We Shall

---

[9] *Uncle Sam:* Popular personification/nickname for the United States.

Overcome." Expand the civil-rights struggle to the level of human rights, take it into the United Nations, where our African brothers can throw their weight on our side, where our Asian brothers can throw their weight on our side, where our Latin-American brothers can throw their weight on our side, and where 800 million Chinamen are sitting there waiting to throw their weight on our side.

Let the world know how bloody his hands are. Let the world know the hypocrisy that's practiced over here. Let it be the ballot or the bullet. Let him know that it must be the ballot or the bullet.

When you take your case to Washington, D.C., you're taking it to the criminal who's responsible; it's like running from the wolf to the fox. They're all in cahoots together.... No, take Uncle Sam to court, take him before the world.

By ballot I only mean freedom. Don't you know... that the ballot is more important than the dollar? Can I prove it? Yes. Look in the UN. There are poor nations in the UN; yet those poor nations can get together with their voting power and keep the rich nations from making a move. They have one nation—one vote, everyone has an equal vote. And when those brothers from Asia, and Africa and the darker parts of this earth get together, their voting power is sufficient to hold Sam in check. Or Russia in check. Or some other section of the earth in check. So, the ballot is most important....

I would like to say, in closing, a few things concerning the Muslim Mosque, Inc., which we established recently in New York City. It's true we're Muslims and our religion is Islam, but we don't mix our religion with our politics and our economics and our social and civil activities—not any more. We keep our religion in our mosque. After our religious services are over, then as Muslims we become involved in political action, economic action and social and civic action. We become involved with anybody, anywhere, any time and in any manner that's designed to eliminate the evils, the political, economic and social evils that are afflicting the people of our community....

Our gospel is black nationalism. We're not trying to threaten the existence of any organization, but we're spreading the gospel of black nationalism. Anywhere there's a church that is also preaching and practicing the gospel of black nationalism, join that church. If the NAACP is preaching and practicing the gospel of black nationalism, join the NAACP. If CORE is spreading and practicing the gospel of black nationalism, join CORE. Join any organization that has a gospel that's for the uplift of the black man. And when you get into it and see them pussyfooting or compromising, pull out of it because that's not black nationalism. We'll find another one. . . .

We will work with anybody, anywhere, at any time, who is genuinely interested in tackling the problem head-on, nonviolently as long as the enemy is nonviolent, but violent when the enemy gets violent. We'll work with you on the voter-registration drive, we'll work with you on rent strikes, we'll work with you on school boycotts—I don't believe in any kind of integration . . . [but] we will work with you against the segregated school system because it's criminal, because it is absolutely destructive, in every way imaginable, to the minds of the children who have to be exposed to that type of crippling education.

Last but not least, I must say this concerning the great controversy over rifles and shotguns. The only thing that I've ever said is that in areas where the government has proven itself either unwilling or unable to defend the lives and the property of Negroes, it's time for Negroes to defend themselves. Article number two of the constitutional amendments provides you and me the right to own a rifle or a shotgun. It is constitutionally legal to own a shotgun or a rifle. This doesn't mean you're going to get a rifle and form battalions and go out looking for white folks, although you'd be within your rights—I mean, you'd be justified; but that would be illegal and we don't do anything illegal. If the white man doesn't want the black man buying rifles and shotguns, then let the government do its job. That's all. . . .

. . . No, if you never see me another time in your life, if I die in the morning, I'll die saying one thing: the ballot or the bullet, the ballot or the bullet.

If a Negro in 1964 has to sit around and wait for some cracker senator to filibuster when it comes to the rights of black people, why, you and I should hang our heads in shame. You talk about a march on Washington in 1963, you haven't seen anything. There's some more going down in '64. And this time they're not going like they went last year. They're not going singing "We Shall Overcome." They're not going with white friends. They're not going with placards already painted for them. They're not going with round-trip tickets. They're going with one-way tickets.

And if they don't want that non-nonviolent army going down there, tell them to bring the filibuster to a halt. The black nationalists aren't going to wait. Lyndon B. Johnson is the head of the Democratic Party. If he's for civil rights, let him go into the Senate next week and declare himself. Let him go in there right now and declare himself.

Let him go in there and denounce the Southern branch of his party. Let him go in there right now and take a moral stand—right now, not later. Tell him, don't wait until election time. If he waits too long, brothers and sisters, he will be responsible for letting a condition develop in this country which will create a climate that will bring seeds up out of the ground with vegetation on the end of them looking like something these people never dreamed of. In 1964, it's the ballot or the bullet. Thank you.

All of Us Should Be Critics of Each Other
1964

In this interview excerpt from late 1964, Malcolm persisted in voicing criticism of some of the tactics of King and like-minded civil rights leaders. However, Malcolm was much less inflammatory than in his former attacks on middle-class integrationists. He still rejected committing unconditionally to nonviolence (he was far from alone in the freedom struggle by this time in doing so). This statement, like others found in these late-era documents, illustrates Malcolm's dramatic religious, ideological, and political shifts but also the still considerable continuity in his thought.

... *Crane:* Integration offends you. You don't believe in the use of that word. You prefer to think of it as brotherhood.... But in the old days you didn't believe in brotherhood, you believed in pure strict separation, didn't you?

Malcolm X: Whenever I opened my mouth, I always said that... the Honorable Elijah Muhammad—teaches us thus and so. And I spoke for him. I represented him. I represented an organization and organizational thinking. Many of my own views that I had from personal experience I kept to myself.... Since things came about that made me doubt his integrity... I think for myself....

From Malcolm X interview by Les Crane, 2 Dec. 1964; printed in Bruce Perry, ed., *Malcolm X: The Last Speeches* (New York: Pathfinder Press, 1989), 86–88.

I believe that it is possible for brotherhood to be brought about among all people, but I don't delude myself into dreaming or falling for a dream that this exists before it exists. Some of the . . . leaders of our people in this country always say that they, you know, they believe in this dream. But while they're dreaming, our people are having a nightmare, and I don't think that you can make a dream come true by pretending that that dream exists when it doesn't.

Crane: You've been a critic of some of the Negro leadership in this country—Martin Luther King, Roy Wilkins, Abernathy, and others—have you changed in your feelings toward them of late?[1]

Malcolm X: I think all of us should be critics of each other. Whenever you can't stand criticism you can never grow. I don't think that it serves any purpose for the leaders of our people to waste their time fighting each other needlessly. I think that we accomplish more when we sit down in private and iron out whatever differences that may exist and try and then do something constructive for the benefit of our people. But on the other hand, I don't think that we should be above criticism. I don't think that anyone should be above criticism. . . .

. . . And in situations like Mississippi, places like Mississippi where the government actually has proven its inability to protect us—and it has been proven that ofttimes the police officers and sheriffs themselves are involved in the murder that takes place against our people—then I feel, and I say . . . that our people should start doing what is necessary to protect ourselves. This doesn't mean that we should buy rifles and go out and initiate attacks indiscriminately against whites. But it does mean that we should get whatever is necessary to protect ourselves in a country or in an area where the governmental ability to protect us has broken down—

Crane: Therefore you do not agree with Dr. King's Gandhian philosophy—

Malcolm X: My belief in brotherhood would never restrain me in any way from protecting myself in a society from a people whose disrespect for brotherhood makes them feel inclined to put my neck on a tree at the end of a rope. [*Applause*] . . .

---

[1] Roy Wilkins, head of the NAACP; Ralph Abernathy, King's close colleague in the SCLC.

My Voice Helped Save America
1965

The following excerpts from the closing pages of the Autobiography *contain a number of remarkable and significant statements from the time very near Malcolm's death. These include his intimations that America was redeemable and that Malcolm dreamed that he might play a part in its salvation. He affirmed the essential unity of purpose in his and King's activities: exposing and fighting white racism. Malcolm's sense of how little time he had left is especially poignant; as he predicted here, he never lived to see his book appear in print.*

... Sometimes, I have dared to dream to myself that one day, history may even say that my voice—which disturbed the white man's smugness, and his arrogance, and his complacency—that my voice helped to save America from a grave, possibly even a fatal catastrophe.

The goal has always been the same, with the approaches to it as different as mine and Dr. Martin Luther King's non-violent marching, that dramatizes the brutality and the evil of the white man against defenseless blacks. And in the racial climate of this country today, it is anybody's guess which of the "extremes" in approach to the black man's problems might *personally* meet a fatal catastrophe first—"non-violent" Dr. King, or so-called "violent" me....

Every morning when I wake up, now, I regard it as having another borrowed day. In any city, wherever I go, making speeches, holding meetings of my organization, or attending to other business, black men are watching every move I make, awaiting their chance to kill me. I have said publicly many times that I know that they have their orders. Anyone who chooses not to believe what I am saying doesn't know the Muslims in the Nation of Islam....

Anyway, now, each day I live as if I am already dead, and I tell you what I would like for you to do. When I *am* dead—I say it that way because from the things I *know*, I do not expect to live long enough to read this book in its finished form—I want you to just watch and see if I'm not right in what I say: that the white man, in his press, is going to identify me with "hate."

The Autobiography of Malcolm X, 385, 388–89.

He will make use of me dead, as he has made use of me alive, as a convenient symbol of "hatred"—and that will help him to escape facing the truth that all I have been doing is holding up a mirror to reflect, to show, the history of unspeakable crimes that his race has committed against my race....

Yes, I have cherished my "demagogue" role. I know that societies often have killed the people who have helped to change those societies. And if I can die having brought any light, having exposed any meaningful truth that will help to destroy the racist cancer that is malignant in the body of America—then, all of the credit is due to Allah. Only the mistakes have been mine.

A Martin Luther King Jr. and Malcolm X Chronology (1925–1968)

Martin Luther King Jr. (MLK)	Malcolm X (MX)
BIRTH THROUGH EDUCATION	BIRTH THROUGH INCARCERATION
	1925 *May 19* MX born in Omaha, Nebr., to Earl and Louise Little.
	1928 *November* Little family's home burned down in Lansing, Mich.
1929 *January 15* MLK born in Atlanta, Ga.	
	1931 *September* Father killed by streetcar; rumored murdered by white supremacists.
	1939 *January* Mother committed to state mental hospital in Kalamazoo, Mich.
	Tells eighth-grade teacher he wants to be a lawyer; teacher calls it "no realistic goal for a nigger."
1940 Graduates from Howard Elementary School in Atlanta.	**1940** Lives in various foster homes in Lansing area.
1940–44 Attends Atlanta University Laboratory School two years and then Booker T. Washington High School in Atlanta.	**1941** *February* Moves in with older sister Ella in Boston.
	1941–45 Moves around, mostly between Boston, Detroit, and New York City; holds various jobs (often on railroads) such as a waiter and shoeshine; more and more engages in petty crime.

Martin Luther King Jr. (MLK)

BIRTH THROUGH EDUCATION

1944–48 Attends Morehouse College, Atlanta; receives B.A. in Sociology.

RELIGIOUS TRAINING AND ASCENT

1948 *February* Ordained; made associate pastor of Atlanta's Ebenezer Baptist Church (pastored by father, MLK Sr.).

1948–51 Attends Crozer Theological Seminary in Pa., is student body president and valedictorian as senior; receives Bachelor of Divinity degree.

1951–54 Attends Boston University; earns Ph.D.

1953 Marries Coretta Scott in Marion, Ala.

1954 *April* Becomes pastor of Dexter Avenue Baptist church in Montgomery, Ala.

Malcolm X (MX)

BIRTH THROUGH INCARCERATION

1946 *January* Arrested in Boston; charged with larceny, breaking and entering, and possession of firearms.

February Starts serving prison sentence in Charlestown Prison, Mass.; starts reading program in prison library.

RELIGIOUS CONVERSION AND ASCENT

1947 Starts conversion to Nation of Islam (NOI) and teachings of Elijah Muhammad (EM).

1952 Paroled from prison; gets X name from NOI, making him Malcolm X.

1953–54 Becomes and ascends as an NOI minister. In order, appointed assistant minister in Detroit Temple No. 1, then first minister of Boston Temple No. 11, of Philadelphia Temple No. 12, and of New York Temple No. 7; spearheads successful NOI evangelism and start of new temples around country.

1954 *May 17 Brown v. Board of Education of Topeka, Kansas.* Supreme Court bans racial segregation in public schools.

1955 *December 1* Rosa Parks arrested for disobeying segregation seating rules on bus in Montgomery, Ala.

Martin Luther King Jr. (MLK)

FROM PREACHER TO
CIVIL RIGHTS LEADER

1955 *December 5* MLK becomes president of the Montgomery Improvement Association (MIA), to lead African Americans' boycott of Montgomery's city buses.
December 8 MLK delivers the first mass address of the Montgomery movement at Holt Street Baptist Church.
1956 *January 26* MLK is arrested and jailed on a trumped-up speeding charge.
January 30 MLK's home is bombed; he convinces angry blacks gathering outside to leave peacefully.

1956 *November 13* Supreme Court rules Alabama's bus segregation laws unconstitutional.

December 20 MIA ends boycott; MLK is among first riders on Montgomery's newly desegregated buses.
1957 *February 14* MLK becomes president of new Southern Leaders Conference Civil Rights organization, later named the Southern Christian Leadership Conference (SCLC).
March King travels to Ghana to attend Independence ceremonies.
May 17 King gives "Give Us the Ballot" speech to over 30,000 people at Prayer Pilgrimage for Freedom in Washington, D.C.

Malcolm X (MX)

FROM NOI MINISTER
TO BLACK RIGHTS LEADER

1957 *April 14* NOI member severely beaten by New York police and kept in jail; MX leads large group to police station and demands prisoner's release to a hospital.
October MX hospitalized for heart attack in New York City.

1957 *August 29* Congress passes Civil Rights Act of 1957, establishing U.S. Commission on Civil Rights and Civil Rights Division of U.S. Justice Department.

Martin Luther King Jr. (MLK)

FROM PREACHER TO
CIVIL RIGHTS LEADER

Malcolm X (MX)

FROM NOI MINISTER
TO BLACK RIGHTS LEADER

1957 *September* Violence erupts during court-ordered desegregation of Central High School in Little Rock, Ark. President Eisenhower sends federal marshals to escort nine black students into school.

1958 *June 23* MLK meets with President Eisenhower in Washington, D.C.

September MLK publishes first book, *Stride toward Freedom: The Montgomery Story.*

September 20 MLK stabbed at book signing in Harlem; in danger of dying, recovers.

1959 *February* MLK starts trip to India as guest of Prime Minister J. Nehru.

1958 *January 14* MX marries NOI member Betty X (formerly Sanders, later Shabazz).

1959 *July* MX spends most of month touring Egypt, Mecca, Iran, Syria, and Ghana as EM's ambassador.

July 13–17 Documentary on NOI, "The Hate That Hate Produced," by Mike Wallace, airs for five days on WTNA-TV in New York; begins making Malcolm and NOI widely known.

1960 *March 3* MX is interviewed by William Kunstler, along with Rev. William H. James, on topic "Is Black Supremacy the Answer?" on New York WMCA radio show, "Pro and Con"; in following years, MX will have many such on-air debates with civil rights activists and supporters.

1960 *January 24* MLK, having already left Dexter Avenue Baptist Church in Montgomery, becomes co-pastor, with MLK Sr., of Ebenezer Baptist Church in Atlanta.

February Student sit-ins to desegregate lunch counters begin in Greensboro, N.C.; spread rapidly from there.

June 22 MLK meets with Democratic presidential candidate John F. Kennedy.

1960 *April 15–17* Student Nonviolent Coordinating Committee (SNCC) is formed.

1960 *September 22* Interstate Commerce Commission declares segregation illegal in interstate transportation facilities.

Martin Luther King Jr. (MLK)	Malcolm X (MX)
FROM PREACHER TO CIVIL RIGHTS LEADER	FROM NOI MINISTER TO BLACK RIGHTS LEADER

October MLK arrested in Atlanta sit-in, sentenced to four months hard labor at a state penitentiary for violating probation on a prior traffic conviction; John Kennedy phones concern to Mrs. King, and brother Robert Kennedy speaks with judge in case; King released; Kennedy wins key black votes in 1960 election.

1961 *May 4* Freedom riders leave Washington, D.C., by bus to publicize and protest segregation in southern interstate transportation facilities.

1961 *May 21* MLK addresses freedom riders and local supporters at First Baptist Church in Montgomery, Ala.; federal marshals intervene when a white mob threatens meeting.

December Albany Campaign begins with marches and mass meetings; MLK accepts Albany Movement president William Anderson's request for support.

1962 *Spring–August* Albany Campaign progresses then finally fails due to internal disunity, lack of visible police repression, and weak federal support.

October 16 MLK meets with President Kennedy, urges him to make a second Emancipation Proclamation ending racial segregation; Kennedy declines.

1963 *April–May* SCLC's Birmingham Campaign for desegregation ongoing.

1961 *April 27* NOI member Ronald Stokes is killed and six members injured by police in Los Angeles; EM sends MX to L.A.; over next weeks MX denounces atrocity widely in L.A. and New York media.

1962 *May* MX's interview in *Playboy* magazine appears; also is interviewed on television by James Baldwin.

Martin Luther King Jr. (MLK)

FROM PREACHER TO
CIVIL RIGHTS LEADER

Malcolm X (MX)

FROM NOI MINISTER
TO BLACK RIGHTS LEADER

April MLK disobeys an injunction for first time by refusing to halt all racial protests; while in prison, writes "Letter from Birmingham Jail."

May After weeks of peaceful protest amid violent repression making national and world news, Birmingham leaders agree to a desegregation plan; motel where King is staying and his brother's home are bombed.

June 11 President Kennedy makes a nationally televised speech supporting "moral issue" of black equality; a week later asks Congress to pass broadest civil rights law ever.

June 11 MLK meets with President Kennedy, who privately warns MLK about FBI surveillance of him and urges him to cut ties with alleged ex-Communists working for him, Jack O' Dell and Stanley Levison. King initially dismisses both but later resumes contact with Levison.

June 22 President Kennedy meets with King and other civil rights leaders in White House to try to dissuade them from going forward with March on Washington planned to rally support for the administration's civil rights bill.

August 28 Over 250,000 people gather before the Lincoln Memorial at the March on Washington; King gives "I Have a Dream" speech.

September King's second book, *Strength to Love,* is published.

1963 *August 28* MX attends, as highly critical observer and commentator, the national civil rights March on Washington.

Martin Luther King Jr. (MLK)	Malcolm X (MX)
FROM PREACHER TO CIVIL RIGHTS LEADER	FROM NOI MINISTER TO BLACK RIGHTS LEADER
September 15 Four black girls killed in a bomb blast at Sixteenth Street Baptist Church in Birmingham, Ala.; MLK delivers eulogy. *October 20* Attorney General Robert Kennedy authorizes FBI wiretaps on King's home and, later, on SCLC's phones.	*November 10* MX delivers "Message to the Grassroots," his most influential speech to date, in Detroit at Northern Negro Grass Roots Leadership Conference.

1963 *November 22* President John F. Kennedy assassinated in Dallas, Tex.

	December 1 At New York rally, MX says that the slain president "never foresaw the chickens would come home to roost so soon," violating EM's directive against comments on assassination. *December 4* EM suspends MX from ministry for 90 days, ostensibly for MX's comments.
1964 *February–June* St. Augustine Campaign. *February* SCLC responds to Robert B. Hayling's plea for aid when white violence nearly destroys local Civil Rights movement in St. Augustine, Fla.	**1964** *January 15* MX spends week with boxer Cassius Clay (later Muhammad Ali) in fighter's training camp in Miami, Fla. *March 8* MX announces break with EM and NOI and plan to start a black nationalist political organization. *March* MX announces formation of the Muslim Mosque, Inc.

1964 *March 26* MX and MLK meet in person, for only time, in U.S. Capitol in Washington.

April Mississippi Freedom Democratic Party (MFDP) founded to challenge the regular (segregationist) Mississippi delegation to the 1964 National Democratic Convention.	*April–May* MX travels to Middle Eastern nations under name Malik El-Shabazz. Travels in Africa; is feted by African heads of state, speaks at universities and on radio and TV.

Martin Luther King Jr. (MLK)	Malcolm X (MX)
FROM PREACHER TO CIVIL RIGHTS LEADER	FROM NOI MINISTER TO BLACK RIGHTS LEADER
	April MX sends home "Letter from Mecca," telling how his hajj experience made him aware that racism was not inevitable and that Islam could cure white America's racism.
May 31 MLK arrives in St. Augustine, Fla. *June* King's third book, *Why We Can't Wait,* published. *June 30* King leaves St. Augustine, calling it the "most lawless" city he had ever seen; returns to Atlanta. *July 2* King and other civil rights leaders attend White House signing ceremony of 1964 Civil Rights Act, banning racial discrimination in public accommodations, education, and employment.	*May 24* MX returns to New York and at airport press conference gives new views on race and politics. *June 28* MX announces formation of the Organization of Afro-American Unity (OAAU) as political organization; says OAAU will do "whatever is necessary to bring the Negro struggle from the level of civil rights to the level of human rights."
July MLK and SCLC launch People to People tour of Mississippi to help SNCC and CORE in Mississippi Freedom Summer.	*July 2* MX in telegram to MLK offers to send armed blacks to defend civil rights workers in St. Augustine.

1964 *June 21* On eve of SNCC's Mississippi "Freedom Summer" voter registration project, civil rights workers James Chaney, Michael (Mickey) Schwerner, and Andrew Goodman are reported missing after arrests in Philadelphia, Miss.; their bodies are found on August 4.
1964 *July* Violence breaks out in Harlem and six other northern cities.

	July–November MX travels abroad under name Malik El-Shabazz; attends African Summit Conference and asks the delegates to challenge the U.S. at the United Nations for violating African Americans' human rights; by mid October he has visited eleven nations, talked with eleven heads of state, and spoken to most of their legislatures.
December 10 MLK receives Nobel Peace Prize in Oslo, Norway; his selection had been announced in October.	

Martin Luther King Jr. (MLK)

FROM PREACHER TO CIVIL RIGHTS LEADER

1965 *January–March* Selma Campaign for voting rights.

March 21–25 Selma–Montgomery march. MLK leads 300 marchers from Selma to Montgomery, Ala.; addresses more than 30,000 people in rally at state capital.

Malcolm X (MX)

FROM NOI MINISTER TO BLACK RIGHTS LEADER

1965 *February* MX speaks with Coretta Scott King in Selma; attends First Congress of African Organizations in London; house in New York is firebombed in early-morning hours; MX and his family are evicted from (same) home, owned by NOI.

February 21 MX shot several times while speaking at an OAAU rally in the Audubon Ballroom in New York; one NOI man is arrested; MX pronounced dead on arrival at hospital.

February 27 1,500 people attend MX's funeral service at Faith Temple Church of God in Christ, NYC; actor Ossie Davis delivers eulogy; MX buried at Ferncliff Cemetery, Hartsdale, New York.

1965 *March 26* Stokely Carmichael of SNCC helps organize in Lowndes County, Ala., the Lowndes County Freedom Organization, which becomes known as the Black Panther Party.

1965 *November 5* New York Times praises publication of *The Autobiography of Malcolm X* (written with Alex Haley); calls it "eloquent statement."

August 6 MLK and other civil rights leaders attend White House signing ceremony of the 1965 Voting Rights Act.

August 11 Los Angeles's largest black ghetto, Watts, explodes in widespread riot; Chicago blacks also take to streets; MLK arrives in Los Angeles to see damage and urge peace and calm.

1966 *January 7* MLK announces SCLC Chicago Campaign to combat slums and end discrimination in housing and de facto segregation in city.

Martin Luther King Jr. (MLK)	Malcolm X (MX)
FROM PREACHER TO CIVIL RIGHTS LEADER	FROM NOI MINISTER TO BLACK RIGHTS LEADER

June 17 SNCC chairman Stokely Carmichael in Greenwood, Miss., uses controversial slogan "Black Power" to summarize black goals and demands; debate ensues between nationalistic young militants and MLK and more moderate civil rights forces over wisdom of slogan and tactics.

July–August SCLC Chicago Campaign.

July 10 MLK addresses rally at Soldiers Field, attended by 30,000–45,000, to inaugurate campaign; presents movement's proposals to Mayor Richard Daley for turning Chicago into an "open city" for housing; Daley angrily rejects demands.

August SCLC marches for open housing in Chicago; MLK, while leading march into white Chicago's Southwest side, is hit with brick hurled by angry whites. In "Summit Agreement," MLK, Chicago Freedom Movement, and Mayor Daley agree on measures to increase open housing in Chicago.

1966 *June 17* James Meredith shot and wounded as he begins march from Memphis, Tenn., to Jackson, Miss., to protest continuing denial of black voting rights. Next day SCLC, SNCC, and CORE vow to continue Meredith march.

1966 *Summer* Another "long hot summer" of racial violence; rioting erupts in over twenty northern cities.

1966 *July* Rioting occurs in Chicago's west side ghetto.

1966 *October* Huey Newton and Bobby Seale found the Black Panther Party in Oakland, Calif.

1966 *December 1* SNCC officers vote to expel whites from organization membership.

Martin Luther King Jr. (MLK)

FROM PREACHER TO
CIVIL RIGHTS LEADER

1967 Harper & Row publishes King's fourth and last book, *Where Do We Go from Here: Chaos or Community?*

March 28 MLK leads 5,000 protesters in antiwar march in Chicago.

April 4 MLK makes his major antiwar speech, "Beyond Vietnam," at New York City's Riverside Church.

April NAACP, moderate civil rights leaders, and press criticize King for mixing civil rights with antiwar movement.

April 15 MLK marches and speaks against Vietnam War at United Nations building in New York.

November 28 At staff retreat, MLK calls for radically restructuring American society and outlines plans for SCLC's upcoming Poor People's Campaign.

Malcolm X (MX)

FROM NOI MINISTER
TO BLACK RIGHTS LEADER

1967 *June 13* Thurgood Marshall named first African American on the Supreme Court.

1967 *Summer* Widespread urban racial violence.

1968 *January* SCLC approves plan for the Washington Spring Project (Poor People's Campaign); SCLC field-workers recruit poor volunteers from rural South for Washington project; FBI adds MLK to list of "black nationalist hate groups" targeted by its COINTELPRO (counterintelligence program) for undercover disruption and harassment of King.

February 12 Plans for the Washington Spring Project are finalized.

Martin Luther King Jr. (MLK)   Malcolm X (MX)

FROM PREACHER TO CIVIL RIGHTS LEADER	FROM NOI MINISTER TO BLACK RIGHTS LEADER

March 28 MLK leads march in support of striking sanitation workers in Memphis, Tenn.; to MLK's dismay, march ends in rioting by some people.

April 3 In mass meeting at Memphis's Bishop Charles J. Mason Temple, King delivers "I Have Been to the Mountaintop," his last speech.

April 4 MLK is assassinated, shot on his room balcony in Memphis's Loraine Hotel; worst yet rioting erupts in many U.S. cities; President Johnson declares April 7 a day of national mourning.

April 9 MLK buried in Atlanta.

1968 *April 11* Congress passes (largely as tribute to MLK) 1968 Civil Rights Act outlawing racial discrimination in housing.

May–August SCLC's Poor People's Campaign (PPC): May 11, "Resurrection City" camp set up near Lincoln Memorial; June 19, PPC climaxes in interracial march of 50,000; June 24, Resurrection City closed by authorities; August 6, PPC moves to Republican National Convention in Miami; campaign ends without achieving goal of new federal antipoverty measures.

Questions for Consideration

1. How different or similar in social origins were King and Malcolm? How may their differences in experiences and backgrounds help explain their differences of view?
2. What was King's ultimate social goal and ideal?
3. What types of specific demands and goals did the mass demonstrations and public campaigns that King helped lead have? How did King's main programmatic objectives change over time?
4. On what grounds does King present nonviolence as the best tool of social struggle and means of effecting change?
5. What was Malcolm's overall social goal? When a member of the Nation of Islam? Later?
6. What did Malcolm mean by black nationalism? What did King think of black nationalism? Did King reject all aspects of it?
7. What were Malcolm's views about revolution? By what means, did he argue, could or should oppressed peoples achieve their freedom?
8. What, to Malcolm, was the nature of whites and of America?
9. What did King think about the nature of America and of its future?
10. What was King's style of "critical patriotism"? Did Malcolm believe that blacks should identify as Americans?
11. What were the main points of the critiques Malcolm and King each made of the other's positions?
12. How different was the post-Mecca/post–Nation of Islam, or "new," Malcolm of 1964–65 from the earlier Malcolm? How did his ideas and feelings change about such things as white people, the value of African Americans seeking civil rights and participating in American politics, and the potential redeemability of America? Did all his views change, or were there areas of continuity?
13. Was there a "new," more radical Martin Luther King during his last couple of years? After about 1965, what evils was he mainly addressing and what sorts of reforms in U.S. society and foreign policy was he calling for?

14. During their respective end periods, how did King grow less optimistic and Malcolm more so about the possibilities for major improvements in America?
15. How did Malcolm and King each display heightened internationalism in their late periods?
16. In what ways and areas did King's and Malcolm's views significantly converge during each one's last year or two? Did they ever bridge all their disagreements?
17. What do you think of the argument that King and Malcolm's essential unity as spiritually inspired leaders and black freedom fighters ultimately outweighs their differences?

Selected Bibliography

BOOKS AND ARTICLES

Albert, Peter J., and Ronald Hoffman, eds. *We Shall Overcome: Martin Luther King Jr. and the Black Freedom Struggle.* New York: Pantheon Books, 1990.

Ansbro, John J. *Martin Luther King Jr.: The Making of a Mind.* Maryknoll, N.Y.: Orbis Books, 1982.

Asante, Molefi Kete. *Malcolm X as Cultural Hero and Other Afrocentric Essays.* Trenton, N.J.: Africa World Press, 1993.

Baldwin, James. "Malcolm and Martin." *Esquire* 77, no. 4 (April 1972): 94–97, 195–96, 198, 201.

Baldwin, Lewis V. "A Reassessment of the Relationship between Malcolm X and Martin Luther King Jr." *Western Journal of Black Studies* 13, no. 2 (Summer 1989): 103–13.

———. "Malcolm X and Martin Luther King Jr.: What They Thought about Each Other." *Islamic Studies* 25, no. 4 (Winter 1986): 395–416.

———. *There Is a Balm in Gilead: The Cultural Roots of Martin Luther King Jr.* Minneapolis: Fortress Press, 1991.

———. *To Make the Wounded Whole: The Cultural Legacy of Martin Luther King Jr.* Minneapolis: Fortress Press, 1992.

Baldwin, Lewis V., with Rufus Burrow Jr., Barbara A. Holmes, and Susan Holmes Winfield. *The Legacy of Martin Luther King Jr.: The Boundaries of Law, Politics, and Religion.* Notre Dame, Ind.: University of Notre Dame, 2002.

Baldwin, Lewis V., and Amiri Yasin Al-Hadid. *Between Cross and Crescent: Christian and Muslim Perspectives on Malcolm and Martin.* Gainesville: University Press of Florida, 2002.

Bennet, Lerone, Jr. *What Manner of Man: A Memorial Biography of Martin Luther King Jr.* New York: Pocket Books, 1968.

Boesak, Allan. *Coming In Out of the Wilderness: A Comparative Interpretation of the Ethics of Martin Luther King Jr. and Malcolm X.* Kampen, Nederland: Theologische Hogeschool der Gereformeerde Kerken, n.d.

Branch, Taylor. *Parting the Waters: America in the King Years, 1954–63.* New York: Simon & Schuster, 1988.

———. *Pillar of Fire: America in the King Years, 1963–65.* New York: Simon & Schuster, 1998.

Breitman, George. *The Last Year of Malcolm X: The Evolution of a Revolutionary.* New York: Pathfinder Press, 1967.

Breitman, George, Herman Porter, and Baxter Smith, eds. *The Assassination of Malcolm X.* New York: Pathfinder Press, 1976.

Carson, Clayborne, ed. *The Autobiography of Martin Luther King Jr.* New York: Warner Books, 1998.

———. "A 'Common Solution': Martin and Malcolm's Gulf Was Closing, but the Debate Lives On," *Emerge* 9, no. 4 (Feb. 1998): 44–46, 48–52.

———. *Malcolm X: The FBI File.* New York: Carroll & Graf, 1991.

Carson, Clayborne, et al., eds. *The Papers of Martin Luther King Jr.* Vol. 1, *Called to Serve, January 1929–June 1951.* Berkeley: University of California Press, 1992.

———. *The Papers of Martin Luther King Jr.* Vol. 2, *Rediscovering Precious Values, July 1951–November 1955.* Berkeley: University of California Press, 1994.

———. *The Papers of Martin Luther King Jr.* Vol. 3, *Birth of a New Age, December 1955–December 1956.* Berkeley: University of California Press, 1997.

———. *The Papers of Martin Luther King Jr.* Vol. 4, *Symbol of the Movement, January 1957–December 1958.* Berkeley: University of California Press, 2000.

Carson, Clayborne, and Peter Holloran, eds. *A Knock at Midnight: Inspiration from the Great Sermons of Reverend Martin Luther King Jr.* New York: Warner Books, 1998.

Carson, Clayborne, and Kris Shephard, eds. *A Call to Conscience: The Landmark Speeches of Dr. Martin Luther King Jr.* New York: Warner Books, 2001.

Clark, Kenneth B., ed. *King, Malcolm, Baldwin: Three Interviews.* Middletown, Conn.: Wesleyan University Press, 1985.

Clarke, John Henrik, ed. *Malcolm X: The Man and His Times.* New York: Collier Books, 1969.

Cone, James H. *Martin & Malcolm & America: A Dream or Nightmare?* Maryknoll, N.Y.: Orbis Books, 1991.

———. "The Theology of Martin Luther King Jr." *Union Seminary Quarterly Review* 40, no. 4 (1986): 21–36.

Davis, Ossie. "Why I Eulogized Malcolm X." *Negro Digest* 15, no. 4 (Feb. 1966): 64–66.

DeCaro, Louis A., Jr. *Malcolm and the Cross: The Nation of Islam, Malcolm X, and Christianity.* New York: New York University Press, 1998.

———. *On the Side of My People: A Religious Life of Malcolm X.* New York: New York University Press, 1996.

Downing, Frederick L. *To See the Promised Land: The Faith Pilgrimage of Martin Luther King Jr.* Macon, Ga.: Mercer University Press, 1986.

Dyson, Michael E. *I May Not Get There with You: The True Martin Luther King Jr.* New York: Free Press, 2000.

———. *Making Malcolm: The Myth and Meaning of Malcolm X.* New York: Oxford University Press, 1995.

Erskine, Noel L. *King among the Theologians.* Cleveland: Pilgrim Press, 1994.

Essien-Udom, E. U. *Black Nationalism: A Search for Identity in America.* New York: Dell, 1964.

Fairclough, Adam. *To Redeem the Soul of America: The Southern Christian Leadership Conference and Martin Luther King Jr.* Athens: University of Georgia Press, 1987.

Frady, Marshall. *Martin Luther King Jr.* New York: Viking Press/Penguin Putman, 2002.

———. "Reflections: The Children of Malcolm." *New Yorker* (12 Oct. 1992): 64–72, 74–81.

Gallen, David, ed. *A Malcolm X Reader: Perspectives on the Man and the Myths.* New York: Carroll and Graf, 1994.

———, ed. *Malcolm X: As They Knew Him.* New York: One World/Ballantine Books, 1992.

Garrow, David J. *Bearing the Cross: Martin Luther King and the Southern Christian Leadership Conference.* New York: William Morrow, 1986.

———. *Protest at Selma: Martin Luther King Jr. and the Voting Rights Act of 1965.* New Haven, Conn.: Yale University Press, 1978.

———. *The FBI and Martin Luther King Jr.: From "Solo" to Memphis.* New York: W. W. Norton, 1981.

———, ed. *Martin Luther King Jr. and the Civil Rights Movement.* 18 vols. Brooklyn, N.Y.: Carlson, 1989.

Goldman, Peter. *The Death and Life of Malcolm X.* Urbana: University of Illinois Press, 1979.

Halberstam, David. "The Second Coming of Martin Luther King." *Harper's* (Aug. 1967): 39–51.

Haley, Alex. "Alex Haley Remembers Malcolm X." *Essence* 14, no. 7 (Nov. 1983): 52–54, 118, 122.

———. "Interview: Malcolm X." *Playboy* (May 1963): 53–54, 56–60, 62–63.

———. "Interview: Martin Luther King Jr." *Playboy* (Jan. 1965): 65–68, 70–74, 76–78.

Harding, Vincent. *Martin Luther King: The Inconvenient Hero.* Maryknoll, N.Y.: Orbis Books, 1996.

Ivory, Luther D. *Toward a Theology of Radical Involvement: The Theological Legacy of Martin Luther King Jr.* Nashville: Abingdon Press, 1997.

Jenkins, Robert L., and Mfanya Donald Tryman, eds. *The Malcolm X Encyclopedia.* Westport, Conn.: Greenwood Press, 2002.

King, Coretta Scott. *My Life with Martin Luther King Jr.* 1969. Reprint, New York: Henry Holt, 1993.

———, ed. *The Words of Martin Luther King Jr.* New York: Newmarket Press, 1987.
King, Martin Luther, Jr. *Strength to Love.* 1963. Reprint, Philadelphia: Fortress Press, 1981.
———. *Stride toward Freedom: The Montgomery Story.* New York: Harper & Row, 1958.
———. *The Measure of a Man.* 1959. Reprint, Philadelphia: Fortress Press, 1988.
———. *The Trumpet of Conscience.* San Francisco: Harper & Row, 1967.
———. *Where Do We Go from Here: Chaos or Community?* Boston: Beacon Press, 1968.
———. *Why We Can't Wait.* New York: Harper & Row, 1964.
"King and Roy: On Malcolm's Death." *New York Amsterdam News,* 27 Feb. 1965, 27.
"King Views Malcolm X as Tragic." *New York Amsterdam News,* 28 Mar. 1964, 35.
"King's Kwips: King on Malcolm X." *Pittsburgh Courier* (Georgia edition), 25 May 1963, 1.
Kly, Y. N., ed. *The Black Book: The True Political Philosophy of Malcolm X (El-Hajj Malik El-Shabazz).* Atlanta: Clarity Press, 1986.
Lentz, Richard. *Symbols, the News Magazines, and Martin Luther King.* Baton Rouge: Louisiana State University Press, 1990.
Lewis, David L. *King: A Critical Biography.* New York: Praeger, 1970.
Lincoln, C. Eric *The Black Muslims in America.* 1961. Reprint, Trenton, N.J., and Grand Rapids, Mich.: Africa World Press and William E. Eerdmans, 1994.
———, ed. *Martin Luther King Jr.: A Profile.* New York: Hill and Wang, 1986.
Malcolm X. *By Any Means Necessary: Speeches, Interviews, and a Letter by Malcolm X,* ed. George Breitman. 12th ed. New York: Pathfinder Press, 1970.
———. *February 1965: The Final Speeches,* ed. Steve Clark. New York: Pathfinder Press, 1988.
———. *Malcolm X: The Last Speeches,* ed. Bruce Perry. New York: Pathfinder Press, 1989.
———. *Malcolm X on Afro-American History.* New York: Pathfinder Press, 1988.
———. *Malcolm X Speaks: Selected Speeches and Statements,* ed. George Breitman. New York: Grove Press, 1982.
———. *Malcolm X Talks to Young People: Speeches in the U.S., Britain and Africa,* ed. Steve Clark. New York: Pathfinder Press, 1991.
———. *The End of White World Supremacy: Four Speeches by Malcolm X,* ed. Imam Benjamin Karim. New York: Seaver Books, 1971.
———. *The Speeches of Malcolm X at Harvard,* ed. Archie Epps. New York: William Morrow, 1968.

Malcolm X, with Alex Haley. *The Autobiography of Malcolm X.* New York: Ballantine Books, 1999.

McCloud, Aminah B. *African American Islam.* New York: Routledge, 1995.

Oates, Stephen B. *Let the Trumpet Sound: The Life of Martin Luther King Jr.* New York: Harper & Row, 1982.

Perry, Bruce. *Malcolm: The Life of a Man Who Changed Black America.* Barrytown, N.Y.: Station Hill Press, 1991.

Perry, Theresa, ed. *Teaching Malcolm X.* New York: Routledge, 1996.

Sales, William W., Jr. *From Civil Rights to Black Liberation: Malcolm X and the Organization of Afro-American Unity.* Boston: South End Press, 1994.

Smith, Ervin. *The Ethics of Martin Luther King Jr.* New York: Edwin Mellen Press, 1981.

Smith, Kenneth L. "The Radicalization of Martin Luther King, Jr.: The Last Three Years." *Journal of Ecumenical Studies* 26, no. 2 (Spring 1986): 270–88.

Smith, Kenneth L., and Ira G. Zepp Jr. *Search for the Beloved Community: The Thinking of Martin Luther King Jr.* Valley Forge, Pa.: Judson Press, 1974, 1988.

T'Shaka, Oba. *The Political Legacy of Malcolm X.* Chicago: Third World Press, 1983.

Ward, Brian, and Tony Badger, eds. *The Making of Martin Luther King Jr. and the Civil Rights Movement.* New York: New York University Press, 1996.

Washington, James M., ed. *A Testament of Hope: The Essential Writings and Speeches of Martin Luther King Jr.* New York: HarperCollins, 1986.

———, ed. *I Have a Dream: Writings and Speeches That Changed the World.* San Francisco: HarperCollins, 1992.

Watley, William D. *Roots of Resistance: The Nonviolent Ethic of Martin Luther King Jr.* Valley Forge, Pa.: Judson Press, 1985.

Wolfenstein, Eugene V. *The Victims of Democracy: Malcolm X and the Black Revolution.* New York: Guilford Press, 1993.

Wood, Joe, ed. *Malcolm X in Our Own Image.* New York: St. Martin's Press, 1992.

ARCHIVES AND PAPERS COLLECTIONS

The two largest holdings of original papers and documents by King are the Archives of the Martin Luther King Jr. Center, Atlanta, Ga., and the Martin Luther King Jr. Papers, Special Collections Department, Mugar Library, Boston University, Boston, Mass.

The Martin Luther King Jr. Papers Project at Stanford University, in collaboration with the King Center in Atlanta, Clayborne Carson director and editor-in-chief, amasses, organizes, researches, annotates, and publishes copies of King's papers. This papers project is the largest and best source of King papers; its volumes, databases, and other products are unsurpassed in scholarly quality.

Notable archival holdings of Malcolm primary materials include the Malcolm X holdings of the Archives of the Schomburg Center for Research in Black Culture, New York. There is as yet no single Malcolm X primary materials collection comparable to the Stanford King Papers Project, but the Malcolm X Papers Project recently begun by Columbia University's Institute for Research in African American Studies, Manning Marable, director, in collaboration with members of the Shabazz family, holds great promise.

FILMS, VIDEOTAPES, AUDIOTAPES, AND RECORD ALBUMS

Bell & Howell Close-Up: Walk in My Shoes. Features Malcolm X speaking at Uline Arena, Washington, D.C., 25 June 1961; broadcast originally on ABC-TV, 19 Sept. 1961. Video in Museum of Television and Radio, New York.
Like It Is. Videotaped interview with Malcolm X by Gil Noble. WABC-TV, New York, Nov. 1963. King Center Archives, Atlanta.
Martin Luther King Jr.: A Personal Portrait. Videotape. Carroll's Marketing and Management Service, Goldsboro, N.C., 1966–67.
Martin Luther King Jr.: An Amazing Grace. McGraw-Hill Films, Del Mar, Calif., 1978.
The Early Days. Taped sermon by Martin Luther King Jr., Mt. Pisgah Baptist Church, Chicago, 27 Aug. 1967. King Center Archives, Atlanta.
The Hate That Hate Produced. CBS News documentary, New York, 1959.
The Martin Luther King Commemorative Collection. MPI Home Video, 1988.
The Wisdom of Malcolm X. Malcolm X at Nation of Islam Rally, 10 Aug. 1963, New York. Rahway, N.J.: Audiofidelity Enterprises, n.d.

ACKNOWLEDGMENTS

Langston Hughes. "America" stanza from *The Collected Poems of Langston Hughes.* Copyright © 1994 by The Estate of Langston Hughes. Used by permission of Alfred A. Knopf, a division of Random House, Inc.

Excerpts from the *Playboy* Interview: Martin Luther King Jr. *Playboy* magazine (January 1965). Copyright © 1964, 1992 by Playboy. Reprinted with permission. All rights reserved.

Martin Luther King Jr. "I Have a Dream." Copyright 1963 Dr. Martin Luther King Jr., copyright renewed 1991 Coretta Scott King. Reprinted by arrangement with the Estate of Martin Luther King Jr., c/o Writers House as agent for the proprietor, New York, NY.

Martin Luther King Jr. Excerpts from "Pilgrimage to Nonviolence," "Why Jesus Called a Man a Fool" (Sermon at Mt. Pisgah Missionary Baptist Church, Chicago, 1967), "The Ethical Demands for Integration," "The American Dream," "Stride Towards Freedom," "The Nightmare of Violence," "Beyond Vietnam 1967," "Where Do We Go From Here." Copyright Martin Luther King 1963, copyright renewed 1991 Coretta Scott King. Reprinted by arrangement with the Estate of Martin Luther King Jr., c/o Writers House as agent for the proprietor, New York, NY.

Malcolm X. "The Black Revolution" and "God's Judgment of White America." Copyright © 1971 by Merlin House, Inc./Seaver Books. Reprinted from *The End of White World Supremacy: Four Speeches by Malcolm X,* edited by Imam Benjamin Karim, published by Seaver Books, New York, NY. Reprinted by permission.

Malcolm X. Excerpts from "God's Judgment of White America," "The White Man Is a Devil," "Black Bodies with White Heads!" "My Voice Helped to Save America," "Nightmare," "Vicious as Vultures," "Mr. Ostrowski," "Conked," "Caught," "Saved," "Press Conference on Return from Africa," "Sincere Whites (That Coed Again)" from *The Autobiography of Malcolm X* edited by Malcolm X and Alex Haley. Copyright © 1964 by Alex Haley and Malcolm X. Copyright © 1965 by Alex Haley and Betty Shabazz. Used by permission of Random House, Inc.

Malcolm X. Excerpts taken from "An Interview by A. B. Spellman" (pp. 1–13), "The Founding Rally of the OAAU" (pp. 33–67), and "The Homecoming Rally of the OAAU" (pp. 133–56) from *By Any Means Necessary* by Malcolm X. Copyright © 1970, 1992 by Betty Shabazz, Bruce Perry, and Pathfinder Press. Reprinted by permission.

Malcolm X. Excerpts taken from "Message to the Grassroots" (pp. 15–29), "The Ballot or the Bullet" (pp. 35–58), and "The Black Revolution" (pp. 59–72) from *Malcolm X Speaks* by Malcolm X. Copyright © 1965, 1989 by Betty Shabazz and Pathfinder Press. Reprinted by permission.

Malcolm X. Excerpts taken from "Whatever Is Necessary to Protect Ourselves." Interview with Les Crane (pp. 79–85) from *Malcolm X: The Last Speeches* by Malcolm X. Copyright © 1989 by Betty Shabazz, Bruce Perry, and Pathfinder Press. Reprinted by permission.

Index

Abernathy, Ralph, 177
Affirmative Action (AA), 25–26
Africa, 123, 162, 186
African Americans. *See also* Civil Rights movement; integration; oppressed people; racism; segregation
   career restrictions, 51–52
   conditions of, 104–7
   contributions of, 149–50
   criminal justice system and, 53–55, 78–80
   cultural pride of, 148, 150–51
   economic rights of, 91, 94–95, 104–5, 151
   freedom for, 148–50
   hatred and, 109–10
   house Negroes and field Negroes, 128–30
   human rights of, 157–59, 173–74, 188
   independence of, 71–72
   international freedom and independence movements, 92, 122–23, 162, 165
   Islam and, 8–9
   middle-class, 117, 127–28
   oppression of, 84, 118–21, 167–69
   poverty of, 148–52
   pro-integration, 127–28
   raped by whites, 108–9, 126
   responses to oppression, 118–21
   segregation effects, 60–63, 78–79
   self-respect and dignity of, 66–67, 83, 104–7, 118–21, 134–35, 149–51
   separation of, 2
   Uncle Toms, 127, 130
   urban, 3, 91–92
   Vietnam war and, 140–41
   violence against, 97–98
   voting power of, 165–66, 168–70
African Summit Conference, 187
Afro-American's Right to Self-Defense, The (Malcolm X), 96–98
Alabama Christian Movement for Human Rights, 75, 76
Albany Campaign, 184

Ali, Nobel Drew, 8
All of Us Should Be Critics of Each Other (Malcolm X), 176–77
American Can Have a Bloodless Revolution (Malcolm X), 164–65
American dream
   King's views on, 102–7
   Malcolm X's views on, 102, 107–16
American Revolution, 99
Amos, 85
Anderson, William, 184
Aquinas, Saint Thomas, 80
Augustine, Saint, 79
Autobiography of Malcolm X, The (Malcolm X), viii, 23, 46, 47–56, 108, 157, 178, 188
Autobiography of Religious Development, An (King), 34–39

Back to Africa movement, 47, 48. *See also* Marcus Garvey
Baldwin, James, 14, 184
Baldwin, Lewis, 19, 22, 24
Ballot or the Bullet, The (Malcolm X), 165–76
Betty X (also Betty Sanders, Betty Shabazz), 183
Beyond Vietnam (King), 138–47, 190
Bible
   African Americans in, 69
   Nation of Islam doctrine and, 68–69, 114–15
Birmingham (Alabama) Campaign (SCLC)
   bombing of Sixteenth Street Baptist Church in, 100*n*, 186
   demonstrations by schoolchildren in, 135*n*
   Letter from Birmingham Jail (King), 74–90
   police department, 88–89
Black Bodies with White Heads (Malcolm X), 127–28
Black Legion, 48

201

black nationalism, 3, 6, 12, 23
  Civil Rights movement and, 171–76
  integration vs., 20
  King's views on, 90–91, 121–24
  Malcolm X's views on, 71–72, 101
  Muslim Mosque, Inc. and, 174–75
  sincere whites and, 160–61
Black Panther Party, 188, 189
Black Power, 23, 90, 117, 148, 189
Black Revolution, The (Malcolm X), 67–70
black supremacy, 109–10, 183
Boston University, 34
Boutwell, Albert, 78
boycotts, 3, 4, 43, 95, 182
Boyle, Sarah Patten, 85
Braden, Ann, 85
Brown v. Board of Education of Topeka, 3, 153*n*, 181
Bryant, William Cullen, 155–56, 156*n*
Buber, Martin, 61, 80
Bunyan, John, 85

California Civil Rights Initiative (CCRI) (also called Prop. 209), 26
capitalism, 154
Carmichael, Stokely (Kwame Ture), 90, 188, 189
Carson, Clayborne, 20
Castro, Fidel, 142
Chaney, James, 187
Chicago Campaign (SCLC), 137, 188, 189
Chicago Freedom Movement, 189
China, 167
Chinese Revolution, 100
Christian church
  denunciation of, by Nation of Islam, 117–18
  early Christians, 81
  human worth and, 64
  King's disappointment with, 86–88
  racial injustice and, 82–83
Christianity and the Social Crisis (Rauschenbusch), 42
civil disobedience, 81
Civil Rights Act of 1964, 1, 104, 131–32, 137, 185, 187
Civil Rights Act of 1968, 190
Civil Rights movement
  black nationalism and, 171–76
  human rights and, 157–59, 173–74
  King's defense of protest activities, 74–90
  King's role in, 6
  Malcolm X reaches out to, 13–14
  Montgomery bus boycott and, 3, 4, 43, 182
  Nation of Islam and, 12
  voting rights, 165
  white control of, 132–33
Clark, Kenneth B., 134–35
communism, 154, 185
Cone, James, 19

Congress of Racial Equality (CORE), 131, 133*n*, 167, 174–75, 187, 189
"conked" hair, 52–53
Connerly, Ward, 26
Connor, Eugene "Bull," 77, 78, 88
Constitution, U.S., 94, 97
"convergence" school, 21
Crozer Theological Seminary, 34
Crane, Les, 176–77

Dabbs, James McBride, 85
Daley, Richard, 189
Davis, Ossie, 14, 149, 188
Declaration of Independence, 59, 88
de facto school segregation, 93
democratic ideals
  King's views on, 2
  Malcolm X's views on, 2
Democratic Party, 168, 170
desegregation. *See also* integration; segregation
  integration vs., 59, 63, 64–65
  Little Rock High School, 183
  in Montgomery, Alabama, 182
Dixiecrats, 169, 170
Douglass, Frederick, 59
Dyson, Michael Eric, 24, 25

Eastland, James O., 169
Ebenezer Baptist Church, 4
Eisenhower, Dwight D., 183
Eliot, T. S., 88–89
El-Shabazz, El-Hajj Malik, viii, 186, 187
Emancipation Proclamation, 104, 184
employment, 151
equality
  Declaration of Independence and, 59
  of the races, 63–64
Ethical Demands for Integration, The (King), 58–67

"Farce on Washington," 128, 137
Fard, W. D., 8
Farmer, James, 131, 133
Federal Bureau of Investigation (FBI), 185, 186, 190
field Negroes, 128–30
filibusters, 132, 171
First Congress of African Organizations, 188
Fosdick, Harry Emerson, 65
Fourteenth Amendment, 170*n*
freedom
  for African Americans, 148–50
  integration and, 61–62
  national heritage and, 88
freedom riders, 84, 111, 184
French Revolution, 99

Gandhi, Mohandas, 4, 43, 66
Garvey, Marcus, 6, 47, 48, 49

INDEX

gerrymandering, 171
God
   destruction of white America by, 114–16
   human worth and, 64
   King's belief in, 45
   racial justice and, 88
God's Judgment of White America (Malcolm X), 113–16
Golden, Harry, 85
Goldman, Peter, 16
Goodman, Andrew, 187
Great Society, 148

Halberstam, David, 21
Haley, Alex, viii, 23, 33, 121, 188
Harding, Vincent, 24
hate
   King and, 153
   Malcolm X and, 109–10, 178–79
"Hate That Hate Produced, The," 183
Hayling, Robert B., 186
Hitler, Adolf, 81
house Negroes, 128–30
Hughes, Langston, 141
Hugo, Victor, 95
human rights, 157–59, 173–74, 187
Hungarian freedom fighters, 81

"I Have a Dream" speech (King), 24–25, 103–7, 185
"I Have Been to the Mountaintop" speech (King), 191
I May Not Get There with You: The True Martin Luther King Jr. (Dyson), 25
I'm Not a Racist (Malcolm X), 162–63
Independence, Not Separation (Malcolm X), 70–72
independence, of African Americans, 71–72
India, 43, 44
integration. *See also* desegregation
   desegregation vs., 59, 63, 64–65
   freedom and, 61–62
   King's views on, 2, 57–67
   legal system and, 65–66
   Malcolm X's views on, 2, 57, 127–28, 176–77
   nationalism vs., 20
   nonviolent action and, 120–21
   northern liberals and, 112
   separation vs., 57–62, 68
international freedom and independence movements, 92, 122–23, 162, 165
interracial brotherhood, 157–59, 176–77
Interstate Commerce Commission, 183
Islam, 113–16, 160–61, 166

Jackson, Jesse, 24
James, William H., 183
Jesus Christ, 82, 84–85
John, Saint, 146
Johnson, Lyndon, 97–98, 138, 175–76, 191

justice system, racial injustice in, 53–55, 78–80

Kant, Immanuel, 61
Kennedy, John F., 131–32, 145, 183, 184, 185, 186
   Malcolm X's remarks on, 113
Kennedy, Robert, 184, 186
King, Coretta Scott, 14, 18, 125–26, 181, 188
King, Martin Luther, Jr.
   on American dream, 102–7
   arrested, 184
   assassination of, 191
   attitudes toward Malcolm X, 2, 13–14, 117, 121–24, 123–26
   attitudes toward middle-class blacks, 117
   attitudes toward whites, 102–3
   background, 3–5, 18, 33–34
   beliefs, 58
   birth, 180
   on black nationalism, 90–91, 121–24
   chronology, 180–91
   communication skills, viii
   contrasted with Malcolm X, vii, 2–3, 10, 13–14, 16–18, 19–22
   convergence with Malcolm X's thinking, 18, 21–22, 136–56
   defense of protest activities by, 74–90
   disappointment with church, 86–88
   disappointment with white moderates, 81–86
   discouragement of, 137–38
   education, 36, 39, 180–81
   family, 3–4, 35–36, 38
   FBI surveillance of, 185, 186, 190
   goals of, 14–15, 57
   "good cop/bad cop" relationship with Malcolm X, 19–20
   integration views, 2, 57–67
   Malcolm X's attitudes toward, 2, 117–18, 130–31, 133, 134–35, 176–77, 178
   marriage, 181
   meeting with Malcolm X, 1–2, 186
   militancy of, 18, 20
   mythic status of, 22–26
   on nonviolent resistance, 40–46, 66–67, 73–96
   patriotic style, 102
   photos, 5, 7
   racism and, 38–39
   religious beliefs, 2, 20, 39, 40–46, 166
   religious development, 34–39, 181
   role in Civil Rights movement, 6
   temperament, 17
   Vietnam war opposition, 138–47, 190
   on violence, 90–92, 105, 121–26, 152–53
   on violence used in self-defense, 93–94
   white Americans and, 6, 23
   wins Nobel Peace Prize, 187
   words used out of context, 25

King, Martin Luther, Jr. (cont.)
  writings and statements
    Autobiography of Religious Development, An, 34–39
    Beyond Vietnam, 138–47, 190
    On Black Nationalists and Malcolm X, 121–24
    Ethical Demands for Integration, 58–67
    "I Have a Dream" speech, 24–25, 103–7, 185
    "I Have Been to the Mountaintop" speech, 191
    Letter from Birmingham Jail, 74–90, 185
    Nightmare of Violence, The: Regarding the Death of Malcolm X, 123–26
    Nonviolence: The Only Road to Freedom, 90–96
    Pilgrimage to Nonviolence, 40–46
    Strength to Love, 185
    Stride Toward Freedom: The Montgomery Story, 183
    Three Responses of Oppressed Groups, 118–21
    Where Do We Go from Here? 147–56, 190
    Why We Can't Wait, 187
King, Martin Luther, Sr., 3–4, 36, 183
King Is the White Man's Best Weapon (Malcolm X), 134–35
Korean war, 100*n,* 167
Ku Klux Klan, 6, 47–48, 81, 153
Kunstler, William, 183

Lee, Spike, 23
legal system
  integration and, 65–66
  racial injustice, 53–55, 78–80
Letter from Birmingham Jail (King), 74–90, 185
Levison, Stanley, 185
liberal theology, 40–41
Lincoln, Abraham, 85
Little, Earl, 6, 46, 47–50, 180
Little, Louise, 6–7, 8, 46, 49–51, 180
Little, Malcolm, 6–8. *See also* Malcolm X
  name change, viii, 9, 181
Little, Philbert, 54–55
Little, Reginald, 54–55
Little Rock High School, 183
Lomax, Louis E., 167
Lowndes County Freedom Organization, 188
Lumumba, Patrice, 126
Luther, Martin, 85

Malcolm X
  on America, 102, 107–16
  assassination, 123–26, 188
  attitudes toward King, 2, 117–18, 130–31, 133, 134–35, 176–77, 178
  attitudes toward middle-class blacks, 117
  attitudes toward whites, 103, 107–12, 162–63
  background, 6–8, 18, 33–34
  birth, 180
  on black nationalism, 71–72, 101
  break with Nation of Islam, 12, 70–71, 156
  childhood home burned, 6, 48
  chronology, 180–88
  Civil Rights movement and, 13–14
  communication skills, viii, 10–12, 16
  "conked" hair, 52–53
  contrasted with King, vii, 2–3, 10, 13–14, 16–18, 19–22
  convergence with King's thinking, 18, 21–22, 136–37, 156–79
  conversion to Nation of Islam, 8–9, 54–56, 181
  conversion to Sunni Islam, viii, 12, 156
  criminal years, 8, 53–55, 180–81
  education, 9
  family, 46, 47–51, 180
  funeral, 188
  "good cop/bad cop" relationship with King, 19–20
  heart attack, 182
  impacts of, 9–12, 23–24, 178–79
  imprisonment, 8, 54–55, 181
  on independence, 71–72
  on integration, 2, 57, 127–28, 176–77
  on interracial brotherhood, 157–59, 176–77
  on Kennedy assassination, 113
  King's attitudes toward, 2, 13–14, 117, 121–24, 123–26
  marriage, 183
  meeting with King, 1–2, 186
  ministries, 181
  name change, viii, 9, 181
  as Nation of Islam spokesman, 9–10
  on nonviolent resistance, 2, 73–74
  offers armed defense to King, 13–14, 187
  photos, 11, 15
  religious beliefs, 20–21, 46, 56, 113–16, 160–61, 166
  on revolution, 99–101
  on right to self-defense, 13–14, 74, 96–98, 134–35, 187
  on separation, 2, 57, 67–70, 71–72
  skin color, 49
  strengths of, vii
  temperament, 17
  violence advocated by, 2, 73–74, 74, 83, 96–98, 134–35
  welfare system and, 50–51
  white Americans and, 10, 23, 47–55, 112, 160–61
  writings and statements
    Afro-American's Right to Self-Defense, The, 96–98

INDEX

All of Us Should Be Critics of Each Other, 176–77
American Can Have a Bloodless Revolution, 164–65
Autobiography of Malcolm X, The, viii, 46, 47–56, 108, 157, 178, 188
Ballot or the Bullet, The, 165–76
Black Bodies with White Heads, 127–28
Black Revolution, The, 67–70
God's Judgment of White America, 113–16
I'm Not a Racist, 162–63
Independence, Not Separation, 70–72
King Is the White Man's Best Weapon, 134–35
"Letter from Mecca," 187
Message to the Grassroots, 99, 128–33
My Voice Helped Save America, 178–79
Press Conference on Return from Africa, 157–59
On Revolution, 99–101
Sincere Whites (That Coed Again), 160–61
White Man Is a Devil: Statements on Whites, The, 108–12
man
 human rights, 157–59, 173–74, 187
 innate worth of, 59–61
Mao Zedong, 142
marches, 7, 95, 103–4
March on Washington for Jobs and Freedom, 7, 103–4, 131–33, 185
Marshall, Thurgood, 190
Martin & Malcolm & America (Cone), 19
Marx, Karl, 4, 154
Mau Mau, 100
McGill, Ralph, 85
Meredith, James, 89, 189
Meshach, 81
Message to the Grassroots (Malcolm X), 99, 128–33, 186
middle-class blacks, 117, 127–28
Mississippi Freedom Democratic Party (MFDP), 186
Mississippi Freedom Summer Project, 165, 187
Montgomery (Alabama) bus boycott, 3, 4, 43, 181–82
Montgomery Improvement Association, 4, 182
Morehouse College, 31
Moses, 114–15
Muhammad, Elijah, 8, 12, 46, 70–71, 83, 109, 114, 134, 176, 181, 184
 separation and, 68–70
Muslim Mosque, Inc., 12, 71–72, 96, 174
My Voice Helped Save America (Malcolm X), 178–79

National Association for the Advancement of Colored People (NAACP), 131, 174, 190
National Baptist Convention, 4
National Liberation Front (Vietcong), 139*n*
Nation of Islam, 2, 3, 6, 46, 83, 178, 181
 Civil Rights movement and, 12
 denunciation of Christians by, 117–18
 King's views on, 121
 Malcolm X as spokesman for, 9–10
 Malcolm X's break with, 12, 70–71, 156
 Malcolm X's conversion to, 8–9, 54–56, 181
 separation and, 67–70
Nehru, J., 183
neo-orthodoxy, 41–42
Newton, Huey, 189
Niebuhr, Reinhold, 41, 78
Nightmare of Violence, The: Regarding the Death of Malcolm X (King), 123–26
Nixon, E. D., 4
Nobel Peace Prize, 187
Nonviolence: The Only Road to Freedom (King), 90–96
nonviolent resistance
 boycotts, 3, 4, 43, 95, 182
 disagreement over, 21–22
 Gandhi and, 43
 for international issues, 44
 King's views on, 40–46, 66–67, 73–96, 152–53
 King's workshops on, 76–77
 Malcolm X's views on, 2, 73–74
 marches, 7, 95, 103–4
 by oppressed people, 120–21
 self-worth of African Americans and, 66–67
 sincere whites and, 161
 steps in, 76
 violence and, 13–14, 20, 84, 90–96, 121–24, 168–69, 172–73, 175–76, 177
Northern liberals, Malcolm X's views on, 111–12

O'Dell, Jack, 185
On Black Nationalists and Malcolm X (King), 121–24
On Revolution (Malcolm X), 99–101
oppressed people. *See also* African Americans
 acquiescence by, 118–19
 nonviolent resistance by, 120–21
 responses of, 118–21
 violence by, 119–20
 voting rights and, 166–76
Organization of Afro-American Unity (OAAU), 12, 96, 161, 162, 187

pacifism, 45
Pan-Africanism, 162

INDEX

Parks, Rosa, 181
Paul, Saint, 85
Pilgrimage to Nonviolence (King), 40–46
Playboy magazine, 121, 184
police departments
   Birmingham, Alabama, 88
   violence by, 172
Poor People's Campaign, 137, 165, 190, 191
poverty
   of African Americans, 104, 148–54
   in urban areas, 14
Powell, Adam Clayton, 166
Prayer Pilgrimage for Freedom, 182
Press Conference on Return from Africa (Malcolm X), 157–59
Protestant liberalism, 41–42

racial equality, 63–64
racial imperialism, 92
racial injustice
   Christianity and, 82–83
   identifying, 76
   legal system and, 53–55, 78–80
   nonviolent resistance and, 78
racism
   King's experiences with, 18
   King's views on, 38–39
   Malcolm X's experiences with, 6, 47–55
   Malcolm X's views on, 46, 79, 103, 162–63
   of northern liberals, 111–12
   of Southerners, 111
   violence and, 98
   of white Americans, 38–39, 59, 103, 118
Randolph, A. Philip, 132, 133
rape, by whites, 108–9, 126
Rauschenbusch, Walter, 42
religion
   King's beliefs, 2, 20, 39, 40–46, 166
   King's religious development, 34–39, 181
   liberal theology, 40–41
   Malcolm X's beliefs, 2, 20–21, 46, 56, 113–16, 160–61, 166
Republican Party, 168
Resurrection City, 191
Reuther, Walter, 133
revolution
   King's views on, 146–47
   Malcolm X's views on, 99–101, 164–65
Richardson, Gloria, 131
riots, 152, 187, 188, 190, 191
Robinson, Jo Anne, 4
Russian Revolution, 100
Rustin, Bayard, 16

Sanders, Betty (also Betty X, Betty Shabazz), 183
satyagraha, 43
school segregation
   de facto, 93
   Little Rock, 183

Schwerner, Michael (Mickey), 187
Scott, Coretta, 181
Seale, Bobby, 189
segregation. *See also* desegregation
   effects on African Americans, 60–63, 78–79
   illegality of, 172
   innate worth of man and, 60–61
   of interstate transportation facilities, 183, 184
   King's interest in, 42
   police preservation of, 88, 172
   schools, 93, 183
   as "social leprosy, 62–63
   unjustness of, 80
   violence against, 172–73
self-defense, violence used in, 13–14, 74, 93–94, 96–98, 134–35, 187
Selma (Alabama) Campaign, 13–14, 165, 188
separation
   Back to Africa movement, 47, 48
   integration vs., 57–72, 68
   Malcolm X's views on, 2, 57, 67–70, 71–72
   Nation of Islam and, 10, 67–70
Shabazz, Betty (also Betty Sanders, Betty X), 183
Shuttlesworth, Fred, 76
sin, man's inclination for, 41
Sincere Whites (That Coed Again) (Malcolm X), 160–61
skin color
   of Malcolm X, 49
   rape by whites and, 108–9
"slave names," viii, 9
slavery
   house Negroes and field Negroes, 128–30
   innate worth of man and, 61
   psychological inheritance of, 17
   rape, 108–9
Smith, Lillian, 85
social ethics, 42–43
social philosophy, 42–43
Socrates, 77, 81, 82
Socratic method, 77*n*
Southern Christian Leadership Conference (SCLC), 4, 13–14, 75, 90, 102, 131, 135*n*, 137, 141, 147, 182, 186–91
   Albany Campaign, 184
   Birmingham Campaign, 184
   Chicago Campaign, 137, 188, 189
   Poor People's Campaign, 65, 137, 190, 191
   Selma Campaign, 13–14, 165, 188
   St. Augustine Campaign, 186, 187
Southern white racism, 111
Spellman, A. B., 70*n*
St. Augustine, Florida, Campaign, 186, 187
Stokes, Ronald, 184

Strength to Love (King), 185
Stride Toward Freedom: The Montgomery Story (King), 118, 183
Student Nonviolent Coordinating Committee (SNCC), 12, 13, 90, 165, 187, 189
Sunni Islam, viii, 12, 156

Temple, Charles J. Mason, 186, 187, 191
Three Responses of Oppressed Groups (King), 118–21
Tillich, Paul, 61, 80
Tolstoy, Leo, 62
Ture, Kwame, 90

Uncle Toms, 127, 130
United Nations, 173–74, 187
Universal Negro Improvement Association (UNIA), 6, 47
urban areas
 ghettos, 3, 91–92
 poverty, 14
 riots, 152, 187, 188, 190, 191

Vietcong, 139*n*
Vietnam war
 African Americans and, 140–41
 King's opposition to, 92, 138–47, 190
violence
 advocated by Malcolm X, 2, 73–74, 83, 96–98, 134–35
 against African Americans, 97–98
 black nationalism and, 121–24
 King's views on, 90–92, 105, 121–26, 152–53
 by oppressed peoples, 119–20
 racism and, 98
 as response to oppression, 119–20
 revolution and, 99–101
 against segregationists, 172–73
 urban riots, 152, 187, 188, 190, 191
 used in self-defense, 13–14, 74, 93–94, 96–98, 134–35, 187
 Vietnam war and, 140–47
 voting rights vs., 168–69
 when nonviolent resistance fails, 13–14, 84, 121–24, 168–69, 175–76, 177
 by whites, 186
voter registration, 187
voting rights, 165–76
 African American voting power, 168–70
 government conspiracy against, 168–71

violence vs., 168–69
Voting Rights Act of 1965, 137, 188

Wallace, Mike, 183
war
 Korea, 100*n*, 167
 nonviolence and, 44
 as racist imperialism, 92
 Vietnam, 92, 138–47, 190
 World War II, 100*n*
Warren, Earl, 78*n*
Washington Spring Project, 190, 191. *See also* Poor People's Campaign
Watts riot, 152, 188
welfare system, 50–51
Where Do We Go from Here: Chaos or Community? (King), 147–56, 190
white Americans
 black nationalism and, 121
 Civil Rights movement and, 132–33
 collective nature of, 110
 destruction of, 69–70, 113–16
 as devils, 69–70, 107–12
 fears of African Americans, 17
 King's attitudes toward, 102–3
 King's disappointment with, 81–86
 King's relationships with, 6, 23
 Malcolm X's advice to, 112, 160–61
 Malcolm X's attitudes toward, 103, 107–12
 Malcolm X's relationships with, 10, 23, 51–52, 54–55
 northern liberals, 111–12
 oppression by, 166–69
 racism of, 18, 38–39, 103, 159
 rape of blacks by, 108–9, 126
 "sincere," 158–59, 160–61
 SNCC and, 189
 Southerners, 111
 violence against, 69–70, 91–92, 113–16
 violence by, 186
White Citizens Councils, 81, 153
White Man Is a Devil: Statements on Whites, The (Malcolm X), 108–12
white nationalism, 101
Why We Can't Wait (King), 187
Wilkins, Roy, 131, 132, 177
Williams, A. D., 3
World War II, 100*n*

Zeitgeist, 84, 122